Barack Obama

Barack Obama

A LIFE IN AMERICAN HISTORY

F. Erik Brooks and MaCherie M. Placide

Black History Lives

An Imprint of ABC-CLIO, LLC
Santa Barbara, California • Denver, Colorado

Library of Congress Cataloging-in-Publication Data

Names: Brooks, F. Erik, author. | Placide, MaCherie M., author.
Title: Barack Obama : a life in American history / F. Erik Brooks and
  MaCherie M. Placide.
Description: Santa Barbara : ABC-CLIO, [2019] | Series: Black history lives
  | Includes bibliographical references and index. |
Identifiers: LCCN 2019026821 (print) | LCCN 2019026822 (ebook) | ISBN
  9781440859137 (hardcover) | ISBN 9781440859144 (ebook)
Subjects: LCSH: Obama, Barack. | Presidents—United States—Biography. |
  United States—Politics and government—2009-2017. | Presidents—United
  States—Election—2008. | Political campaigns—United
  States—History—21st century. | Legislators—United States—Biography.
  | African American legislators—Biography. | United States. Congress.
  Senate—Biography. | Racially mixed people—United States—Biography.
Classification: LCC E908 .B76 2019 (print) | LCC E908 (ebook) | DDC
  973.932092 [B]—dc23
LC record available at https://lccn.loc.gov/2019026821
LC ebook record available at https://lccn.loc.gov/2019026822

ISBN: 978-1-4408-5913-7 (print)
      978-1-4408-5914-4 (ebook)

23 22 21 20 19   1 2 3 4 5

This book is also available as an eBook.

ABC-CLIO
An Imprint of ABC-CLIO, LLC

ABC-CLIO, LLC
147 Castilian Drive
Santa Barbara, California 93117
www.abc-clio.com

This book is printed on acid-free paper ∞

Manufactured in the United States of America

Contents

Series Foreword

The Black History Lives biography series explores and examines the lives of the most iconic figures in African-American history, with supplementary material that highlights the subject's significance in our contemporary world. Volumes in this series offer far more than a simple retelling of a subject's life by providing readers with a greater understanding of the outside events and influences that shaped each subject's world, from familial relationships to political and cultural developments.

Each volume includes chronological chapters that detail events of the subject's life. The final chapter explores the cultural and historical significance of the individual and places their actions and beliefs within an overall historical context. Books in the series highlight important information about the individual through sidebars that connect readers to the larger context of social, political, intellectual, and pop culture in American history; a timeline listing significant events; key primary source excerpts; and a comprehensive bibliography for further research.

Preface

Indeed the election of President Barack H. Obama as the forty-fourth president of the United States of America was a remarkable event and a poignant example for future politicians and leaders of all races. It has been well documented that many African Americans of all ages and classes did not believe that they would ever see an African American elected president of the United States. The March 2008 cover of *Ebony Magazine* confirmed the notion that most blacks questioned if an African American could be elected president. The cover has a picture of Barack Obama with the caption reading, "In Our Lifetime: Are We Really Witnessing the Election of the Nation's First Black President?"

Initially, I must admit I was a nonbeliever. I did not believe that any African American candidate could raise enough money to finance a presidential run. Growing up in a ruby-red state like Alabama and with George C. Wallace as my governor for most of my childhood, I was also not convinced an African American candidate could gain enough support from white America to win the U.S. presidency; I proudly say I was wrong. It was not until Barack Obama won the Iowa caucuses that my doubt subsided and I began to believe an African American had a chance to become the president of the United States. My parents were lifelong Alabamians born in the 1940s, who had witnessed firsthand discrimination and who were doubtful much longer than I was. But as soon as Obama strung together a few primary wins and a groundswell of enthusiasm and support grew across the country, they were all in for Obama.

My coauthor of this book, MaCherie Placide, notes that her mother, who was battling diabetes, would not see Barack Obama become president of the United States. However, after observing Barack Obama's address at the 2004 Democratic National Convention in Boston, Massachusetts, MaCherie stated that her mother was now convinced that he could become the first black man to become president of the United States. She recalls her mother watching the convention on television, and on the television appeared a tall, slim African American man who confidently walked up to the podium to deliver the keynote address. As he spoke, we heard phrases such as "grateful for the diversity of my heritage," "aware that my parents' dreams live on in my two precious daughters," and "I stand here knowing that my story is part of the larger American story." My coauthor remembers how she and her mother both stopped in their tracks to listen to the charismatic man behind the podium. Having very little information, MaCherie's mother continued to pepper her with questions: "What is his name?" "Where is he from?" and "Why haven't I heard of him before?" Obama's voice boomed from the television, "Well, I say to them tonight, there's not a liberal America and a conservative America; there's the United States of America." At the conclusion of this address and the rousing applause that followed, MaCherie's mother commented, "That black man might become president one day."

On November 4, 2008, Barack Obama was elected president of the United States. MaCherie reflected on her mother's revelation and wished her mother could have witnessed this historical moment happen. The Obama presidency represented the hope and faith of black people's advancement and progress. MaCherie also notes her mother came from a generation who experienced the depth of de jure and de facto segregation and discrimination. A large segment of her mother's generation were suspicious when it came to issues regarding race and they had difficulty seeing the world through a "lens of change." Therefore, seeing an African American as president of the United States was more dream than reality; therefore, MaCherie was shocked when her mother commented, "Obama could become the first black president!"

Professor and author Michael Eric Dyson noted in his work, *The Black Presidency,*

> Obama's presidency represents the paradox of American representation. Obama represents all of us because he stands as a symbol of America to the world. He also represents to the American citizenry proof of progress in a nation that has never embraced a black commander in chief. Yet a third sense of representation has a racial tinge, because Obama is also a representation of a black populace that, until this election, had been excluded from the highest reach of political representation. (Dyson 2016, xi)

Barack Obama has set the model for future generations to follow. He is a great father, a great husband, a great politician, and a great president. His presidency has made many scholars reexamine American politics, political influence, and racial attitudes in the United States. While this work is about Barack Obama, it is not to glorify him. The purpose of the work is to provide information about Barack Obama's life from birth through child-hood and adulthood. The work also provides an account of Obama's family background, education, personal and professional influences, struggles, accomplishments, and contributions. This work also provides a timeline of events and primary documents associated with Obama.

1

Early Life

In 1960, the parents of the forty-fourth president of the United States met. Barack Hussein Obama Sr. first encountered Stanley Ann Dunham while they were students in a Russian language class at the University of Hawaii in Manoa. Obama had been born in Kenya, while Stanley Ann Dunham was born in Wichita, Kansas. She was better known as "Ann." Ann was an anthropologist who specialized in economic anthropology. Her first impression of the young man from Kenya was that he was handsome, principled, and very intelligent. Ann told her parents about the bright young Kenyan that she had met, and her parents insisted that she invite him over for dinner. Upon meeting him, her parents were equally impressed with the young man.

On their first official date, Barack Obama and Ann Dunham were to meet at the library. Obama was late. While waiting, Ann decided that she would catch a quick suntan and reclined and relaxed. She fell asleep waiting for Obama. After Ann's nap, Obama, along with three friends, arrived. Obama, who had a reputation for braggadocio, promptly boasted to his friends that Ann was a good woman because she waited for him even though he was late (Meacham 2008).

Ann had been an independent thinker even as a child and would take her own course of action even if it conflicted with the mores of the time. She was a liberal, thinking that was a product of her parents, Stanley Armour Dunham and Madelyn Lee Payne. Ann's parents were from

Wichita, Kansas, and were free spirits who liked to pursue new adventures. There seemed to be no seminal foundation to their liberal perspectives. They had not had much contact with African Americans except for a few who had crossed their paths. Her parents' liberal racial views and an incident involving a black playmate helped shaped Ann's lifelong view on race.

In 1960, Barack Obama Sr. and Ann Dunham had made plans to get married. Obama wrote home to his father, Onyango, to tell him about his engagement. Onyango Obama was not happy about Barack Obama's choice to marry a white woman. Onyango believed that white people's customs and priorities were too starkly different from those of African people. He also did not believe that Ann would come to live in Kenya after the marriage. Underlying Onyango's anxiety about the impending marriage was the belief that it was Obama's duty to return to Kenya and help provide solutions to fix Kenya's troubled government.

Ann's parents enjoyed Barack Obama's company, and they liked it when he discussed and analyzed politics and government. Obama's pursuits apparently began to rub off on Ann's father, who took an interest in the racial dynamics of the United States and the political discourse of the time. Like Obama's father, Ann's parents also had concerns about the marriage, specifically about the treatment their daughter would receive in the United States because she was married to a black man from Africa. During this time in U.S. history, most states outlawed marriages between a white person and black person. These laws were not changed until after the U.S. Supreme Court's ruling in the *Loving v. Virginia* case in 1967.

Hawaii was a progressive state, so the young couple was joined in a civil ceremony in 1961. Barack Hussein Obama Jr. was born on August 4, 1961. He was born at the Kapiʻolani Medical Center for Women and Children in Honolulu, Hawaii. He weighed eight pounds and ten ounces at his birth. The name Barack means "blessed" in Swahili and in Arabic, Hussein means "beautiful" (G. Thomas 2008, 17). Many of his family members nicknamed him "Barry" or "Bar" as a term of endearment. He would be called Barry until he attended law school.

Obama Sr. completed his studies in economics at the University of Hawaii in 1962, earning his bachelor of arts in three years. He was an ambitious student and excelled academically. A student organizer, he helped found the International Students Association on the campus. After completing his undergraduate degree, Obama Sr. had the opportunity to further his education at New York University or Harvard University. He chose Harvard because of its renowned reputation, the universal regard as an excellent, world-class university, and the prestige associated with its graduates. Obama Sr. wanted to go to a school that the people in Kenya would recognize as an elite university. He believed this association with Harvard University would prove to the people of his homeland he was

---

STANLEY ANN DUNHAM

Stanley Ann Dunham, better known as Ann Dunham, was the mother of Barack Obama, the forty-fourth president of the United States. Her father always wanted a son, and thus he named her after him even though "Stanley" is not a traditionally feminine name. Ann Dunham was born in Wichita, Kansas, but lived her formative years in several states including Hawaii, California, Texas, and Washington. She began to go by her middle name, Ann, while she was an undergraduate student at the University of Hawaii. While there, she met Barack Obama Sr., who was from Kenya and attending the university on an international fellowship. Dunham and Obama began dating, and after some months, Dunham became pregnant. Obama and Dunham were married in a private civil ceremony in February 2, 1961. On August 4, 1961, Barack Obama Jr. was born.

Dunham was liberal in her view of the world. She married a black man at a time when nearly two dozen states in the country still had laws against interracial marriage. After her divorce from Barack Obama Sr., she and her son moved to Jakarta, Indonesia, during an anticommunist uprising. In Indonesia, she continued to instill her values and strongly influence his view of the world. Ann Dunham died of cancer in 1995 at age fifty-two.

---

indeed a success. He was offered financial assistance to attend Harvard, but it was not sufficient to cover of the cost of his family. He saw that leaving his family was a necessary sacrifice to becoming a success.

While Barack Sr. was advancing his graduate studies at Harvard University, Ann and Madelyn kept abreast of the Mau Mau Rebellion and the fight for independence in Kenya. Madelyn feared that if Ann moved to Kenya with Obama Sr. after he completed his studies at Harvard, she might be killed. Madelyn believed that she was too young to be called "Granny" or "Grandma," so she insisted that young Barack call her *tutu*, the Hawaiian word for "grandparent." Tutu was later shortened and morphed into "Toot" (Obama 2004, 7). Toot's fears about her daughter moving to Kenya would be put to rest. By the time Obama Sr. had finished his doctoral studies, Ann had decided that she no longer wanted to be married.

The younger Obama did not have a close relationship with his father. His mother and grandfather told him stories to shape his knowledge of his absent father. Many of the stories portrayed Barack Obama Sr. as a legendary figure or a social justice superhero. These versions combined tall tales and outright lies, fueling the younger Obama's construction of a mythical portrayal of his father, which he would later discover was not an accurate picture. There were many grand stories of Barack's father, who had a larger-than-life personality and seemed to never be embarrassed about anything.

The only time that Toot could remember Obama Sr. ever being embarrassed was at his induction into the prestigious honor society, Phi Beta Kappa, at the University of Hawaii. Obama Sr. showed up to accept this great honor in blue jeans and an animal-print shirt, while other attendees dressed in tuxedos. Obama Sr. had a deep baritone voice, great oratory skills, and regal aura even in the face of racism.

On one occasion, Obama Sr. and Gramps went to a restaurant and encountered a white patron who did not like black people. This man exclaimed loudly that he did not want a black person to sit next to him. He even used a racial epithet. Instead of exacting violence on the customer, Obama Sr. approached the man and launched into lecture on self-respect, human rights, and the ills of racism. After this compelling and convincing lecture, the man felt so guilty that he gave Obama Sr. one hundred dollars. This incident confirmed the confidence of Obama Sr. He exuded confidence in all matters; his maternal grandfather advised young Barack to embrace this quality if he wanted to be successful.

While the stories of Obama's exploits grew to mythical proportions, his grandfather served as Barack's surrogate father. In the absence of Barack's biological father, his grandfather attempted to fill this void. He made certain Barack knew he was unique, a special person. He even stretched the truth to ensure young Barack had healthy self-esteem and grew to be as confident as his biological father. Young Barack was a novelty in Hawaii.

BARACK OBAMA SR.

The father of the first African American president of the United States, Barack Obama Sr. was a native of Kenya. As a young child, he went to the village school, where he immediately was acknowledged for his strong mathematics skills. These early skills would assist him in pursuing a career as an economist. In 1959, Obama Sr. went to study at the University of Hawaii, where he stood out for his impeccable dress and his public speaking skills. A year after he enrolled at the University of Hawaii, he met Stanley Ann Dunham, a white seventeen-year-old girl who was originally from Kansas. After dating Obama for a short period, Dunham gave birth to Barack Obama Jr. on August 4, 1961, in Honolulu, Hawaii. Obama Sr. left a year later to attend Harvard University for a graduate fellowship in economics. In 1964, Dunham filed for divorce. Obama Sr. returned to Kenya, which had just gained its independence from England. He got a job in management with a private company and eventually worked in the public sector in Kenya. The last time the future president saw his father was when he was ten years old, when Obama Sr. returned to the United States in 1971. In 1982, Obama Sr. was killed in a car accident. He was forty-six years old at the time of his death.

Because he had a lighter skin tone, many tourists mistook him as a native Hawaiian. His grandparents were protective of young Barack and attempted to shield him from overt racism. Some people who did not know Barack's ethnicity or racial composition would make racist comments. Barack's grandparents gave a tongue-lashing to anyone treated him unfairly because of his African heritage and race. They were somewhat successful in safeguarding him from the effects of U.S. racism during the early part of his life in Hawaii.

Obama Sr. left Hawaii when his son was two years old. Barack felt a continual void in his life from his missing father. Like others who grow up missing a parent, he questioned why his father had left. He used stories of his father's exploits and artifacts to piece together memories of his father. On one occasion as teenager, Barack discovered a photograph accompanying an article in the local Hawaiian newspaper upon his father's graduation. Because he had no real sense of who his father truly was, he fixed his eyes and intently stared at the photograph and the article. In the photograph his father appeared poised, noble, and regal, as if he were an ambassador for the entire continent of Africa. In the article Obama Sr. issued a verbal reprimand to the University of Hawaii for not promoting cultural understanding and for some instances of overt discrimination on campus. In this article, Obama did not mention his son or his son's mother, and young Barack wondered why.

Reading became a passion for young Barack. Reading strengthened his imagination and became a foundational skill for the great orator he would become. Barack often looked at popular magazines. He thumbed through these magazines, looked at the photographs, and fantasized about the story before reading it. He liked being creative and dreaming about the things he saw in the photographs and read about in the articles.

On one of his father's extended visits to Hawaii, these tensions spilled over. Friction persisted between Obama Sr. and Ann Dunham. Obama Sr. had a domineering personality, and he made overbearing demands on his son and wife. One evening, young Barack turned on the television to watch the Christmas classic cartoon, *How the Grinch Stole Christmas*, and an impassioned argument ensued. His father claimed that young Barack had watched too much television and should go study. His mother attempted to explain it was almost Christmas vacation and the holiday animated movie was his favorite. The elder Obama insisted Barack should study, and if he had completed all of his current lessons, he should read ahead and prepare for lessons scheduled for after his holiday break. Young Barack went to his room and continued to watch television, but he could hear his grandparents, mother, and father arguing. His grandfather insisted it was his house and Obama had no right to come in and bully his grandson and everyone else. Obama insisted they were spoiling his son and not instilling discipline. The next day, Barack's mother attempted to explain that his father was not a bad person, but perhaps just a little too stubborn. These intermittent arguments continued throughout Obama's stay in Hawaii and would be a negative factor and a source of tension throughout the remainder of the Obamas' marital relationship. The couple officially divorced in 1964. Obama Sr. would go on to multiple marriages and have several children from these relationships. He was killed in an automobile accident in 1982.

At age six, Barack's mother married Lolo Soetoro, an Indonesia man, and the family moved to Indonesia in 1967. Lolo means "crazy" in Hawaiian. Some people in Barack's family thought this translation was hilarious. As a child, he attended schools operated by both Catholics and Muslims. Barack enrolled in St. Francis of Assisi Catholic School in Jakarta in 1968 but would later transfer to Besuki Public School. Barack lived in Indonesia until 1971. His life in Indonesia was quite different from the life he had known in Hawaii. Lolo's house was filled with exotic animals, and Lolo gave Barack an ape as a pet.

It took Barack about six months to learn the language of Indonesia and the country's customs. He made friends with people mostly from Indonesian's working class. Barack befriended children of farmers, servants, and low-level bureaucrats and connected with other children who enjoyed reading comic books. He tried his best to fit in with other children but was a little shy because of his U.S. accent, which became a source of laughter for other children, but he remained an easygoing child, which allowed him to make friends. He was physically bigger than most of the other children; he was overweight and was darker than the other children at his school.

Barack's food palate and taste buds changed while living in Indonesia. The cuisine of Indonesia was different from what he had experienced in the United States. In Indonesia, rice was a main course, the mainstay of the diet of most of the population of the country. Lolo taught Barack how to eat small raw chili peppers with rice. He was also introduced to dog, snake, and roasted grasshoppers as a part of some meals.

Barack frequently corresponded with his grandparents through letters, recording the events of his life so he could keep his grandparents abreast of his developments. He also hoped these letters would prompt his grandparents to send him U.S. food goodies such as chocolate and peanut butter. Barack's letters did not report all of the things he witnessed in Indonesia. He did not tell his grandparents about the great poverty or widespread illnesses he witnessed in Indonesia. He did not want them to worry about him and his mother.

Barack's mother made sure education remained a focal point in his life. She knew education was a passport to a better life for people of color. Therefore, she made sure he kept up on mastering the English language by

INDONESIA

"Indonesia is a part of me." These words were proclaimed by former U.S. president Barack Obama when he delivered his speech during the Fourth Congress of Indonesian Diaspora Network in Jakarta, Indonesia, in 2017. At age six, Obama moved to Indonesia with his mother and Indonesian stepfather, Lolo Soetoro, in 1967. The couple split up a few years later, and Barack Obama moved back to Hawaii at age ten to live with his grandparents. Obama maintains he has never forgotten the years he spent in Indonesia. Indonesia is the fourth most populated country in the world and the world's largest democracy. It also has the largest Muslim population in the world. This country is made up of a chain of islands between Asia and Australia. With Indonesia's current population growth, it is on course to overtake the United States and become the third largest country before 2044. Indonesia's people are diverse. There are more than three hundred languages spoken in Indonesia, and its landscape ranges from cosmopolitan urban cities to rural villages. Indonesia's capital city is Jakarta. The country consists of thirty-one provinces, one autonomous province, one special region, and one national capital district. In 2009, when Obama accepted the Nobel Peace Prize, a statue of a ten-year-old Barack Obama was commissioned and placed in Jakarta Park. On his 2017 trip to Indonesia, Obama was greeted by a crowd of thousands, including leaders, students, and business people.

waking him at five o'clock each morning to read and follow lessons. One morning in particular when Barack did not want to wake up and was reluctant to do his English lessons, his mother impressed upon him that getting up early was not easy for anyone and being diligent in his pursuit of education would be beneficial in the long run. Eventually, Barack would go and live with his grandparents in Hawaii. Lolo and Ann had a child. Maya Kasandra Soetoro, Barack's sister, was born on August 15, 1970. She spent several years with her brother in Indonesia and Hawaii, but they would later grow up in separate homes. After Ann and Lolo divorced in 1980, he remarried. Maya graduated from Punahou School in Honolulu, Hawaii, in 1988. As a testament to Ann's commitment to education of her children's individual success, Maya showed her intellectual prowess and received a bachelor of arts from Barnard College, a master of arts from New York University and a doctor of philosophy from the University of Hawaii at Manoa.

In 1971, Barack was sent to live with his grandparents in Hawaii. His mother was concerned about the level and quality of education her child was receiving in Indonesia. Because of their socioeconomic status and privilege, Barack's grandparents, Stanley and Madelyn, were able to use their connections to get Barack admitted to the prestigious Punahou

School. Punahou is a private preparatory school in Honolulu, Hawaii. Barack attended Punahou Prep School from fifth grade until he completed his high school education. While in high school, Barack's mother divorced Lolo and returned to Hawaii and began studying cultural anthropology. She later returned to Indonesia to conduct field research.

Barack developed a profound affection for basketball that continued through adulthood. His love for the sport is probably due to a gift of a basketball his father gave him as a child one Christmas. Basketball also became an escape from reality. Even with the example of his maternal grandfather Barack still sought African American men as role models. His grandfather took him to see a University of Hawaii basketball game. The Hawaii basketball team's five starting players were black. Barack was star struck by the players. After witnessing the team in action, he began to practice and play pickup games on a local recreational court. Eventually, he began to play with African American men on the courts at the University of Hawaii. On the court and under the tutelage of these men, Barack learned a few lessons. He learned about developing mental and physical toughness. He also learned how to play basketball with flair and swagger. Basketball soon became the sport that would garner his full attention. In high school, Barack was an average student because he was not living up to his full academic potential. He played on the school's basketball team and was nicknamed "O-Bomber" by some of his classmates. He benefitted from a multiplicity of cultures that he drew upon to aid in his personal development. Barack made the varsity basketball team as a left-handed backup forward. During his senior year, in 1979, Panahou High School defeated Moanalua High School to win the Hawaiian State Championship.

After a pickup game with some African American young men who had done a lot of trash talking during the game, one of his assistant basketball coaches used a racial epithet. The assistant coach muttered within the hearing distance of Barack and some of his other black teammates that they should not have lost to a bunch of "n******." In what might been bottled-up frustration from navigating his own racial identity, Barack confronted his coach. The coach erroneously tried to explain that there are "black people" and there are "n******." The passionate debate continued but ended when Barack called the coach ignorant and walked out of the gym.

His grandfather began to take Barack to the bars and watering holes he frequented, and he began to meet a wider range of individuals. Frank, one of his grandfather's drinking buddies, became somewhat of a mentor to Barack. Barack's grandparents had not interacted with many black people, so it was almost impossible for them to understand their plight. Barack learned the complexity of race in the United States from older African Americans living in Hawaii. For African Americans in the United States, understanding the norms of white people and society is a matter of survival. However, for many white people knowing the some of the intricacies of black culture is at best a diversion. Moreover, Barack found that his grandparents may have believed some of the negative stereotypes presumed about African Americans.

In one instance, his grandparents got into a heated argument because a panhandler approached his grandmother. His grandmother was afraid. Barack could not understand why his grandmother was afraid and why his grandfather was upset and why this incident caused such a disruption. The panhandler was a black man. He was stunned that his grandparents could harbor such racist sentiments and a deep-seated fear of black people. After a while, Frank began discussing racism and other racial issues with Barack. Through these candid conversations, Frank began to show Barack the nuances and complexities associated with race in United States. Since his grandparents were raising him, they could not share the same perspective and insight as Frank could about how to be a black man. Frank was also a poet and would share some of his poetry at their drinking sessions.

Barack began to hang out with other African American boys and older men. He learned about soul music and artists like Stevie Wonder, Marvin Gaye, and Earth, Wind, and Fire. The men and boys with whom he developed a comradery and a connection with seemed to be angry with all white people because of the racial injustices and the treatment of African Americans in the United States. Some of the injustices and racial slights were real and some were perceived. Whether the injustices were real or perceived, they caused conflict within Barack. How could he dislike all white people? His mother was white and his grandparents were white. He could not bring himself to dislike white people. His mother and grandparents had set an example of being accepting of people of all racial and cultural identities.

In high school, he began to read books by African American authors, including Langston Hughes, Richard Wright, and Malcolm X. Barack concluded that only Malcolm X left solutions to reconciliation between black people and white people. Malcolm X's works appealed to him because they offered Malcolm's perpetual re-creation of himself and his image. He also liked that Malcolm was able to eventually reconcile the fact that whites could live beside him as brothers in Islam. This gave Barack hope that blacks and whites could reconcile their racial differences.

In high school, Barack and his friends often commiserated over how Hawaiian girls preferred not to date black boys. Through his network of college friends, Barack kept up with the happenings at the University of Hawaii and where the "black" parties were being held. Their conversations also encompassed the racism they experienced on the island. They discussed their perceptions that their coaches were slighting them because they felt pressure to have to play white players even if they were not as good as the black players. Barack conceded that part of the problem was there were not many African American females in Hawaii and that made it more difficult, but he did not hold that all girls on the island were racist. He even noted that some girls may have just wanted someone who looked like their fathers or brothers. As for the coaches, Barack stated that it may have been a clash of cultures, the black athletes' style clashing with the coaches' style of play. Attempting to be the voice of reason in the conversation, Barack urged his friend to be introspective and suggested that his friend might not have been getting playing time because he was a smart-aleck. Barack did not have all of the answers during these discussions on racial matters, but he did note that it was very complicated and there were not any simple solutions. Barack struggled trying to find himself and to function as a black man in America and to understand what that truly meant.

Throughout his time in high school, Barack was bright but was not living up to his full intellectual potential. Barack's mother, an academic, challenged him. She confronted him about his attitude and the lack of preparation for his future. After high school, he did not have a particular university in mind to attend. He chose to attend Occidental College mainly because he had met a young woman from Brentwood, a high income suburb on the west side of California, who was student at the college while she was vacationing in Hawaii.

One of his grandfather's friends asked what he expected to get out of college. Barack did not really know why he was going to college. This seemed to anger his grandfather's friend, because he believed that the universities miseducated African Americans by making them ashamed of their heritage and the race.

> They want to leave your race at the door. They train you to want what you do not need. They will train you to forget what you already know. They train you to manipulate your words so you don't know what anything means anymore. They tell you about equal opportunity and the American way. They will give you a corner office and invite you to fancy dinners. They will tell you that you are a credit to your race, until you actually want to start running things, and then they will yank your chain and let you know that you are a well-trained, well-paid n*****. (Obama, *Dreams*, 2004, p. 97)

The gentleman was not trying to persuade Barack not to go to college, but he was telling him to keep his eyes open and stay conscious to issues affecting black people. Staying conscious would be easier said than done.

2

Undergraduate Student

Barack Obama studied at Occidental College in Los Angeles, California, from the fall of 1979 through the spring of 1981. In 1981, he transferred to Columbia University in New York. Occidental College is a liberal arts college founded in 1887, one of the oldest liberal arts colleges on the West Coast. It is the home of one of the first chapters of Phi Beta Kappa and one of the original campuses where Upward Bound got its start. The school is deeply rooted in high academic achievement and community service. About thirty-two students from his high school graduating class attended schools in the Los Angeles, California, area. Four of his classmates from high school joined him at Occidental College.

When Barack Obama arrived at Occidental, it reminded him of Punahou, but it was nonetheless unsettling. His time at Occidental College was significant in his development, a time of discovery. He explored and worked through the complexities of his cultural identity. Obama's residence was a collection of people from all walks of life. Obama represented a bit of all of the groups, and this contributed to his ability to relate and get along with everyone who lived in the residence hall. Obama moved in with two roommates: Paul Carpenter, a white student from Southern California, and Hasan Chandoo, a Pakistani who grew up in London. Obama and his roommates were all approximately the same height, about six feet, one inch, and about the same weight, 160 to 170 pounds. They called each other by their last names. During Obama's time at Occidental College, he began to take his studies more seriously. Occidental was where he first began to experience a transformational call and to believe there was a specific purpose and destiny for his life.

There were people from various social economic backgrounds, races, and ethnic groups. Most of the college classmates thought Obama was cool and collected and had everything together. He was laid-back, a smooth operator, but it was an act because of turmoil about his identity. Because he loved playing basketball, most of his friends could not believe he was an avid smoker. He jokingly stated he smoked cigarettes to keep his weight down and he would quit when he got married because it would be okay to pick up weight when you get married (Maraniss 2012, p. 345). Obama was somewhat health conscious, so he took up jogging. Although he did not play on the basketball team at Occidental, he regularly played pickup games of students against faculty members. He would continue to play pickup games even as he served as president of the United States.

At Occidental College, Obama was quiet during class discussions, but this would change significantly by the time he reached Harvard Law School, where he was verbose and expressive. When he did speak in his undergraduate classes, his remarks were thoughtful. Intellectually, Obama could tangle with some of the upperclassmen in debates and made his points in a logical and intellectual way. These skills were unusual for an undergraduate student. He seemed to have a natural talent inherited from his parents—or perhaps from the hours young Barack spent reading and engaging in imaginative thinking. His eclectic childhood, international travel, and life abroad provided him with maturity and a better worldview than a lot of undergraduate students.

During Obama's undergraduate academic studies, he would work hard for a stretch and then play hard. He was laid-back in his approach to life, which bled into his academic studies. He would often wait until just a day or two prior to deadlines to finish his papers, but he still managed to make good grades. Obama was a talented undergraduate student but put in minimum effort on his assignments.

Many of Obama's newly minted professors had participated in the antiwar and civil rights movements of the 1960s and 1970s. These sentiments and philosophies spilled over into their teaching, which most likely influenced Obama. At Occidental College, professors had an unmistakable learning philosophy: listen, analyze, and decide. This philosophy affirmed Obama's natural learning methods and sharpened the skills used in his professional life. Obama connected to students who looked lonely or were considered misfits.

Because of his dad's position with the Kenyan government and his mother's insistence he keep up with these issues, Obama knew African politics and African political leaders. He struck up friendships with some

African students. Obama studied and tutored some of them in his political science classes. The African students developed a kinship with Obama, and they began to call him their brother. He confided in the African students how much he wanted to visit his father's homeland and discover his father's roots and learn more about him and thus learn more about himself.

After Obama's first year of school, he moved into a small two-bedroom apartment with Hasan Chandoo. Chandoo, in his senior year, was three years older than Obama, but Obama was probably the more mature and serious student. Chandoo's family owned a shipping enterprise. He and Obama were not living a luxurious lifestyle as college students, but they made time for fun by throwing parties and listening to music. Obama never ate much; he usually ate cereal for meals. Obama and Chandoo would refer to each other as brothers.

In his undergraduate studies, Obama constructed a persona to keep from being viewed as a sellout. Even with this constructed persona, some African American students questioned the authenticity of his blackness and whether he supported black causes, identified culturally as black, or socialized with other black people. Many of the African American students viewed Obama's history and narrative as different from their own and from the experience of most black Americans and therefore either did not consider him black, or at least not black enough. When he initially began his political career, he would face these sentiments again from some members of the African American community, who believed he was not black enough to represent them.

There were very few black students at Occidental, so they easily identified each other and bonded. The black students at Occidental were either working class or middle class, but few had a multicultural perspective like Obama's. He did not have a neocon black-nationalist view of the world; he believed blacks should not exclude white people but engage with all individuals regardless of their race. He was not antiwhite. Some students referred to him as the "Oreo," but there was a loose bond among black students to the extent that they exchanged hellos and passing glances on campus. Some of his classmates considered Obama a "floater" who moved fluidly from social group to social group and from political group to political group but never showed a full allegiance to any one group (Maraniss 2012, p. 376).

The black students at Occidental College functioned as a tiny tribe; they lived relatively close to each other and were usually communal in their interactions. When they traveled on campus, rarely did they travel alone but moved about campus in groups of twos, threes, or more. During his freshman year, Barack Obama lived in the campus residence halls. Like many of those he had had with his friends in Hawaii, discussions centered on race and racism. The complaints and perceived slights were the same.

Although many were weary of race being the dominant theme of their communal discussions, that always seemed to be the case. When pressed by fellow black students about his upbringing, he would try to avoid those conversations because he did not grow up in the predominately black cities like Compton or Watts. Some students at Occidental seemed to not want to be viewed or labeled as black; they preferred to be called biracial or multiracial. These students did not want to have to choose. Barack noticed that some students talked about embracing all of the multiracial makeup while avoiding being classified or identified as black. Moreover, these individuals avoided interacting with black people. Barack wanted to embrace multiculturalism and interact with people from various backgrounds and racial and cultural identities, but he did not want to be viewed as a sellout. He began hanging around students who were more Afrocentric in their dealings. The grandfather of one of the most conscious students was a Garveyite, and his older sister was a member of the Black Panther Party. Barack did not exactly feel comfortable around the student because unlike this student, he could not trace his family lineage to any of the United States' great black social movements. During his sophomore year, he enrolled in political science courses and had conversations with campus political activists. Obama joined Occidental's activist network—shades of his father's involvement as a student at the University of Hawaii.

According to his book *Dreams from My Father*, he consciously chose to begin to use his given name after a conversation with a politically conscious woman. She convinced him that his given name, Barack, was a beautiful name and that he should no longer go by his nickname, Barry.

He was an intelligent and serious student and a good athlete. Obama not only bonded with the black students on campus but also forged relationships with Latino, white, and international students.

Politics had taken an unyielding hold on Barack Obama. His eclectic array of friends and political leanings are evident through his involvement with groups of Marxist professors, structural feminists, and punk-rock poets. He was active in many social and political groups including a group that pushed for U.S. corporations to divest from South Africa during the apartheid movement of the 1980s.

During his sophomore year, he was nominated for the prestigious, competitive Truman Scholarship. The award was founded in 1975 and named for the thirty-third U.S. president, Harry S. Truman. It is given to students who desire a career in public service and leadership. Obama was not selected for the Truman Scholarship. This now seems stunning given his life of public service and becoming the first African American president of the United States.

Obama's life experiences provided him with the ability to connect across economic, racial, and cultural divides. They informed his outlook

EARTH, WIND, AND FIRE

The musical group Earth, Wind, and Fire has sold over 100 million albums worldwide. The group fused a combination of jazz, soul, funk, and R&B to create a distinct musical sound. The group was founded in 1969 when Maurice White, Wade Flemons, and Don Whitehead collaborated as a songwriting team composing songs and commercials in the Chicago area. During these collaborations, they created a band, and when Maurice White relocated to Los Angeles, California, he renamed the band after looking at an astrological chart and incorporating the astrological elements for Earth, Wind, and Fire. In addition to White, Flemons, and Whitehead, Maurice recruited Michael Beal on guitar, Leslie Drayton, Chester Washington, and Alex Thomas on horns, Sherry Scott on vocals, percussionist Phillard Williams, Philip Bailey on drums and vocals, and his younger brother Verdine on bass.

In 1971, the band released its first album and got to number 24 on the soul charts. In 1973, the group reached new heights with its album release *Head to the Sky*. Though the group has a number of memorable hits, some of the most memorable are "Shining Star," "Boogie Wonderland," "After Love Is Gone," "September," "Serpentine Fire," "Reasons," "That's the Way of the World," and "Let's Groove Tonight." Barack Obama listed Earth, Wind, and Fire as one of his favorite music groups. In 2009, the group was celebrating its fortieth anniversary and in February 2009, Earth, Wind, and Fire performed in the East Room of the White House. Like many baby boomers, Obama grew up listening to the band's popular tunes as the soundtrack of their lives. Along with Stevie Wonder's song, "Signed, Sealed, Delivered," various Earth, Wind, and Fire tunes could be heard at many of Obama's presidential campaign events. When founding member Maurice White died in 2016, Obama stated, "With his brothers and bandmates of Earth, Wind and Fire, Maurice fused jazz, soul, funk and R&B into a quintessentially American sound that captured millions of fans around the world. Their playlist is timeless, the one that still brings us together at birthdays and barbecues, weddings and family reunions."

on life as a citizen of the world. His preferences in music also exhibited his eclectic predilections and his ability to appreciate various genres. His musical tastes ranged from soul music, blues, and classical to rock and roll. He listened to the music of Earth, Wind, and Fire, Billie Holiday, and Jimi Hendrix, to name a few. While at Occidental, Obama wore hats cocked to the side as a fashion accessory. While he believed a cocked hat gave him flair, it symbolized his desire be noticed and to be cool.

While he sought attention through hats, his interest in politics continued to grow, and his political acumen began to develop. It was further refined at Columbia University and Harvard Law School, where he began to develop his political chops. He developed an exceptional listening ear and discovered an uncanny ability to read people. It was here that he learned to adjust his playbook according to what the situation called for. This ability allowed him to move seamlessly from one group to another, backing this cause or that cause. His intellectual curiosity and his ability to accommodate various people and situations allowed him to show interest and express his preference to work behind the scenes of the causes he supported. He also worked with the Student Coalition at Occidental College, who were pushing to get the college's board of trustees to divest all of the university's holdings in companies who had business relationships and work with South Africa.

During Black History Month of 1981, he gave one of his first public speeches as a part of a skit. It was a speech about the imprisonment of Nelson Mandela. The speech was part theater and part political speech. Students dressed as police were supposed to take Obama away toward the conclusion of the speech, symbolizing the establishment attempting to stamp out the struggle for freedom in South Africa and the United States. Obama launched into the speech in the cadence and rhythm of Martin Luther King Jr. His emotions poured into the speech, and he appeared to channel a charismatic evangelist. The audience enthusiastically responded to the speech, and it exceeded the expectations of those who had asked him to participate in the protest. For days and weeks, he received compliments on his speech. Obama experienced what it is like to move and motivate an audience through the craft of public speaking and his own words. It allowed him to control his rage and to not react to his bottled-up anger. Obama contemplated the perception of black anger. In his book, *Dreams from My Father*, Obama wrote,

> At best, these things were a refuge; at worst a trap. Following this maddening logic, the only thing you could choose as your own withdrawal into a smaller and smaller coil of rage, until being black meant only the knowledge of your own powerlessness, of your own defeat. And the final irony: Should you refuse this defeat and lash out at your captors, they would have a name for that too, a name that could cage you just as Paranoid, Militant, Violent. N*****. (*Dreams*, 2004, p. 85)

While at Occidental, Obama wrote short fiction and poetry for a literary magazine called the *Feast*. The *Feast* was sponsored by the Department of English and was published semiannually. Two of Obama's poems appeared in the semiannual *Feast*. This was where he first began to use his given name, Barack, on the works published in the magazine.

At the end of his sophomore year, many of Obama's close friends were graduating and moving on from Occidental College. Some were moving to new international destinations; others were starting graduate or professional school at Ivy League institutions. Obama decided to transfer to another university. He reasoned that he needed more; Occidental did not have many black professors and mentors, and an Ivy League institution's brand was recognizable and well respected internationally. His time at Occidental had seemed like an extension of his high school experiences. Desiring to be engaged in the black American experience on a deeper level, Obama relocated to New York City and transferred to Columbia University to complete his undergraduate studies.

Columbia is an elite academic institution, founded as King's College by royal charter of King George II of England. Columbia University is the fifth oldest college in the United States. Obama sought the prestige of an Ivy League university just as his father had when he chose Harvard University several decades earlier.

The decision to transfer to Columbia University did not come lightly and there may have been a tinge of regret about the move. He was twenty years old and classified as a junior when he transferred during the fall of 1981. Obama did not have a real connection to his new college home. He was a political science major with a concentration in international relations. Columbia was an epicenter for discussion of foreign policy and featured faculty like Zbigniew Brzezinski, a former national security adviser, and Zalmay Khalilzad, a U.S. ambassador to the United Nations. Michael L. Baron was Obama's thesis adviser and wrote him a recommendation for law school. Baron recalled Obama as intelligent, thoughtful, and one of the best two students in the class (Scott, October 30, 2007). Obama wrote his thesis on Soviet nuclear disarmament. Though Obama was intelligent, Baron never could imagine that Obama would become the president of the United States. Because of his maturity and the gravity of his conversation, some students assumed that Obama was a graduate student at Columbia. Obama graduated from Columbia University but opted out of participating in the commencement exercises.

While the years in New York were pivotal, Obama also felt isolated there. He struggled to unearth his true self. He was lonely, and he often passed time contemplating how to right the wrongs of the world. He also felt disconnected from his friends and family during this time. He felt he lacked religious structure and the family support needed to feel secure. To steady himself, he became an avid runner and found solace in reading African American classic literature. He began reading the black literary classic *The Invisible Man*, by Ralph Ellison, which was published in 1952 and centers on social and intellectual issues of the early twentieth century. The book explores themes of black national identity, blacks and Marxism, and reformist racial policies. Obama's autobiography, *Dreams from My Father*, appears to be slightly modeled after the literary structure of *The Invisible Man*, and some characters in the book may be based on composites of individuals. Some of Obama's friends remembered him carrying around a frayed copy of the book for two or three months, whipping it out

MALCOLM X AND *THE AUTOBIOGRAPHY OF MALCOLM X*

Malcolm X was a U.S. Muslim minister and human rights activist. He was a fearless advocate for the rights of African Americans. He was born Malcolm Little in Omaha, Nebraska, in 1925. Earl Little, Malcolm's father, was an outspoken Baptist minister who supported Black Nationalist leader Marcus Garvey. Malcolm's father received numerous death threats because of his outspokenness. Malcolm's father was killed under suspicious circumstances when he was hit by a streetcar in Lansing, Michigan, in 1929. Some people suspect his father was killed by white supremacists because of his outspoken advocacy against racist behavior and white supremacy. The local police ruled Malcolm's father's death a suicide. Malcolm's mother had an emotional breakdown after the death of her husband and was later institutionalized at a mental health facility. In 1946, Malcolm X was convicted of burglary and spent just over six years in prison. While in prison, he converted to Islam and the Nation of Islam. Upon leaving prison in 1952, Malcolm attended the local Nation of Islam mosque and actively sought out new converts. He quickly became a favorite of the leader of the Nation of Islam, Elijah Muhammad, who promoted him to minister prior to dispatching him to Boston and Philadelphia to establish new mosques.

In 1963, Malcolm's relationship with Elijah Muhammad was seriously fractured. Muhammad suspended him for publically commenting on President John F. Kennedy's assassination when he stated it was a case of the "chickens coming home to roost." The following year, Malcolm announced his split from the Nation of Islam, converted to traditional Islam, and took on the name El-Hajj Malik El-Shabazz. *The Autobiography of Malcolm X* was published in 1965. Malcolm X and writer Alex Haley collaborated to write this work through a series of in-depth interviews recorded between 1963 and 1965. Malcolm X was assassinated on February 21, 1965, at the Audubon Ball Room in upper Harlem, New York. Thomas Hagan, one of the gunmen, was wounded at the Audubon Ballroom where Malcolm X was assassinated. Hagan was beaten by the crowd before police arrived. The police who took Hagan into custody stated Hagan had a pistol with four unused bullets. Witnesses at the scene identified Nation of Islam members as the gunmen, but Hagan refused to confirm the identities of the other gunmen. All three men were convicted in March 1966 and sentenced to life in prison. Thomas 13X Johnson and Norman 3X Butler maintained their innocence. *The Autobiography of Malcolm X* has become a classic and essential reading for high school students. Barack Obama discussed the impact of Malcolm X's autobiography on his life and identity in, *Dreams from My Father.*

and reading it during periods of inactivity. This was an intense period where Obama was struggling with issues of his self-identity.

During his time at Columbia University, he decided to stop dabbling with marijuana. He would consciously identify and embrace his blackness but continue to rise above the divide of cultural, racial, and societal margins. He also moved toward embracing universal truths and moral precepts as a method of gaining stability.

While at Columbia, Obama's father was killed in a car accident in 1982. Barack's Aunt Jane telephoned from Nairobi, Kenya, and told him about the death. He called his mother, who wailed upon hearing the news. He also called a half brother in Boston. This conversation was awkward, and Barack soon hung up. He believed Barack Obama Sr. was a misunderstood man. His father's death did conjure up thoughts of Kenya, his father's homeland. He wanted to visit and get acquainted with his family in Kenya. He wrote a letter of condolences to his family in Kenya; however, he did not attend his father's funeral.

Obama did not attend his undergraduate commencement exercises. After graduating in 1983, he had hoped to get hired by civil rights organizations or as a staffer for African American elected officials. He was unsuccessful in securing long-term employment, so he took a series of temporary management jobs, during which he learned something valuable. One such job was with the New York City Fire Department, managing entry-level and temporary low-level workers. He noticed that managers and workers did not converse on a personal or intimate level. There seemed to be a wall of separation between the two groups. Most of the managers were white,

---

STANLEY AND MADELYN DUNHAM

Stanley and Madelyn Dunham were a white couple from the Midwest who settled in Honolulu, Hawaii. They were Barack Obama's maternal grandparents. For a time, they were the primary caregivers for their grandson, Barack Obama. Obama grew up in Hawaii with his grandparents Stanley Dunham, a furniture salesman, and Madelyn Dunham, who worked in a bank. The Dunhams were married against the wishes of Madelyn's parents. In several speeches during Obama's presidential run, he often talked about his grandparents. He shared stories about his grandfather's enlisting after Pearl Harbor and his grandmother's work at a bomb assembly line making B-29 bombers during the war. He also talked about after the war how his grandparents studied on the GI Bill and bought a house through a government assistance program. Stanley Dunham died in 1992.

When Obama launched his presidential campaign, Madelyn Dunham was too frail to travel but she kept up with her grandson's campaign through the media in Hawaii. At age 86, Madelyn died on November 2, 2008, just two days before Obama was elected President of United States. Obama learned of her death while campaigning in Jacksonville, Florida. Obama acknowledged in his acceptance speech at the Democratic National Convention that his grandmother and grandfather were the rock on which his character and future were built.

and most of the workers were African Americans and Latinos. And this may have caused the divide. Obama felt drawn to converse with the workers. Perhaps he felt more comfortable around the workers than he did with management.

During his time in New York, Obama was also employed at Business International as a junior employee doing research and writing reports. When not at work, Obama became a solitary wanderer searching for his purpose. He later found work at the New York Public Interest Research Group, a nonprofit organization that promotes consumer, environmental, and government reform. His assignment was at City College in Harlem, and his salary was a mere $10,000 for mobilizing student volunteers. He spent his time attempting to convince minority students to recycle and worked on other kitchen table issues like mass transit, tuition, and financial aid. As he busied himself working in New York City, he still longed for a connection to a place, to something that would connect to the world of his father, which he still knew very little about.

During his time in New York, Obama connected with his sister, Auma, in 1988. He was in search of his roots and decided on a visit to Kenya to connect with his father's side of the family. He flew into Nairobi's Kenyatta International Airport and was picked up by his sister, Auma Obama. Auma was the daughter from Obama's father's marriage to Kezia. Auma drove a Volkswagen Beetle that was operable but badly in need of repair. In his book, *Dreams from My Father*, he gave a vivid description of the car. "Unfortunately, the engine had come down with a tubercular knock and the muffler had fallen off on the way to the airport. As we sputtered out onto a four lane highway, Auma clutching the steering wheel with both hands, I couldn't keep from laughing" (p. 306).

Auma Obama has also become successful. She earned a doctorate at Bayreuth University in 1996 and had earned a master's degree in Heidelberg, Germany, in 1987. She attended the German Film and Television Academy in Berlin, Germany, and helped operate a NGOI called Sauti Kuu Foundation, which provides assistance to orphans and those struggling with poverty. Obama would return to Kenya in 2006 as a U.S. Senator, and while as president of the United States in 2009 and 2013.

Obama developed a relationship with his sister, and this helped him to unite and become familiar with his father's side of his family, giving him a connection to his heritage and the continent of Africa. During this period of Obama's life, he was still seeking his self-identity. During his college years, some people characterized Obama as introverted and sometimes eccentric, perhaps due to his search for his self-identity. He would become the first African American president of the United States and the first president with an undergraduate degree from Columbia University.

3

Community Organizer

While Obama was introduced to organizing in New York at City College, he was indoctrinated in the world of community organizing when he moved to Chicago, Illinois. In 1985, Barack Obama moved there for employment opportunities and landed a job as a community organizer. He found himself concerned and fascinated by all of the problems that plagued inner-city Chicago. He was also intrigued by the inner workings of city politics of his new city. He worked as a grassroots community organizer for three years. It was in Chicago where Obama gained a real sense of community for the first time. In addition to having a sense of family, he discovered how the political machines work in Chicago. Ultimately, Obama fell in love with the city of Chicago.

Community organizing involves motivating a specific group of people to take collective and direct action to change a particular policy or policy action of an administrative body. This administrative body may be any level of government, a corporation, or nonprofit entity. Saul Alinsky is credited with developing the modern playbook for community organizing. Most of his organizing efforts were aimed at helping the working poor and improving the conditions of those living in poverty. Alinsky stepped into the labor movement by organizing Chicago stockyard workers, and his organizing efforts expanded and included efforts organizing poor communities in California and New York.

His book, *Rules for Radicals: A Pragmatic Primer for Realistic Radicals*, was published in 1971. This seminal work provides a textbook of strategies that can be applied in large-scale community organizing. Alinsky aimed to steer people he organized toward confrontation. He urged them to tackle little issues and after the organizer had gained the group's confidence, then challenge bigger issues. The ultimate goal was to teach organizers how to strategize and encourage people to advocate and take actions on their own and on behalf of their own community cause.

Obama took to heart and applied Alinsky's key principles of meticulously planning for meetings with power brokers and allowing residents to be in the forefront while the organizer took a background presence. With his disposition, he found direct confrontation difficult and hell-raising uncomfortable. Obama believed that his time as a community organizer qualified him to become president of the United States. It certainly made him a great campaigner and would be a great skill when he became president. He worked as a community organizer from 1985 until 1988, when he decided to attend law school at Harvard University.

Gerald Kellman, a veteran organizer who was originally from New York, had been working in blue-collar neighborhoods of all ethnic groups. Kellman began organizing in the 1960s when he advocated for laid-off factory workers on the far South Side of Chicago. Kellman organized many workers in the Wisconsin area and in the Chicago area, especially around the Altgeld Gardens housing projects and the Roseland neighborhood. The majority of the residents of these two places were African American. Kellman and the other white organizers found it difficult working in these communities because the residents did not trust them because they were white. Kellman needed an African American organizer to overcome the coldness shown to their organizing efforts. He was specifically looking for someone who had the ability to organize in the African American community and connect with the African American neighborhoods in Chicago.

Kellman ran an employment advertisement, and Obama responded. Obama did not indicate on his application that he was African American. After a brief telephone conversation, Kellman hired Obama, and though he did not know much about community organizing, he accepted the job. Initially, Kellman did not realize Obama was African American. At some point during the telephone conversation, he came to this realization, but it did not matter because he had determined Obama was intelligent and engaging and genuinely interested in social issues (Maraniss 2012, p. 508). Barack Obama impressed the board members with his intellect and maturity, although he was only twenty-four years old. His starting salary was a paltry thirteen thousand dollars, with another two thousand dollars thrown in as an allowance for his beat-up car (Moberg 2007). Kellman hired Obama to organize for the Developing Communities Project (DCP), based in communities on the far South Side of Chicago. At his first organizing meeting, held at St. Helena Catholic Church, many who attended thought it was strange that a man so young would be interested in helping them.

Obama organized and focused mainly on poverty and economic opportunities for residents of the African American communities of Altgeld Gardens and Roseland (Judis 2008). Altgeld Gardens is a part of the Chicago Housing Authority. It consisted of just under two thousand units built in 1945. The federal government had built apartments as a place to house African American military veterans after World War II, making it one of the first housing projects in the United States. The housing project is named after John Peter Altgeld, a former governor of Illinois.

Altgeld Gardens was plagued by poverty, drug violence, and turf wars. The housing project was surrounded by landfills, a sewage treatment plant, and the Calumet River, which had a history of environmental problems. Residents affectionately called this neighborhood "The Gardens," and it was situated in the middle of a food desert, without any close proximately to a grocery store. When Obama became president, he had firsthand knowledge of the issues plaguing the poor because of his experience organizing in these poor communities.

Obama's other primary area to organize was Roseland. The Roseland neighborhood is also located on the far South Side of Chicago. It was a poverty-stricken area and one of the most dangerous areas in the city. The neighborhood had declined from its beginnings as a middle-class neighborhood. During his presidential run, Obama recalled how his time in Roseland shaped his views and values. Roseland began as a Dutch community during the 1840s, the name taken from the beautiful flowers that had sprung up in this area. The Pullman Land Association created a larger community through the 1920s and 1930s. Between 1965 and 1975, the racial demographics of Roseland changed (Thomas 2006). As factories moved out and inflation increased, poverty gripped the area. By the mid-1980s, Roseland had receded into steep economic decline (Thomas 2006). Roseland continues to struggle to recover from the many years of economic decline. Obama's job was to help the people in these deprived areas to regain resources that had eluded them.

Obama did not have any real connections to these predominately African American communities, so he had to decide on the best method to ease the residents' skepticism and gain their trust. Obama conducted one-on-one interviews to assess the needs of the residents, find their important issues, and then prioritize those issues. Obama realized he needed to build relationships with community leaders and church pastors if he was to make inroads within the communities. Obama wanted to build a wide alliance of churches in the Chicago. Having a nonreligious, secular upbringing, Obama was hampered in making inroads with African American churches because he was not a member of any church. Many of the pastors openly asked if him if he was a member of a church.

In most large cities, there is a strong network of African American churches whose congregations work together on various causes. They also share worship services and other programs. To gain entry into this network, oftentimes a pastor must endorse or vouch for a person unknown to this community. When Obama replied he was not a member of a particular church, it made pastors more reluctant to encourage members to participate in his community organizing efforts. Many of the pastors he met gave him the sage advice "to find a church home" (Obama, *Dreams*, 2004, pp. 273–74). Church membership would help him succeed as an organizer. After visiting several churches, Obama became a member of the Trinity United Church of Christ; its pastor was Rev. Dr. Jeremiah A. Wright Jr.

Trinity United Church of Christ was founded in December 1961 with a congregation committed to black liberation theology and social justice. Trinity was formed after the merger of the Congregational Christian, Evangelical, and Reformed denominations to form the United Church of Christ in 1952. Trinity United was the first predominately black United Church of Christ in the Illinois region. In 1972, Dr. Jeremiah Wright became pastor, its third since the church's founding (New Megachurches 2001, 148–60). Wright sought to build a congregation that was God-conscious, self-conscious, and mission-conscious. According the church's history, under Dr. Wright's leadership, the church grew from 87 members in 1972 to more than 8,000 members in 2008. Like many others, Obama was drawn to the spirited preaching of Dr. Wright and the black liberation theology that Dr. Wright prescribed in his sermons. Obama became a member of Trinity United Church but resigned in 2008, when controversy ensued after a sermon Wright had preached was circulated online. Dr. Wright had claimed that Hillary Clinton, Obama's Democratic Party opponent, was a member of the white establishment. In another sermon Dr. Wright said, "God damn America . . . for killing innocent people" (Politico Staff 2008). The comments from these sermons made some people uncomfortable and provided political fodder for white conservative talk radio. In a statement, Obama affirmed he vehemently disagreed with the comments made in Dr. Wright's sermon. He stated he had not heard any hate speech or racist rhetoric during his time as a member of Trinity United. Pastor Wright retired from Trinity in 2008.

Barack Obama is credited with organizing people who were initially skeptical but coalesced around his incredible organizing ability and oratory skills. Most of the people in the communities Obama organized believed that he was hardworking, trustworthy, dedicated, diligent, intelligent, confident, and a humble person. He helped win employment training, playgrounds, and other public services for the communities assigned to him.

Obama organized the community to have asbestos removed from the apartments of Altgeld Gardens. Asbestos can cause lung cancer and mesothelioma. Initially, the officials lied about asbestos being in their apartments, and later they attempted to delay the removal of the hazardous material. Long-time resident of Altgeld Gardens, Hazel Johnson, and several other women helped Obama gain a foothold in the community. Johnson had been documenting residents' health problems since her husband's death in 1969. She did much of the work of pushing for cleanup of hazardous building materials (Trice 2010). Johnson and Obama would strategize at her kitchen table, and the two made a formidable team. Obama's most significant achievements as a community organizer were the expansion of Chicago's summer job program and asbestos removal from the area's oldest housing projects. During his time as a community organizer, Obama realized there was more to life than making money but that community organizing could not solve all of society's problem and social ills.

In community organizing, he found his life's calling in public service. He developed lifelong relationships, discovered his political identity, and found a church home. He learned many political strategies and tools by watching Chicago's first African American mayor, Harold Washington, during the 1980s. He learned how to develop a cogent and coherent campaign message and the importance of storytelling to move people. Obama returned to visit Altgeld Gardens while on the campaign trail in 2008. He had throngs of news crews and journalists with him. He visited a local school and took pictures with young students. He promised he would return for a follow-up visit, but disappointed many residents of the "Gardens" when he failed to return during his eight years as president. In 2015, the Chicago Housing Authority had planned to demolish several crumbling units in Altgeld Gardens, even though some residents opposed the move. As evidence of the economic depravity of this community during Obama's visit, the lone remaining business in this community was a liquor store.

Obama believed he had reached his career ceiling as a community organizer. He was restless and decided to attend law school. His years as a grassroots organizer were an education of a lifetime and good preparation for political campaigning. He has stated that it was more salient than anything that learned at Harvard Law School. He displayed the lessons and skills learned as a community organizer during his presidential campaign. Obama kept connected to the Developing Communities Project and even worked out of their office building when he organized a voter registration drive in 1992. During the 2008 Republican Party convention in St. Paul, Minnesota, Sarah Palin, governor of Alaska and Republican vice presidential

---

HAROLD WASHINGTON

Harold Washington only met Barack Obama once, but Washington was a major influence on the future president's political life. If Harold Washington had never been mayor of Chicago, it is possible Barack Obama would not have been president of the United States. After Obama completed his undergraduate degree at Columbia University in New York, he was looking to advance his career and embrace his identity as a black man.

Obama desired to live and work in Chicago, Illinois, because it was a city where African Americans appeared to have charge of their own political destiny. This was due in part to the election of Harold Washington as mayor of Chicago. During the 1980s, Harold Washington was the most prominent black elected official in America. When looking for a job in the public sector, Obama wrote a letter to the city government of Chicago inquiring about any employment vacancies. No one responded to his inquiry but when he saw an employment advertisement for a community organizer in Chicago, he did not hesitate to apply for the position in part because he wanted to live in Chicago. Years later while accepting the Congressional Black Caucus's Harold Washington Award, Obama stated, "I originally moved to Chicago in part because of the inspiration of Mayor Washington's campaign."

When the Developing Communities Project, for which Obama worked, persuaded the city to open an employment training office on Michigan Avenue in Roseland, Washington attended the dedication of the office, and Obama got the opportunity to shake hands with and greet his political idol. Washington's mayoral administration showed it was possible for an African American politician to get elected and govern effectively. As a result of Washington's political success in Chicago, the city was seen as a place where a young black politician could be ambitious and pursue his dreams. In 1995, when Barack Obama began his political career, he wanted to follow in Washington's political pathway. Obama had the blueprint all laid out. First, he was going to run for the general assembly, where Washington served from 1965 to 1980. Second, he would run for Congress. Lastly, he would become the mayor of Chicago. Barack Obama's first foray into politics was "Project VOTE!" This organization sponsored a voter registration drive that aimed to add 150,000 blacks to the rolls in 1992. The registration drive was modeled on the voter registration drive that led to Washington's election as mayor of Chicago. This drive also assisted Carol Moseley Braun to be elected as the first African American woman to the U.S. Senate in 1992.

---

nominee, used a national platform to respond to Democratic operatives who questioned her qualifications as a small town mayor as a legitimate credential to run the country. Palin retorted by taking a shot at Obama's qualifications as an organizer: "I guess a small-town mayor is sort of like a community organizer . . . except that you have actual responsibilities" (Weeks 2008). Palin's retort was effective. Despite his experience as an

Illinois state legislator and a U.S. senator, it forced Obama to defend against Palin's verbal jab and showcase his qualifications for the highest office in the land.

During Barack Obama's time in Chicago, he continued to develop his political chops by observing the inner workings of the city of Chicago and Illinois state politics. In many ways, if Harold Washington had not been elected mayor of Chicago, Obama would have not been president of the United States. The two only met once, but Washington's position as mayor became a blueprint for Obama's success. Washington's victory showed Obama and other African American politicians how to run successful campaigns, govern during a divisive period, and obtain the highest office of the land.

Obama had his political career all worked out. He had planned to follow in Harold Washington's footsteps. He wanted to run for General Assembly and for Congress, and then run for mayor of Chicago. In an interview on the anniversary of Washington's death, Obama specifically said, "Watching him as a larger-than-life figure and seeing the impact he had on the confidence of the African American community, the hopefulness of the community, it had a lasting impact on me. And I suspect that was the first time when I fully appreciated the potentials of a political figure, not just to pass laws, but also to change people's attitude about themselves" (Corley 2007). Many of the themes from Washington's speeches can be heard in Obama's speeches and other writings. Moreover, many of the same strategies like mobilization of voters became hallmarks for both men. Both men connected to people who had been who hadn't voted before.

Obama became the director of Illinois Project Vote. The national organization was founded in Washington, DC, by Sandy Newman, a lawyer and civil rights activist. The organization focused on registering mainly African American voters. Project Vote operated mainly on the East Coast and the DC area at the time Harold Washington was elected. Project Vote made donations to support voter registration drives in predominately African American wards in Chicago, but the leadership of Project Vote did not open a branch in Chicago because there were an infrastructure and other mobilization mechanisms in place, and they did not want to compete with them. Project Vote did have an indirect hand in Harold Washington's victory. After Washington's death and Carol Moseley Braun's surprising primary victory, it became easier for Project Vote to directly mobilize voters. Project Vote began looking for someone to head up its Chicago operations, and the thirty-year-old Barack Obama emerged as a perfect fit. Within a few months, he had recruited a staff and had signed up numerous volunteers. By then Obama had established and built relationships with churches and community organizations. This helped him to sign up and train more than seven hundred deputy voter registrars (Hayes 2008).

CHICAGO, ILLINOIS

Chicago, Illinois, became Barack Obama's adopted hometown when he accepted employment as a community organizer in 1985. He chose the city as the site for his presidential library, specifically in Jackson Park on the South Side of Chicago. The present location of Chicago began as a mission site started by Father François Pinet, a Jesuit priest. The mission was abandoned in 1700. Jean Baptiste Point du Sable, a Haitian, built the first permanent settlement at the mouth of the Chicago River in 1779. The word "Chicago" is derived from a French rendering of the Native American word *shikaakwa* from the Miami-Illinois tribal language. The original size of Chicago was only three-eighths of a square mile and its population consisted of only about 350 people. In 1835, the area of the town was expanded and the population swelled to about 3,000 people. Just two years later, the city grew to 4,170 people. This growth has slowed during recent years, according to the U.S. census. Chicago lost more than 13,000 people between 2016 and 2017. Chicago's African American population has declined every year since 2005. Today, Chicago is the third most populous city in the United States, behind New York and Los Angeles. In 2016, the estimated population of Chicago, Illinois, was 2.7 million people.

During this time, Obama was juggling several activities. He was working on a book manuscript that was under contract about his background and upbringing, and he continued to lead Project Vote, using his skills as a community organizer to help shape and change Chicago's electoral model to become a star in Illinois politics. While juggling these activities, Obama and the Project Vote efforts both flourished. Media advertisement is the mother's milk of any political campaign, and Obama brokered and secured a deal with Brainstorm Communications, who donated several thousand dollars to support Project Vote's efforts. "It's a Power Thing" became the group's slogan (Jarrett 1992). Soon after the brokering of this deal, airways and buildings were flooded with political advertisements, posters, and memorabilia. Minority business owners also agreed to hold on-site registration drives and to make donations to secure more radio advertisements and posters. Labor unions also assisted by providing additional funding for advertisements. Due to widespread and far-reaching advertisements encouraging African Americans to get out and vote, the African American community was energized and organized. More than 150,000 new African American voters were added to the city of Chicago voter rolls (Reynolds 1993). This was one of the most successful minority voter registration drives in U.S. history. Heading up this push to register more African American voters in the voter rolls in Chicago was Barack Obama.

Increasing the number of voters registered was an old strategy from the civil rights movement. This strategy would be used in Obama's presidential campaign. Prior to Obama heading up Project Vote, the Democratic Party offered money to those who could get new voters to register. After the budget for registered voters was depleted, participation usually waned. The Democratic Party in Chicago recruited minority voters, but had not made a full-scale push to flood its voter rolls. Obama emphasized appealing to the importance of voting and the historical significance of the battle for voting rights for African Americans. He believed that an appeal of this kind, a sense of obligation for African American voters, was more effective than money.

After the Project Vote efforts, Obama returned to teaching his class at the law school at the University of Chicago, working on the manuscript of his memoir, and doing legal work at the Davis Miner, Barnhill, and Galland law firm. After the success of Project Vote under Obama leadership, many began to see a run for public office in his future. In 2017, Project Vote suspended its operation due to lack of funding.

Barack Obama had a twelve-year stint teaching at the University of Chicago Law School. Obama taught law classes at the law school from 1992 to 2004 as a lecturer. He was then promoted to senior lecturer from 1996 to 2004. Senior lecturers are considered members of the law school faculty. The University of Chicago is a private, nondenominational university located in the Hyde Park section of Chicago. The University of Chicago was modeled after Oxford University in England. Obama primarily taught courses in constitutional law and race theory. The room he usually taught in was room 5 in the Harry A. Bigelow Lecture Hall. Obama's office was located in the library in office 603. He wrote most of his best-selling book, *Dreams from My Father*, in this library office. He later moved to office 514 in the library. His teaching evaluations typically ranked very high and students seemed to genuinely like the courses he instructed. In class students were assigned readings of Malcolm X, Dr. Martin Luther King Jr., Robert H. Bork, and Frederick Douglass (Kantor 2008). Obama discussed his love for academia and the law school classroom in his second book, *The Audacity of Hope.*

> I loved the law school classroom: the stripped down nature of it, the high-wire act of standing in front of a room at the beginning of each class with just blackboard and chalk, the student standing taking measure of me, some intent or apprehensive, others demonstrative their boredom, the tension broken by my first question—"What's this case about?"—and the hands tentatively rising, the initial responses and me pushing back against whatever arguments surfaced. (Obama, 2006, p. 84)

Obama had been reluctant to take the position at the University of Chicago because his focus was on writing a book and doing other community organizing work. He was also eyeing a possible run for public office. In spite of Obama's reluctance, the chair of the law school's appointment committee convinced Obama to initially take a two-year position as a law and government fellow. Because of his work as a state legislator, Obama rarely made afternoon faculty meetings in the law school. These meetings allowed professors to bond and get to know each other and the intellectual canons to which they subscribed. Some colleagues saw him as rigid as an intellectual. Some of his colleagues perceived him as aloof and too assured, too ambitious, and perhaps a bit arrogant.

By the mid-1990s, Obama was contemplating a run for public office. He made his intentions known to the dean of the law school at the University of Chicago, who promptly told him he thought it was not a good idea. The dean encouraged Obama to become a tenure track professor in the law school because he recognized his immense talent. As a young lecturer at Chicago Law, he won over his colleagues and students with his skill in the classroom. Obama was known as a master teacher. He was described as sharp, charismatic, evenhanded, and fair. More than once the law school tried to lure him with a tenure-track appointment, which would have meant more scholarly writing and being immersed in the world of academia. In the end, Obama declined becoming a full-time tenure track professor.

Richard Epstein, a former colleague of Obama's at the University of Chicago Law School, was critical of Obama. Epstein believed that Obama did not like to be pushed and did not engage the intellectual community at the school because he was always involved in some side project and kept to himself. Epstein believed that this limited Obama because it did not allow him to debate others who fundamentally disagreed on an intellectual basis (Kantor 2008). Epstein also believed that Obama was good at playing intellectual poker and concealing his real beliefs, which made him too rigid in his thinking.

The law school continued to receive inquiries about Obama's tenure at the school when he was elected as a U.S. senator. The distinction between a lecturer and a senior lecturer position hinges on the employment security associated with the positions. The senior lecturer position is considered more prestigious because those who hold those positions are considered to be members of the law school faculty although they are not tenure track. A lecturer position is considered to be an adjunct professor or an affiliate with the university. After Obama's rise to the presidency, the law school even placed a marker outside Obama's former office and the lecture room where he taught.

4

Law Student and Family Man

Barack Obama made a stellar impression on the faculty and his classmates at Harvard University. From his initial enrollment at Harvard Law, it was obvious that Obama wanted to distinguish himself from the other incoming law students. He was not only concerned with completing his degree; he had loftier intellectual as well as career goals. Professor Laurence Tribe hired Obama as a research assistant during his first year of law school. Professor Tribe rarely hired first-year law students but saw the talent and boundless potential in Obama and therefore hired him on the spot (Mackey 2014). Tribe probably saw Obama's maturity. He was a little older and more experienced than many of his classmates, since he had worked as a community organizer. Later, Obama enrolled in Tribe's constitutional law course and continued to make a name for himself with his academic prowess. Many of the bad study habits he had as an undergraduate were a part of his past. Now, he was a driven student who wanted more than superficial solutions and the intake of information. He wanted to understand how the systems of the world worked and how they could be fixed if they were not functioning correctly. At Harvard Law, many of Obama's classmates observed two sides of the future president of the United States. In the classroom, he was thoughtful, measured, and attempted to get everyone involved in class discussions. On the basketball court during pickup games, he was left-handed, had a pretty good jump shot, and was a notorious trash talker who showed his opponents no mercy on the court.

While some may have called his trash talking arrogance, others noted that he was just adhering to the code of the basketball court in urban and African American communities.

At Harvard Law, Obama studied under acclaimed constitutional law professor Charles Ogletree. In an interview, Professor Ogletree noted he taught both Michelle and Barack Obama. He also noted that Michelle was the star student of the two. In an interview, Ogletree admitted Michelle probably would be a better presidential candidate, and Barack Obama noted that if he had to run for public office against his wife, it would be no question, he would lose (Worley 2017). In discussing Obama's life as a law student, Ogletree noted that he asked great questions and made wonderful contributions but sometimes talked a little too much in class (Shapiro 2012). Ironically, Obama was at Harvard Law School at the same time as future U.S. Supreme Court Justice John Roberts. Obama spoke fondly of Professor Ogletree. "Professor Ogletree was beloved at Harvard Law School." He had heard of Ogletree's efforts to create a safe space for African American law students, relieve their anxiety, and show them the ropes. Ogletree began review and study sessions for African American students. It became known as "Saturday School." Initially, Saturday School was geared for African Americans, but this venture became such a success, law students of all ethnicities began to come there.

CHARLES OGLETREE

Charles Ogletree was a longtime Harvard Law School professor. He taught both Barack and Michelle Obama at Harvard Law. Professor Ogletree earned an undergraduate and graduate degree in political science from Stanford University. At Stanford, he was also a member of America's most prestigious honor society, Phi Beta Kappa. After earning his undergraduate and graduate degrees, he also earned a law degree from Harvard Law School in 1978. He served an eight-year stint in the District of Columbia Public Defender Service.

Between 1982 and 1984, Ogletree began teaching law as an adjunct professor at both Antioch Law School and American University School of Law. In 1989, he joined the faculty of Harvard Law. He was also given responsibility for overseeing Harvard Law School's trial advocacy workshop. He was a dedicated teacher who taught students that law can be a tool for social and political change. Professor Ogletree served as the cochair of the Reparations Coordinating Committee, a group of lawyers and other experts researching a lawsuit based upon a claim of reparations for descendants of African slaves. He authored several books on race and justice, and became a mentor to Barack Obama and Michelle Obama. In 2016, he announced he had been diagnosed with Alzheimer's disease and proclaimed he would work to raise awareness of the disease.

Barack Obama was the first African American to become editor of the *Harvard Law Review.* Harvard Law was consistently ranked in the top ten and was one of the most prestigious law schools in the United States. The *Law Review*'s articles are edited by law students, allowing them to improve legal research methods and review scholarship of new legal arguments. It was first issued in 1887. Editor of the *Law Review* position is the top coveted position for law students at Harvard Law. By being selected to this position, Obama was immediately set on a path to prominence. Former Harvard Law Review editors include a plethora of Supreme Court justices, federal judges, academicians, and U.S. government officials. In the spring of 1990, Barack Obama was elected the first African American to win this coveted and prestigious position. He succeeded Peter Yu, a first-generation Chinese American (Butterfield 1990). As the *Law Review* president, Obama was interested in exploring articles on diversity and inequality.

Obama was slightly older than many of his law school classmates when he began law school at age twenty-seven during the fall of 1988. His maturity along with his eclectic background and diverse experiences made him comfortable with conversing with a wide range of people while he was at Harvard Law. Though he did not openly discuss his complex racial identity, he had become comfortable with it and appeared not to spend as much time pondering it as he had in the past. In law school, Obama displayed many of the qualities that would make him a successful presidential candidate and future U.S. president. He could listen to varying opinions and reach a conclusion. He brought varying factions of people together to accomplish goals (Shapiro 2012).

Obama navigated fractious political disputes taking place on campus. Many students were pushing for the hiring of more black professors at Harvard's law school. Obama also advocated for more black law professors and spoke at one protest rally, but for the most part he labored behind the scenes to support the cause. He did believe some progress had been made on the issue of race at Harvard. He believed his selection as the editor of *Harvard Law Review* was evidence of this progress. He even believed some progress had been made in race relations, but he did not want people to misconstrue that everything was great on U.S. racial fronts, so he spoke publicly at the rally to hire more black professors. He believed more could be done.

Harvard's campus continued to be deeply divided over diversity, not only at the law school but on the entire campus. Central to the debates at Harvard were fights over the use of affirmative action programs to diversify the school's faculty. Professor Derrick Bell was the first African American to obtain tenure at Harvard in 1969. Bell believed Harvard should deliberately recruit and retain more minority faculty members. As a way to bring attention to his cause, Bell decided to forgo his salary to bring attention to this problem. Bell also solicited students to support his cause. Students rallied and protested. Some students even camped out in the dean of the law school's office to push for change.

Though he attempted to avoid this public push, Obama could not escape being drawn into this battle. As a high-profile student, Obama spoke out on behalf of Professor Bell. In 1990, Harvard Law School had 1,600 law students, but there were only five tenured women professors and three African American male tenured professors (Butterfield, April 26, 1990). Due in part to Bell's and students' efforts, Lani Guinier became the first tenured African American woman at Harvard Law School (Sawano 1998).

Obama had mastered maneuvering between various racial groups and various social worlds, regardless of the racial or socioeconomic makeup of these communities. This ability would help him as a future politician and president. In 2005, as a part of their Celebration of Black Alumni weekend, Harvard Law Association honored Barack Obama. Obama was the keynote speaker for the event. Elena Kagan, the dean of Harvard Law School who would later become an associate justice on the U.S. Supreme Court, presented him with a citation.

It is a common for former presidents of the *Harvard Law Review* to serve in high profile clerkships and become federal judges and associate justices on the U.S. Supreme Court. Barack Obama did not plan to seek any of these career options. After he completed law school, he could have pursued any job in the legal profession he wanted. He could have sought a prestigious clerkship or become a rainmaking attorney. Instead, he planned to spend some time working in a private law firm to help pay off some of his student loan debts before returning to Chicago to resume community organizing or make a run in local politics. Before he graduated from law school, during the summer of 1989, Obama took an internship as a summer associate at Sidley and Austin corporate law firm in Chicago (Newton-Small 2008). This law firm has a reputation as one of the best law firms in the United States. Sidley and Austin did not usually hire first-year law students to intern, but Obama's reputation had become well known. Like most summer associate interns, he conducted research for the attorneys in the firm.

By the 1990s, Barack Obama discovered the love of his life, and his shaping as a family man, father, and husband would begin during this period of his life. The story of Michelle Robinson and Barack Obama's romance has been well chronicled. The account of their story is touted as a true love story. The couple met during the summer of 1989, when Barack interned at Sidley and Austin Law in Chicago. Much like his grandparents' stories about his father's exploits, Barack's exploits grew to legendary proportions as well. Obama had gained a reputation at Harvard Law, and people talked about him being a rising star in the legal profession. Martha Minow's dad was a senior partner at Sidley and Austin. She told her father about an immensely talented Harvard University law student named Barack Obama (Mundy, *Michelle*, 2008, p. 105). Ultimately, Obama would be offered and accept an internship with the firm. People could see there was something special about this intern. With the exception of a few people, everyone at the law firm was all abuzz because Obama was coming onboard.

Though she thought Obama's résumé was impressive, Michelle Robinson, a junior associate at the law firm, believed they were making too big of a deal over the new intern. Obama sounded too good to be true, and she would likely not have any kind of interest in him. He would probably be a super nerd or a smooth talker who could charm people and impress them but get very little accomplished. Either way, she would not like him.

Michelle was assigned to be his mentor. They went to lunch and a few outings as a part of the mentoring process. To Michelle's dismay, Obama showed up for lunch wearing an ugly sport coat and smoking a cigarette; she hated cigarettes. There is an old saying you only get one chance to make a first impression and Obama did not make a good one with Michelle.

In speeches and interviews after Barack Obama became president, Michelle talked about her initial impressions. When she met Barack he did not have any money, and she quickly realized that he could not impress her with material things. As she recounted in her book *Becoming*, Obama's car was so dilapidated that a rust hole had formed on the passenger side of the car, and she could see the street through the floorboard while they were riding (Mundy, "When Michelle," 2008) and the car shook violently when he started it. She surmised Obama was not interested in making money.

When he finally asked her on a date, she thought that it would be inappropriate to fraternize with another associate at the firm. There were very few African Americans employed at the law firm, and she did not want to give the appearance she was desperate and dating one of the few black lawyers at the firm. Michelle had resolved to focus on her career. She told her mother when she had completed her first year at the firm that she was going to make her budding career her top priority. In an interview on the *Ellen DeGeneres Show*, Michelle Obama stated, "It was not love at first sight, but it was interest at first sight." Michelle also admitted she had to overcome preconceived notions and a false narrative she had constructed after reading his biographical information. She also noted he was cuter than his photograph. They went to lunch as associates, and her interest was further piqued. After pondering the new associate, she stated, "He was interesting. He was self-deprecating. He was funny and his background was just amazing" (Obama 2018, p. 113). Michelle finally accepted a date with Barack. On their first date, they went to see the Oscar-nominated Spike Lee movie, *Do the Right Thing*, a thought-provoking dramatic comedy that chronicles events that led to a race riot between the residents on

---

DO THE RIGHT THING

Do the Right Thing is a highly acclaimed film, written, produced, and directed by Spike Lee in 1990. The film garnered nominations for the best original screenplay and best supporting actor by the Academy Awards and grossed over $27 million. The Academy's best film award was presented to *Driving Miss Daisy*, which starred Jessica Tandy and Morgan Freeman.

Do the Right Thing is a film that has been regarded as culturally and historically significant and has often been listed as one of the greatest films of all time. The film explores racism and bias in the neighborhood of Bedford-Stuyvesant in Brooklyn, New York, on the hottest day of the year, during which festering racial tensions spark a riot and racial unrest. Spike Lee, Danny Aiello, Ossie Davis, Ruby Dee, Samuel L. Jackson, Richard Edison, Giancarlo Esposito, Rosie Perez, and John Turturro star in this timeless movie. One of the subplots of the movie explores the way some whites celebrate African American stars while detesting poor African Americans. The pioneering hip-hop group Public Enemy's song, "Fight the Power," was a dominant force during this film and became an anthem for the 1990s.

On Michelle Robinson and Barack Obama's first date, they went to see *Do the Right Thing* and visited the Art Institute of Chicago. At a celebration of the twenty-fifth anniversary of the film's release, the Obamas taped a short video tribute for *Do the Right Thing* and Spike Lee. President Obama specifically thanked Spike Lee for helping him impress his future wife on their first date.

---

the hottest day of the year in Brooklyn, New York. After the movie, they also enjoyed Baskin-Robbins ice cream. They were almost busted when they ran into a senior partner at the movie theater. The partner seemed to not care and maybe even approved of the budding romance. Their colleagues reported the pair was immensely smitten with each other.

They would often be seen chatting, oblivious to the world around them. Michelle is not easily impressed, but Barack broke through that wall. On one of their early outings, Barack took her to one of his organizing events at a church in Chicago. Michelle was impressed by his ability to connect with everyday working-class people. She was impressed with Barack's deep-rooted desire to help poor African Americans build a good life and move up the social and economic ladder. His words moved Michelle, and she fell for Barack.

Michelle had graduated from Princeton University and Harvard Law School. Her senior thesis at Princeton centered on the perceptions of African Americans at the university. At Harvard Law, she worked at the university's legal aid bureau. The bureau's mission was assisting those in need with legal services. She handled landlord and tenant issues at the bureau, and her compassion showed through her work. After law school, she faced the prospects of going into public service or legal aid, which offered only modest salaries. She was also recruited by many large corporate law firms. Michelle's humble upbringing influenced her employment decision after law school. She remembered how her parents lived from paycheck to paycheck, and decided to go to work at Sidley and Austin. She rationalized that with a good starting salary and her earning potential over time, she would be able to pay off her student loans.

Michelle's and Barack's educational backgrounds had some similarities, and although their family backgrounds were starkly different, their family values were nearly the same, values they would use to guide their daughters. Michelle grew up in South Side Chicago. She grew up in a strong traditional family unit and graduated from Whitney Young High School, a magnet school in Chicago. Michelle's father, Fraser C. Robinson, suffered from multiple sclerosis but continued to work. Her father battling through his illness showed her an example of great personal resilience. He was a pump worker for the City of Chicago. He supervised the boilers at the water filtration plant. Despite having multiple sclerosis, he rarely missed work. Fraser Robinson walked using two canes for balance and would sometimes struggle getting prepared for work and other daily activities. He was active politically and was a precinct captain for the Democratic Party (Bond-Halbert 2012, p. 54). In 1991, he died from complications of his illness.

Michelle's mother, Marian Shields Robinson, worked as a secretary at a bank until she retired. She was reluctant to move from her cottage in Chicago. Michelle solicited her brother to join forces with her to lobby Marian to move from Chicago to Washington, DC. She finally relented when she was asked to help raise the first daughters and usher them into adulthood. Marian Robinson moved into the White House with the president and first lady, but primarily kept a low profile with the exception of a few public appearances. Michelle noted that her mother was a vital cog in their support network. She lived with almost complete anonymity, and this allowed her to get out and move around Washington, DC, without secret service officers. On these excursions, she was able to see people and engage in discussions about real-life issues. She could provide real-life stories that kept the Obama's from living in a bubble during their time in the White House.

Craig Robinson is Michelle's older brother and the first in the family to attend Princeton University. He was valedictorian of his high school graduating class and was offered both academic and athletic scholarships from other schools, but at his father's urgings, because it was an Ivy League school and had an excellent academic reputation, he decided to attend Princeton University. His father also urged his son to not base his decision on where he would attend school by the family's income, because he knew weighing this factor into his decision would limit his possibilities. Craig's decision to attend Princeton University would undoubtedly influence Michelle's college choice.

When Barack was introduced to Michelle's family, they believed the romance would be short-lived and Barack would not be able to pass Michelle's incredibly high dating standards. They had seen her cast away guys after just a few dates. Michelle invited Barack over for dinner and to meet her family. Michelle's family was impressed with Barack, but they felt sorry for him because they knew he would soon be cast aside like the rest of her suitors. Michelle's family observed Barack and noted he came across as a low-key guy. They were impressed with the way he talked about his family.

Michelle asked her brother to take Barack on the basketball court and see what kind of guy Obama truly was. Craig Robinson believed that you can tell the character of a person by watching him play basketball. He believed when a player got tired, he would revert to the player he truly was. Craig had been a basketball star and a two-time Ivy League player of the year at Princeton in the 1981–82 and the 1982–83 seasons. He was drafted by the NBA's Philadelphia 76ers, but played professionally internationally for two years before returning to the United States to work in business and then begin his basketball coaching career.

After playing basketball with Obama, Craig returned with a good assessment of Barack's game and character. Craig noted that he was quietly confident. Craig Robinson interpreted this as the markings of someone with good self-esteem but not arrogant. He also noted Barack was a team player and was not a ball hog. He followed the rules and played within the flow of the game, Craig reported. Obama passed the ball when it was necessary and made the necessary cuts and screens. Craig was also impressed Barack was not a basketball brownnoser who just passed him the ball because he was dating Michelle.

After dating for a while, Michelle began to pressure Barack about getting married. Barack put her off for a while, arguing that it was a meaningless institution and how they felt about each other was what truly mattered (Mundy, "When Michelle," 2008). Perhaps Barack was simply being coy. Perhaps he did not really want to get married. Michelle knew this excuse for not moving toward marriage would not go over well with her parents. Her parents had been married for thirty years and marriage was an important institution to them. They desired for their daughter to enter into a traditional marriage.

In 1991, Barack took Michelle to Gordon's, an upscale restaurant in Chicago, Illinois. As she had been doing more and more frequently, she pressed him again about his intentions for their future. As Michelle noted in her 2018 best-selling memoir, *Becoming*, Barack began to put her off again arguing that marriage was a meaningless institution. On this night, he was adamant and animated about his disdain for the institution of marriage (Obama 2018, p. 156). This lasted throughout the entire main course. Then a waiter showed up with a dessert platter with her engagement ring on it. Michelle was speechless and a little embarrassed because she had pressed him so hard about marriage. Michelle and Barack were married on October 2, 1992, at Trinity United Church of Christ, and their reception was held at the South Shore Cultural Center, a former exclusive country club that had once prohibited African Americans and Jews from memberships.

Michelle noted though their upbringings were starkly different, she saw the same things in Barack's upbringing that she saw in her own. They had the same values. They believed in forgoing large salaries and giving back. She also believed they could teach these values when they became parents. Michelle noted in an interview, she married Barack because she respected him. Initially, they lived in the top portion of her parents' home in Chicago until they could afford their own place. Early on in the marriage, Michelle was the breadwinner for the family. The couple struggled with infertility and with the help of fertility treatments, she was able to become pregnant.

Barack and Michelle have two children. The oldest child, Malia Ann Obama, was born July 4, 1998, and the couple's second child is Natasha Obama, born June 10, 2001. Obama promised the girls a dog when he decided to run for president of the United States. Finding the right dog for the family became a difficult endeavor. The girls had been angling for a dog for a long time and saw their dad's presidential run as an opportunity. President-elect Obama joked with George Stephanopoulos, saying, "Finding a dog was tougher than finding a commerce secretary" (Rowan and Janis 2009, p. 155). He did fulfill his promise in April 2009. A few months after becoming president, the family adopted a Portuguese water dog. The Obama family named the puppy "Bo." The puppy was a gift from Massachusetts' Senator Ted Kennedy. Bo had white paws and a white front coat. In part, the Obamas chose this breed of dog because of the nonshedding coat and its classification as a hypoallergenic breed. The Obamas got a second dog in 2012. The second dog is named Sunny and is also a Portuguese water dog.

Fatherhood and being a good father are very important to Barack Obama. It was a prevailing theme of his presidency. Because he grew up without contact with his father, he wanted to be an exemplary father. He read aloud to Malia all of the *Harry Potter* book series and read the *Life of Pi* to Sasha. He attended all of his daughters' parent-teacher conferences and by all accounts was an active participant in parenting. At 6:30 p.m., Obama and his wife sat down with the girls for a family dinner without any outsiders. It was almost as if it was a sacred time. Even with his presidential duties, on most days he ate breakfast with his daughters. He attended his daughter's tennis matches, dance recitals, and basketball games. All of the Obamas' activities stop for family time and dinner. He often went back to work after dinner, but his aides did not disturb his quality time with his family.

Being from a family where his father was largely absent, Obama took fatherhood responsibilities seriously. He wanted to provide his girls with a stable father who would be a presence in their lives. His sentiments on fatherhood were spelled out in a Father's Day address at the Apostolic Church of God in Chicago in 2008. He used biblical verses on the Sermon of the Mount found in Matthew 7:24–25 as the foundational text of his message. "Of all the rocks upon which we build our lives, we are reminded today that family is the most important. And we are called to recognize and honor on how critical every father is to that foundation. They are teachers and coaches. They are mentors and role models. But if we are honest with ourselves, too many fathers are M.I.A., too many fathers are AWOL, missing from too many lives and too many homes," Mr. Obama said, to a chorus of approving murmurs from the audience. "They have abandoned their responsibilities, acting like boys instead of men. And the foundations of our families are weaker because of it."

Some believed the tone of his sermon was too negative, too stern, too blunt, and portrayed most African American fathers as deleterious individuals who shucked their responsibilities as fathers. Critics also believed portions of the sermon painted a poor portrait of the African American community as a whole.

In 2010, Obama reflected on fatherhood when he spoke at a Father's Day event in the nation's capital. After speaking, he hosted a fatherhood and mentoring barbeque on the south lawn of the White House. During this event, he discussed how fatherhood impacts children's lives and the responsibilities of fatherhood. At the event, he spoke about the initiative he launched the previous year.

> One year ago this week, we kicked off a national conversation on fatherhood and personal responsibility, and members of our administration fanned out all across the country to hear from fathers and families about the challenges that they face. Secretary Arne Duncan, our Secretary of Education, held a discussion in New Hampshire about the link between fatherhood and educational achievement. Gary Locke talked to fathers in California about balancing the needs of their families with the demands of their jobs. Secretary Shinseki, of Veterans Affairs, held a town hall for military and veteran dads in North Carolina. And Attorney General Holder traveled to Georgia for a forum about fathers in our criminal justice system.

With an assured applause line during his speech, Obama praised single mothers and noted the importance of motherhood.

We can all agree that we've got too many mothers out there forced to do everything all by themselves. They're doing a heroic job, often under trying circumstances. They deserve a lot of credit for that. But they shouldn't have to do it alone. The work of raising our children is the most important job in this country, and it's all of our responsibilities—mothers and fathers.

Taking absent fathers to task with blunt language, Obama admonished fathers for abdicating their duties and for not making responsible choices.

Now, I can't legislate fatherhood. I can't force anybody to love a child. But what we can do is send a clear message to our fathers that there is no excuse for failing to meet their obligations. What we can do is make it easier for fathers who make responsible choices and harder for those who avoid those choices. What we can do is come together and support fathers who are willing to step up and be good partners and parents and providers.

Then Obama touted his nationwide mentoring program. The program's aim was to raise the awareness of responsible fatherhood, while helping fathers who desired to reengage with their families.

And that's why today we're launching the next phase of our work to promote responsible fatherhood—a new, nationwide Fatherhood and Mentoring Initiative. This is a call to action with cities and states, with individuals and organizations across the country—from the NFL Players Association to the National PTA, to everyday moms and dads—we're raising awareness about responsible fatherhood and working to re-engage absent fathers with their families.

During this event, he also laid out a prescription to engage fathers and propose a conglomerate of local and state initiatives and networks to help vulnerable communities to gain the necessary skills to become productive citizens and fully functioning individuals.

As part of this effort, we've proposed a new and expanded Fatherhood, Marriage and Families Innovation Fund. And we plan to seek out and support the very best, most successful initiatives in our states and communities—those that are offering services like job training, or parenting skills classes, domestic violence prevention—all which help provide the kind of network of support for men, particularly those in vulnerable communities.

In one section of the speech, Obama struck a more conciliatory tone in discussing the benefits of having loving relationships between mothers and fathers. He also discussed the benefits of strong marriages.

We're also going to help dads who get caught up. We want to make sure that they're caught up on child support payments and that we re-engage them in their children's lives. We're going to support efforts to build healthy relationships between parents as well because we know that children benefit not just from loving mothers and loving fathers, but from strong and loving marriages as well.

Obama then discussed his administration's efforts to provide jobs for ex-convicts and to remove barriers preventing them from finding gainful employment.

> We're also launching a new transitional jobs initiative for ex-offenders and low-income, non-custodial fathers because these are men who often face serious barriers to finding work and keeping work. We'll help them develop the skills and experience they need to move into full-time, long-term employment, so they can meet their child support obligations and help provide for their families. (Obama, Obama's Father's Day, 2008)

Obama unveiled more of his thoughts on fatherhood and family when he spoke at Morehouse College. On an overcast Sunday in May 2013, President Obama was the keynote speaker at the commencement exercises at Morehouse College, an all-male, historically black college located in Atlanta, Georgia. This commencement speech revealed more about Obama's worldview and his policy aims as president. Dressed in a maroon

---

MOREHOUSE COLLEGE

On May 9, 2013, Barack Obama gave the commencement address at Morehouse College. Morehouse is a private, all-male, historically black college located in Atlanta, Georgia. Augusta Institute, now known as Morehouse College, was founded in Augusta, Georgia, by William J. White and former slave Richard C. Coulter. In 1879, the school was moved to Atlanta, and its name was changed to Morehouse College after Henry L. Morehouse, the corresponding secretary of the American Baptist Home Mission Society. As a historically black college, Morehouse has a strong history of and commitment to educating not only African Americans, but all people who enter through its corridors. It is a small institution with an enrollment of 2,090 undergraduate students.

In 1990, entertainer, businesswoman, and entrepreneur Oprah Winfrey pledged financial assistance to aid one hundred young men to obtain a college degree from Morehouse. She made a financial donation to establish the Oprah Winfrey Endowed Scholarship Fund. Morehouse uses its financial gifts to support deserving students based on academic achievement and financial need. Their financial support covers most of the costs of their education including prior student debt. Among Morehouse College's notable graduates were Dr. Martin Luther King Jr., Spike Lee, Samuel L. Jackson, Julian Bond, Edwin Moses, Howard Thurman, and Maynard Jackson. Two U.S. presidents hold honorary degrees from Morehouse College: Jimmy Carter and Barack Obama.

doctoral gown and armed with broad smile, President Obama also received an honorary doctorate from the college. His commencement speech was interrupted by applause on several occasions. Obama again addressed fatherhood and what it meant to him. Again, some believed he disparaged African American men during his commencement address at Morehouse College. Obama began by talking about noted Morehouse president Benjamin Mays and one the most famed graduates of Morehouse, Dr. Martin Luther King Jr. President Obama made references to both personal and historical events to challenge the audience to strive for greatness and succeed in a global competitive economy. Obama spoke directly to the parents, grandparents, and loved ones of those participating in the commencement ceremonies. He directed the graduates to give their families a celebratory round of applause for providing the support to reach this momentous occasion. President Obama's comedic timing was impeccable, and his jesting solicited big rounds of laughter and applause. He pointed the commencement audience to Morehouse College's illustrious history and tradition of excellence by discussing noted mentor to Dr. Martin Luther King Jr. and sixth president of Morehouse, Benjamin Elijah Mays. He acknowledged the honor the college bestowed on him as an honorary "Morehouse Man" and the folklore associated with being a graduate of the college. Again President Obama was greeted with voluminous laughter from the commencement audience and platform guests. Drawing on the words of wisdom from Benjamin Mays, he challenged the institution to continue to produce honest and responsible men who have a consistent trust factor that can be exhibited in all facets of their lives. Obama directly quoted Mays's saying:

> Benjamin E. Mays, who served as the president of Morehouse for almost thirty years, understood that tradition better than anybody. He said and I quote, "It will not be sufficient for Morehouse College, for any college, for that matter, to produce clever graduates but rather honest men, men who can be trusted in public and private life; men who are sensitive to the wrongs, the sufferings, and the injustices of society and who are willing to accept responsibility for correcting those ills."

President Obama continued to elaborate on the characteristics of individuals who made up the first Morehouse class. He emphasized the self-determination and intestinal fortitude they displayed pursuing an education in the face of such adversity. He also stressed Morehouse's role in training these men for future leadership roles for the African American community and the nation at large. President Obama then turned his attention to Morehouse College's most noted graduate, Martin Luther King, Jr., to showcase Morehouse's educational excellence in training future leaders in all endeavors. He discussed the role Morehouse College played in shaping Dr. King's perspective as a scholar and civil rights leader. He unfurled Dr. King's narrative and Morehouse College's influence on King's life and life's work. Obama also took time to talk about the plight of black men during the era of Jim Crow and state-sanctioned segregation. He encouraged the Morehouse graduates to look to the past. Looking at the obstacles their forefathers endured should provide them courage to persevere. He also pointed them toward the future, noting that it should give them hope and that this knowledge will help give them the endurance to pursue success.

> Now, think about it. For black men in the '40s and the '50s, the threat of violence, the constant humiliations, large and small, the uncertainty that you could support a family, the gnawing doubts born of the Jim Crow culture that told you every day that somehow you were inferior, the temptation to shrink from the world, to accept your place, to avoid risks, to be afraid— that temptation was necessarily strong.

He also pointed to the lineage of strong black leaders that were educated at Morehouse College. He noted the strength and the bravery of these leaders of the past and encouraged others to rise against the challenges of their day and to not fear. Obama recognized that by overcoming these fears, the leaders of the past ultimately opened doors and led to him being elected president of the United States. President Obama also encouraged the Morehouse graduates. He pointed to history but also to some of his presidential accomplishments that made it easier for their generations to accomplish great things.

> So the history we share should give you hope. The future we share should give you hope. You're graduating into an improving job market. You're living in a time when advances in technology and communication put the world at your fingertips. Your generation is uniquely poised for success unlike any generation of African Americans that came before it.

After this wave of encouragement, the president talked about the difficult realities that some black men find themselves in and addressed the scarcity of resources in poor African American communities and his responsibility as president of the United States to assist these communities through public policy. He also reminded the audience that bettering these communities by reducing poverty, providing health care, and better educating citizens is a collective effort. Obama touted his accomplishments in reforming health care and reducing gun violence.

> My job, as President, is to advocate for policies that generate more opportunity for everybody. . . . Policies that create more good jobs and reduce poverty, and educate more children, and give more families the security of health care, and protect more of our children from the horrors of gun violence. That's my job. Those are matters of public policy, and it is important

for all of us—black, white and brown—to advocate for an America where everybody has got a fair shot in life. Not just some. Not just a few.

He then urged the graduates, as Morehouse men, to use their power to help those who are less fortunate than themselves. He implored them to use their collective power and individual power for the greater good and a larger cause. President Obama then took a folksier tone to emphasize his point of benevolence to those who are less fortunate, to give back to those of a lower socioeconomic status, and to use their power to help others in underserved communities. Again he championed his policies. Particularly, he expounded on the benefits of Affordable Care Act also known as Obamacare. He then took a more straightforward and paternal tone to warn the graduates about making excuses for not achieving goals and reaching their full potential as college educated men.

> Which brings me to a second point: Just as Morehouse has taught you to expect more of yourselves, inspire those who look up to you to expect more of themselves. We know that too many young men in our community continue to make bad choices. And I have to say, growing up, I made quite a few myself. Sometimes I wrote off my own failings as just another example of the world trying to keep a black man down. I had a tendency sometimes to make excuses for me not doing the right thing. But one of the things that all of you have learned over the last four years is there's no longer any room for excuses.

He used a common creed used at Morehouse to stress that no one can rest on the laurels of a college degree. The world is competitive and connected, and new graduates would not only be competing against graduates in this country but also with individuals all over the world because of our connectivity. Obama reminded the graduates, it is a mean old world, and the world does not owe them anything. He also urged them not to blame racism or another negative forces or any hardship to impede the progress of their success. He also noted success could be theirs if they worked hard enough.

President Obama then returned to his thoughts on fatherhood and manhood. He encouraged the graduates to be the best fathers they could be and used a personal interjection to underscore the point that one can still be successful even if one comes from an unconventional home. With a raw and personal reflection rarely revealed by President Obama, he disclosed his desire to be a better husband, the best father, and a better man. He beseeched the graduates,

> Be the best husband to your wife, or your boyfriend, or your partner. Be the best father you can be to your children. Because nothing is more important. I was raised by a heroic single mom, wonderful grandparents—made

incredible sacrifices for me. And I know there are moms and grandparents here today who did the same thing for all of you. But I sure wish I had had a father who was not only present, but involved. Didn't know my dad. And so my whole life, I've tried to be for Michelle and my girls what my father was not for my mother and me. I want to break that cycle where a father is not at home, where a father is not helping to raise that son or daughter. I want to be a better father, a better husband, a better man.

President Obama concluded his Morehouse College commencement speech by exhorting graduates to be thankful to the men in their lives who have made sacrifices and been examples for what being a man truly is. He also told the graduates to focus on those things that are really important in life—those things humans think of when they come to their final days.

I know that when I am on my deathbed someday, I will not be thinking about any particular legislation I passed; I will not be thinking about a policy I promoted; I will not be thinking about the speech I gave, I will not be thinking the Nobel Prize I received. I will be thinking about that walk I took with my daughters. I'll be thinking about a lazy afternoon with my wife. I'll be thinking about sitting around the dinner table and seeing them happy and healthy and knowing that they were loved. And I'll be thinking about whether I did right by all of them. So if you've had role models, fathers, brothers like that—thank them today. And if you haven't, commit yourself to being that man to somebody else.

President Obama closed the commencement speech by stating graduates should show concern for all of humanity, no matter the person's race. He encouraged them to seek universal justice for all people and become global citizens who ensure all people have an equal opportunity at success if they are willing to work hard and achieve.

In 2017, Obama described the process of dropping his oldest daughter off at college as akin to having heart surgery. Barack and Michelle helped move Malia into her residence hall room at Harvard University after she completed a gap year following graduating from high school. Obama stated he did well not to cry in front of his daughter but when he returned to the car he did shed a few tears (McDermott 2017). He joked that his Secret Service officers looked straight ahead while pretending not to hear him sniffling and blowing his nose. During his presidency, Obama often spoke about how much fatherhood meant to him. In his presidential farewell address, President Obama told his daughters, "Of all that I've done in my life, I am most proud to be your dad" (Obama, Farewell Speech, 2017).

5

Illinois State Senator

At the age of thirty-five, Obama, a married man and impatient with life, made his first run for public office. At the urging of many of his friends, Obama ran for a seat in the Illinois State Legislature. In 1994, Illinois State Senator Alice Palmer sought to run for the U.S. House of Representative, which created a vacancy in the Thirteenth District of Illinois. Like most traditional politicians, he began his campaign by meeting and talking with anyone who would listen to him. Armed with his experiences as a community organizer and lawyer, Obama believed that getting out to hear what people were talking about was key to mounting a successful political campaign, and therefore he traveled to conventional and unconventional spaces to speak with potential voters. He met people at block club meetings, church socials, beauty shops, barbershops, and on street corners. In speaking with people, he discovered there was blanket skepticism about politics and the political process. He fashioned his campaign message around unity to combat the notion held by many that politics are based on issues that divide people instead of issues that bring people together.

On September 19, 1995, Obama announced his Illinois Senate candidacy to an audience of approximately two hundred people at the Ramada Inn in Chicago's East Hyde Park (Kaergard 2018). A month after his senatorial run announcement, Obama's mother died of cancer at age fifty-two. Despite the loss of his mother, Obama stayed on message and continued to campaign. Obama's constant campaign refrain was, "We have a stake in one another, and that what binds us together is greater than what drives us apart" (Obama 2006, p. 2). His framing of his campaign message on this theme of unity coupled with his charisma propelled him to victory. He handily won the Illinois State Senate seat with about 80 percent of the vote. He defeated Republican Party candidate Rosette Caldwell Peyton, who was seeking office for the first time, and independent candidate David White-head. As Obama's status grew as an incumbent, he faced weaker and weaker Republican Party candidates and handily defeated all of them. He would go on to become a three-term Illinois state senator, winning seats in 1996, 1998, and again in 2002.

As a state senator, Obama showed his proclivity toward bipartisanship. He worked with Democrats and Republicans to create legislation on health care, ethics, and early childhood education programs, as well as state earned income tax credit for the poor. He also took aim at Illinois laws pertaining to prison reform, police brutality, and the death penalty. He worked tirelessly as chairman of the Senate's Health and Human Services Committee to require law enforcement officials to videotape interrogations and confessions in all capital cases after a number of death-row inmates were found innocent. On these issues, he gained support from many of Democratic legislators and had to face resistance from his Republican counterparts. Obama found major opposition from Republican state legislators who supported a tough-on-crime stance and Democratic state legislators who feared being viewed as soft on crime (Scott, July 30, 2007). In particular, he found opposition from varying factions to his proposed legislation on videotaping interrogations. His biggest and most vocal opposition came from law enforcement. Obama's supporters believe opposition of this bill was so visceral because some police officers had become accustomed to routinely using physical force to get leads in solving crimes. Incoming Illinois governor Rod Blagojevich also expressed his opposition for the proposed legislation.

Understanding that moving legislation through the political process sometimes takes social activities to get it done; Obama began to work on key legislators to sway them to his point of view. Because Obama was a Harvard law graduate and did not have deep roots in Illinois, many of his legislative colleagues considered him an elitist and an outsider. They did not consider Obama a regular guy. To combat this notion and move his legislation through the chamber, Obama began engaging in social activities to gently persuade his opponents on the need for this bill. He began playing basketball and poker with them to ensure his concerns were being heard and fully understood. These social events went a long way in getting his points of view across and allowing his colleagues from both political parties to get to know him better. Republicans began to respect him and how seriously he took being a state legislator. One in particular, State

Senator Kirk Dillard, expressed, "Barack had a way both intellectually and in demeanor that defused skeptics" (Peters 2008).

Obama would use this same strategy to defuse his biggest and toughest critics: law enforcement. Just as with his listening tour on the campaign trail for his state political office, he spoke with representatives of many of the law enforcement organizations. He showed them he heard their concerns and empathized with them. He also exhibited political gamesmanship by assisting them with getting other legislation through in exchange for their support. Obama continued to work and persuade others to support his bill. His persuasion proved to be so powerful that the bill passed both houses of the Illinois Legislature. In the Illinois Senate, the bill passed by a convincing vote of 35–0, but work still remained because the governor opposed the legislation and could possibly veto it. Obama began to talk with Blagojevich and was able to get him to sign the bill into law. This made Illinois the first state in the United States to require videotaping of interrogations. Obama's persuasiveness helped him to pass other bills at the state legislature, such as the state's first earned-income tax credit to help working poor as well as the first ethics and campaign finance law. As Illinois Senator Dillard further explained, "Obama has the unique ability to deal the extremely complex issues to reach across the aisle and deal with diverse people. Where many elected officials would see rising above what divides us as rhetoric, Obama lived and believed it!" (Peters 2008).

During his tenure as Illinois state senator, Obama was considered shrewd and practical with the ability to play hardball if needed. He was also viewed as a pragmatist, a legislator willing to compromise to accomplish his policy objectives—and as ambitious. His critics considered him an opportunist. It was clear from the very beginning of his time as a state legislature that he sought a leadership role on high-profile legislative committees or a higher public office. To gain a leadership role, he positioned himself as a protégé of Illinois Democratic senator Emil Jones. Jones, who was a powerful state legislative leader and member of the black Chicago political machine, took Obama under his wing. Jones became a mentor to Obama and helped him get oriented to the inner workings and politics of the Illinois State Legislature. Jones noted Obama could be pushy and impatient at times. This connection to Jones allowed Obama to build a solid record of achievement in the Illinois Senate. In building this record, he exhibited a penchant for reaching across the aisle and negotiating difficult legislation. With the help of Senator Jones, Obama was instrumental in delivering campaign finance reform law in Illinois. Obama's time in the Illinois State Legislature can be summed up by the issues he advocated and provided support for. Obama supported health care issues such as abortion rights, family planning services, and health insurance coverage for contraceptives. He also championed prison reform and gun control. He favored legislation that included a ban on semiautomatic assault weapons and wanted to limit the purchasing of only one handgun per month for individuals. Obama helped pass legislation overhauling Illinois's capital punishment system. He also opposed the use of racial profiling in law enforcement, believing this technique singled out blacks and other minorities. To provide evidence, he pushed for a statewide survey of traffic stops to examine racial profiling. Although law enforcement agencies opposed the legislation, Obama showed empathy and a good listening ear. After meaningful dialogue with law enforcement officers, he accepted some of their suggestions to soothe their fears and improve the bill.

By 1999, Obama had grown restless serving as a state legislator and had turned his attention to looking for a bigger political stage. In 2000, Obama decided to run for a seat in the U.S. House of Representatives. Democratic Party incumbent Bobby L. Rush had served four terms as a member of the House. Rush was a mainstay in congressional politics in Washington, DC, and a formidable opponent. A former Black Panther, a minister, and a veteran of the civil rights movement, Rush was beloved on the South Side of Chicago and had a strong hold on the politics of this area. The constituency of this district was predominantly black, working class, and overwhelmingly loyal to the Democratic Party. A few Chicago City Council members encouraged Obama to challenge for Rush's seat. Obama's close friends and

---

EMIL JONES

Emil Jones was Barack Obama's mentor while he served in the Illinois General Assembly. Jones was raised in one of Chicago's integrated and multiethnic communities. Being raised in a diverse community, he learned about many different traditions and cultures, and this became useful during his political career. Jones was inspired by the 1960 presidential candidacy of John F. Kennedy and volunteered for the campaign. During his time working on the Kennedy political campaign, Jones had a desire to join the call for public service and then began to work in the public sector. Jones served as an assistant for Wilson Frost, who was the only African American alderman to head the City of Chicago's Finance Committee.

In 1972, Jones was elected to the Illinois House of Representatives. He served in the Illinois House for ten years before moving to the Illinois Senate. In 2003, Jones was unanimously selected as minority leader of the Illinois Senate. Jones's political career was on built on the core issues of social justice, fair and adequate funding of public education, and helping the elderly and disadvantaged and working-class citizens. One of Jones's most notable pieces of legislation involved the statewide education curriculum. He successfully got legislation passed that required the teaching of African American and Holocaust history in all schools in Illinois.

close allies with more political cachet with state and local politics warned him not to challenge Rush for this congressional seat. Obama did not listen, and this challenge turned out to be a bad idea, but a great lesson for the future president. Not fully understanding the love and adulation this district had for Bobby Rush, Obama launched a campaign for the U.S. House of Representatives. In what could be considered a bit of arrogance, in Obama's mind, Rush was a lackluster and undistinguished representative. Rush campaigned on his experience as a seasoned political veteran and raised the hopes of the people of the district by declaring that if they voted for him "a better time was coming" (Scott, September 9, 2007).

Barack Obama was thirty-eight years old, teaching at the University of Chicago Law School, and serving as an Illinois state legislator. However, he was virtually unknown to the people who lived in the district, whereas Rush was a hero, celebrity, and legend in the district. Rush was also connected with established politicians in Washington. President Bill Clinton endorsed Rush in this race. Obama also made a political misstep in the political race. During the campaign Bobby Rush's son was murdered on his way from the grocery store, a tragedy that led to an outpouring of sympathy for Rush. Obama suspended his campaign. He and his family went for a brief visit to see his grandmother in Hawaii during the Christmas season. While he was visiting, the Illinois legislature was called back to a special session. On the trip, his daughter Malia got sick, and Obama could not get a flight back to Illinois. He did not return in time and missed a key vote on gun control in the state legislature and the media and his opponent skewered Obama for missing the vote. The bill was defeated by five votes.

After the missed vote, he was portrayed as a person who was not serious about getting things accomplished. Although this assertion was not true, this contributed to Obama's terrible showing in this election. This combination of Obama's voting mishap and President Clinton's endorsement of Rush spelled doom for Obama's House of Representative hopes. On the day of the election, Obama saw firsthand the district's adoration for Rush.

This political race got downright dirty and personal. Rush used Obama's education and his employment at the University of Chicago Law School to portray Obama as an out-of-touch elitist who could not possibly connect with the working-class sensibilities of the people of the district. He also portrayed Obama as overly ambitious and a man who had not paid his dues to the people of the district. Many of the people in the district were turned off by his "fancy education and big law school job at the University of Chicago." Rush even stated, "Obama went off to Harvard and became an educated fool" (Ballasy 2012). In one debate, Rush stated, "Barack reads about civil rights and thinks he knows all about. I helped make that history with my blood, sweat, and tears" (Kleine 2000). Rush also warned the world that the people of his district were not impressed with people who have Eastern elite degrees. Rush's statements signaled to people in the district that Obama was an outsider who did not understand them and their issues.

Evidently, the sullying message took hold with people in the district. Some of the people in the district wondered if Obama was "black enough" to represent their district. Some people in the district even went so far as to ignorantly say Obama was not "hood" enough and was too polished and too intellectual to represent the district. Obama worked the polls and greeted voters on election day. Most voters told Obama that he seemed like a nice guy, with some good ideas, but they were voting for Rush because, "Bobby Ain't Done Nothing Wrong!" (Scott, September 9, 2007). The issues of race and class within the black community were germane to this political race.

Obama lost badly to Bobby Rush. These same kinds of notions would come to play when Obama launched his campaign for president of the United States. In his book *The Audacity of Hope*, Obama noted the loss to Rush was the worst of his political career and filled with a comedy of errors and rookie mistakes. Obama was impressive with one aspect of his campaign. He was a phenomenal fundraiser. He tapped into the pockets of his high-income friends at Harvard Law School and University of Chicago Law, yet his fundraising was not enough to beat the politically savvy Bobby Rush. Rush was reelected by almost 60 percent of the vote. Obama learned a few of valuable lessons with the loss. Though he did not win, he learned that fundraising is truly the mother's milk of politics. He also learned that a candidate can have a total grasp of the issues but that people are looking for hope when they are casting their vote. The theme of hope became a central part of Obama's presidential campaign. He also learned he must connect with voters and use language and stories they could identify with. For a while there were tensions between Rush and Obama.

Despite the loss to Rush, Obama continued his work in the state senate on issues important to him. His tenure in the state senate can be summarized by these victories: Obama successfully cosponsored a prescription drug discount buying club program for seniors and the disabled, voted to end $300 million worth of tax breaks for businesses, voted to endorse embryonic stem cell research, voted against restrictions on public funding of abortion, sponsored a ban on discrimination based on sexual orientation, and sponsored major ethics reform called the Gift Ban Act. In 2004, "Bobby Rush still harbored resentment toward Obama for his earlier challenge" (Scott, September 9, 2007). Rush endorsed M. Blair Hull, a white candidate, when Obama ran for the U.S. Senate. Obama resigned from the Illinois Senate in November 2004 following his election to the U.S. Senate. With all of this success in Illinois politics, Obama arrived on the national scene with his address at the Democratic National Convention.

6

U.S. Senator

With the loss to Bobby Rush for Congress in 2000, Obama was not as sure of himself as a politician. He continued to diligently serve as an Illinois legislator while he looked for political opportunities. With two terms as an Illinois state senator, Obama passed a slew of bills and tackled complex issues like Illinois's death penalty system. Although it seemed all was well, it was not. Obama possessed a restlessness to accomplish more than working as a state legislator and law professor. This restlessness drove Obama to run for the U.S. Senate. As he says in his book, *The Audacity of Hope*,

> An up-or-out strategy was how I described it to my wife, one last shot to test out my ideas before I settled into a calmer, more stable, and better paying existence. And she perhaps more out of pity than conviction agreed to this one last race, though she also suggested that given the orderly life she preferred for our family, I shouldn't necessarily count on her vote. (Obama 2006)

Obama wanted this one last chance to make a significant difference. If he failed to win, he promised to settle into a more stable lifestyle as husband, father, and law professor. A political opportunity came in 2003 and put his lifestyle on hold, when Sen. Peter Fitzgerald decided to retire after just one term in the U.S. Senate. Fitzgerald decided to return to the private sector in business. Fitzgerald had used an estimated $13–$20 million of his personal funds and defeated Carol Moseley Braun for the Senate seat in 1998 (Wilgoren 2003). Meantime, Moseley Braun returned from an ambassadorship in New Zealand and gave thought to reclaiming her U.S. Senate seat, which would put Obama's own plan for the seat on hold. Moseley Braun decided to run for the presidency instead, which placed Obama in a viable position to go after the open senate seat. Open congressional seats without clear-cut and often handpicked successors are very rare. Therefore, there were a multitude of Democratic Party and Republican Party candidates vying for this open seat. Eight Democrat Party candidates competed in the primary, as did eight Republicans. When Obama threw his hat in the ring, no one really thought he had enough clout to pull off a victory in the primary and certainly not a victory in the general election. There were Democratic Party candidates with more statewide name recognition than Obama. Obama faced opponents that included a sitting state comptroller, a business millionaire, chief of staff for Chicago's mayor Richard M. Daley, and a black female health care professional.

Obama went full throttle into the campaign, hiring four young staffers who were ready to work for little money. He opened a small office and

---

Carol Moseley Braun

In 1992, Carol Moseley Braun became the first African American woman to be elected to the U.S. Senate. In 1969, Moseley Braun graduated from the University of Illinois with a degree in political science. After obtaining her undergraduate degree, she earned a law degree from the University of Illinois Law School in 1972. Shortly after earning her law degree, she began working as an assistant U.S. attorney in Chicago in 1973. Moseley Braun held her first political post as a Democratic representative to the Illinois House of Representatives, beginning in 1978. In 1988, she was elected recorder of deeds for Cook County, Illinois, overseeing hundreds of employees as well as the public agency's multimillion-dollar budget.

In 1992, Moseley Braun rose to the national political scene when she ran for the U.S. Senate. Moseley Braun defeated incumbent Democratic Senator Alan Dixon in the Democratic primary and then faced Republican Richard Williamson. Her campaign and term were hampered with allegations of misuse of campaign funds but she was able to pull off the victory and serve as senator. As a senator, Moseley Braun tackled many issues, including women's rights and civil rights. She served on several committees, including the powerful Senate Finance Committee. Moseley Braun continued to support educational reforms and called for more restrictive gun control laws. She lost her next political race and joined the private sector in 2004. After leaving public office for a time, Moseley Braun was appointed the U.S. ambassador to New Zealand and Samoa by President Bill Clinton. In January 2005, Barack Obama was elected to the U.S. Senate seat previously held by Moseley Braun. Obama resigned the post to run for president of the United States in November 2008.

began calling donors to help raise money for his campaign. In the beginning it was difficult. The campaign would hold press conferences and would have either poor attendance or no attendance at all. At the annual St. Patrick's Day Parade in Chicago, Obama's campaign was assigned the very last slot right before the sanitation workers began cleaning up garbage and campaign paraphernalia from lampposts (Norris 2006). Still, Obama did not give up despite the disrespect shown to his campaign. He traveled from ward to ward, county to county, town to town meeting, promoting his campaign and discussing his ideas.

Obama received little if any infrastructure support from Illinois's Democratic Party. He did not have mailing lists or an Internet operation. His support came through an organic campaign of people spreading Obama's ideas through word of mouth. Friends, acquaintances, ordinary people were willing to open their homes or arranged meetings at churches, Rotary Clubs, union halls, or bridge groups to support his campaign. Some meetings were large scale while others were more private at the kitchen table with only two or three people. Obama canvassed from cornfields of Bloomington, Illinois, to fashionable homes on the North Shore of Chicago, to the West Side of Chicago, and listened to people who were friendly, hostile, or indifferent to his campaign. He stayed focused on the issues. He chatted with people about bread-and-butter issues. He talked about local jobs, local schools, the economy, and universal health care.

For any political campaign, fundraising is the key to securing advertising on television and radio. Obama's campaign was bare bones. In the beginning of his campaign, he relied on grassroots support and soft advertising such as guest appearances on television talk shows and radio spots. To gain a foothold in advertising for his campaign, he would need a half a million dollars for a week of advertisement in the Chicago market for the primary race. For the general election, it would take another $15 million. Obama's most formidable primary opponent was M. Blair Hull, who was the founder of the Hull Trading Company. Hull eventually sold the company for $531 million (Dumke 2004). Hull began his campaign posting signs near Obama's home. Hull had beaten Obama to the punch in gaining support from black community leaders, convincing them that he was a champion of inner-city Chicago. Obama convinced large donors to support his campaign, while also appealing to small donors. Obama perfected using technology and the Internet to collect small donations. Small donations from five to ten dollars buttressed the big money donations, and the Obama campaign secured its financial footing for the primary race.

In the early polls, Obama trailed M. Blair Hull but always remained in second place or third, depending on the poll. During the second week of February 2004, Obama trailed Hull in polling data. Just prior to the primary vote, Obama overtook Hull in the polls and never lost control of the polls or the primary. By the second week of March 2004, Obama had closed the gap on Hull and in some polls had surpassed Hull. Negative issues from Hull's divorce became public, and his campaign went into a tailspin and eventually imploded. One week prior to the primary vote, Obama led in most of the polls. A couple weeks prior to the primary, Obama received a couple of high-profile endorsements that propelled him to front-runner status and ultimately a victory. Obama was endorsed by basketball star and icon Michael Jordan and Sheila Simon, the daughter of beloved Illinoisan and late Senator Paul Simon. In March 2004, when the totals were counted, Barack Obama captured the Democratic primary while Jack Ryan captured the Republican primary.

These primary victories set the stage for an interesting set of events that would pave the way for Obama's victory. In the general election, again Obama was the underdog. The vacant seat had previously been controlled by the Republican Party. President George W. Bush, a Republican, was in the White House and could use his influence and the National Committee's support to stump for the Republican candidate and sway voters. The Republicans underestimated the white-hot anger of the electorate, which allowed Obama's message to capture the moment. The Democratic Party shifted its attention and become focused on Republicans and their concentration on international affairs to the neglect of domestic affairs and their perceived policy mistakes. This allowed Obama to bring to the public agenda issues such as health care and a living wage. These were issues he knew very well from his days as a community organizer. Obama knew working class people wanted a living wage and affordable health care that would not cause them to go into bankruptcy if they had a long-term illness. He knew firsthand the benefits of good schools, and he agreed with Americans who believed children should have a good K–12 education. Moreover, a college education should be affordable if not free for all those who wanted to enroll. The preceding, along with other kitchen table issues like clean air and water and neighborhoods safe from crime, were what people wanted addressed, regardless of their political party affiliation. Listening to people and hearing their issues helped Obama hone his political agenda.

Dan Shomon began as Obama's campaign manager but left the campaign after the death of his mother (Remnick 2010, p. 366). Obama turned to David Axelrod, who was not a campaign manager but a political strategist and a media expert. Axelrod began looking for a campaign manager and turned to Jim Cauley. A native Kentuckian, Cauley was a blunt political operative and difficult to impress. On initially meeting Obama, Cauley was not taken with the future president. Cauley had worked with black politicians in the past and had helped many of them get elected to public office in areas where blacks were not the majority of the electorate. Cauley did not want to use many of the strategies and tactics old school black political candidates had utilized in the past. He believed Obama was a midtier candidate at best, but after speaking with him, Cauley was impressed and convinced that he was a candidate with wide appeal. He was convinced Obama was a part of the post–civil rights era black politicians who could appeal to white voters. He realized Obama was progressive and not just a gifted black politician and candidate, but a gifted politician and great candidate in general. He realized Obama "had the juice" (Feltus, Goldstein, and Dallek 2018). He discovered Obama was a part of the next wave of formidable black political candidates who could win a Senate seat as well as the presidency with the right team around them.

Obama's Republican opponent for the general election, Jack Ryan, had his own compelling story that was just as interesting as Obama's. Ryan, a former wealthy investment banker, was a Harvard Law School and Harvard Business School graduate who financed his own political campaign. Ryan also had a look from central casting: tall, handsome, and debonair. Despite his wealth, he left his high-profile position on Wall Street to become an educator and teach in the inner city at an all-black high school for three years. This school had shown a great deal of success placing their graduates in college.

When the general election opened, by all accounts both men were excellent candidates. There were recurring rumors about Ryan's divorce from actress Jeri Ryan. The divorce documents were sealed. The *Chicago Tribune* requested court documents associated with Ryan's child custody case in California. After receiving the documents, the *Chicago Tribune* published them. They contained allegations of sordid details about their sex life (Chase and Ford 2004). Just as in the Democratic primary, Obama was the beneficiary of an opponent's acrimonious divorce proceedings and records. The Republicans pressured Ryan to resign and he decided to withdraw from the Senate race less than a week after the court documents were released.

The Republican Party was left scrambling to find a suitable candidate to replace Ryan on the Republican ticket. The party chose Alan Keyes. Keyes had mounted a weak campaign to become the Republican nominee for president of the United States in 2000. At the time, Keyes did not even live in Illinois. He was a resident of Maryland and had run for the senate in Maryland. This marked the first time in history two black candidates competed for a U.S. Senate seat. Keyes, a master debater, made inroads discussing conservative social issues like abortion, but failed to connect with Illinoisans on issues that really mattered to them. The Republican Party made a terrible error with drafting Keyes as their senatorial candidate. Keyes was not a viable candidate to run for office in a state where he was not a resident. Keyes was no match for Obama. Perhaps remembering the

---

EDWARD BROOKE

In 1966, Edward W. Brooke was the first African American elected to the U.S. Senate and the first since Reconstruction. Brooke served for two terms representing Massachusetts. He was a moderate member of the Republican Party. Brooke positioned himself not only as an African American leader but as a leader of all people in the Commonwealth of Massachusetts. He became a powerful figure on the Appropriations Committee and a considerable force on social and housing policy. He was nonpartisan in his support of various issues and political figures. He was his own man and refused to be a lackey for any political agenda. Brooke did not support Barry Goldwater. However, he supported Richard Nixon's Supreme Court nominees with a racist past but also voted twice against Nixon's nominations for the U.S. Supreme Court. In 2005, President George W. Bush awarded Brooke the Presidential Medal of Freedom. Before his death in 2015, Brooke noted he was "thankful to God" that he lived long enough to see Barack Obama become the nation's first black president of the United States. Brooke was age ninety-five when he died in his home at Coral Gables, Florida. He is buried in Arlington National Cemetery.

---

thrashing he'd received from Bobby Rush and his previous congressional race, Obama campaigned aggressively for the entire length of the campaign season.

In the general election, Obama soundly defeated Republican and former diplomat Alan Keyes. Obama won the general election by the biggest margin ever in an Illinois U.S. Senate race with nearly 70 percent of the vote (Ford and Mendell 2004). Obama collected massive totals in areas where he had lost to Bobby Rush in 2000. With this victory, Obama became the first African American male to be elected as a U.S. senator since Edward Brooke of Massachusetts in 1967. Obama became the second black person elected to the U.S. Senate from Illinois. The first black person elected to the U.S. Senate from Illinois was Senator Carol Moseley Braun. Moseley Braun was elected to the U.S. Senate in 1992.

During the summer of 2004, Obama moved from rising star to bona fide star of the Democratic Party. Barack Obama's keynote address at the Democratic Party National Convention in July 2004 introduced him to the world. The 2004 presidential elections were approaching, and John Kerry secured the presidential nomination for the Democratic Party to challenge President George W. Bush for the presidency. Like most political party loyalists, especially those with great political ambitions, Obama campaigned for Kerry. Obama's political ambitions aside, the two men respected each other and realized they were kindred spirits of sorts. Kerry and Obama's relationship grew after they hit it off while both were visiting

JOHN KERRY

John Kerry did not win in his first bid for Congress in 1972. After this loss, Kerry pursued a law career after graduating from Boston College Law School in 1976. He then began a career in public service that encompassed more than thirty years. His first public service job was as the assistant district attorney of Middlesex County in Massachusetts. After serving in this role, Kerry became lieutenant governor of Massachusetts under Gov. Michael Dukakis. Kerry's public service in the Commonwealth of Massachusetts prepared him for the national political stage.

Kerry won one of Massachusetts's U.S. Senate seats in 1984. He was reelected in 1990, 1996, 2002, and 2008. While serving in the Senate, Kerry earned a reputation for supporting free trade, expansive U.S. foreign and military policy, investment in education, and environmental protection. In 2004, Kerry won the Democratic nomination for president. He made George W. Bush's foreign policy and the Iraq War the focal point of his presidential campaign. During the 2004 presidential campaign, John Kerry asked Barack Obama to speak at the Democratic National Convention in Boston, Massachusetts. After Obama gave a stirring speech, he became a fixture on the political national scene. In December 2012, President Barack Obama nominated Kerry to be his secretary of state, succeeding Hillary Clinton. Obama considered Kerry to be the ideal candidate for the job because of his decades of political experience.

at a vocational center on Chicago's West Side and they met again at a fundraiser at the Hyatt Regency hotel in downtown Chicago. Kerry and Obama developed a bond. When Kerry was considering a keynote speaker for the 2004 Democratic Party convention, he and his strategists and organizers considered several politicians. Kerry's team considered governor of Michigan, Jennifer Granholm, governor of Arizona, Janet Napolitano, governor of Iowa, Tom Vilsack, and Illinois Senator Barack Obama (Berry and Gottheimer 2010).

John Kerry's campaign team concluded that Obama was politically the right choice for the keynote spot because he would help attract African American voters. At the time, Kerry was lagging in the polls and he had received a lukewarm reception from African Americans. The Kerry campaign also believed that Obama's clean-cut and youthful appearance would strike the right tone and provide an optimistic message to the convention. Once the invitation was extended and Obama accepted, he knew he wanted to construct this speech in a way that interwove his personal story with the American story to uplift people's hopes.

Obama diligently worked on his speech. Hour after hour and day after day leading up to the convention, Obama labored, constructing his speech, working on parts on whatever paper he could find when a great sentence or story came to him. He wrote draft after draft. He scribbled on scraps of paper, on the corner of envelopes, on yellow legal pads, and on the top of memos from his aides. He tested his applause lines on anyone who would listen to him. He rehearsed his speech material on his state senate colleagues. He tried out parts of the speech at campaign events and other public events. He continued this trial-and-error approach to speechwriting up to the convention kickoff. On one occasion, Obama came up with a major revision and some new ideas to enhance his speech. He bolted to the men's restroom off the Illinois General Assembly and sat on a toilet to capture his new ideas and write the corrections (Saslow 2008). About a week before the convention, he had a good workable speech but polishing the speech remained. His writing drafts of the speech would continue after the senate day was complete well into the night ending, at one or two in the morning.

Political conventions are orchestrated events with every moment scripted. Political conventions also have tight schedules. Kerry's staff designated Obama only eight minutes for the address. Obama's original draft was twenty-five minutes, so he and his aides worked to scale down the speech into the time allotted. They often disagreed on what content should be cut and what content should remain. Aides would cut out content and Obama would add it back. Because the Kerry campaign had not reviewed the final draft of Obama's speech, they were a little anxious about the content. After the Kerry campaign received a final draft of Obama's speech, they knew it would be a great speech and a memorable moment in the political landscape of U.S. politics. After reading the draft, the Kerry campaign increased Obama's speaking time to seventeen minutes.

Obama and Michelle traveled to the convention and were beseeched with interviews. He sat down for interviews with ABC, NBC, CBS, CNN, Fox News, and National Public Radio. In addition, he did a one-on-one interview with Tim Russert for NBC's *Meet the Press*. Things were going well until it was time to rehearse the address at the Fleet Center. With so many interviews, Obama had strained his voice and had the onset of a case of laryngitis. Obama's rehearsal at the Fleet Center was awkward and unimpressive because he had not been on such a large stage and was not familiar with the workings of a teleprompter. Instead of reading the speech during rehearsal, Obama was winging it and not winging it very well. A staffer coached him and gave him a few pointers of how to master reading from the teleprompter to three competing audiences who would be viewing his address. He would be simultaneously speaking to the screaming party delegates, the giant Jumbotron within the hall, and millions of people who would be glued to their televisions. After a three-hour-long rehearsal, Obama felt comfortable with the task before him. As Obama rested in the

Boston Celtics locker room, members of Kerry's campaign staff watched Obama's charisma and his calm demeanor, and they believed they were in the presence of a special politician.

The day of the speech, Obama had a busy schedule. His schedule began with speaking at a rally sponsored by the League of Conservation Voters followed by interviews with various news media outlets. He flawlessly delivered the talking points the Kerry campaign team had provided. Barack Obama has never been overly concerned with fashion matters and wore a tie that his wife considered a style blunder. Michelle took matters into her own hands and decided that one of Obama's staffer's ties was better. She convinced the staffer to allow Obama to borrow the tie for his speech.

As time grew closer for him to speak, he began to realize the gravity of the moment. A little before his time to go on stage, he began to get nervous. As he wrote in *The Audacity of Hope*, "It wasn't until after he and Michelle were alone backstage he began to get nervous." Michelle hugged him, looked lovingly into his eyes and said, "Just don't screw it up, buddy!" (Obama 2006, p. 359). Alone backstage, Obama summoned up images of his mother, father, grandfather, and grandmother for strength. He also thought about all of his supporters in Illinois. Evidently, these thoughts gave Obama the assurance to emerge onto the stage and for seventeen minutes give the greatest speech of his political life. One of the most memorable sections of the speech would go down in political history and be replayed for years to come:

> It's what allows us to pursue our individual dreams, yet still come together as a single American family: "E pluribus unum," out of many, one. Now even as we speak, there are those who are preparing to divide us, the spin masters and negative ad peddlers who embrace the politics of anything goes. There's not a black America and white America and Latino America and Asian America; there's the United States of America. The pundits, the pundits like to slice and dice our country into red states and blue States: red states for Republicans, blue States for Democrats. But I've got news for them, too. We worship an awesome God in the blue states, and we don't like federal agents poking around our libraries in the red states. We coach little league in the blue states and, yes, we've got some gay friends in the red states. Well, I say to them tonight, there's not a liberal America and a conservative America; there's the United States of America. (Obama, July 27, 2004)

Obama did not shy away from the occasion; he took full advantage of his moment on the world stage. The keynote address earned rave reviews and it was well received by a wide swath of the American public. The speech contained mostly moderate views, which appealed to most Americans. He also had the picture perfect political family, a million dollar smile, and came across as very engaging. After his keynote address, requests for

Obama to speak at engagements skyrocketed. His oratory skills were compared to those of John Kennedy, Ronald Reagan, and Dr. Martin Luther King Jr. After the speech, Obama was mobbed by crowds, yet he was modest about his performance at the convention. He had gained national and international attention with this speech at the Democratic National Convention in Boston. Reporters began asking Obama about a possible run for the presidency in 2008. Understanding deference to the party establishment, he did not directly entertain the question. He understood saying he would make a bid for the presidency so early after the party's presidential loss would be inappropriate. Being a junior U.S. senator, Obama knew the deference associated with being a member and therefore he must appear as an awed and eager apprentice (Remnick 2010, p. 419).

The Obama family had to make adjustments to their living arrangements when he became a U.S. senator. Michelle and his daughters would remain in Chicago, and Obama would rent a one-bedroom apartment near the capitol in a high-rise near Georgetown. With his commitment to being a family man and father, he decided to return to Chicago each weekend to see his family and stay connected with his constituents, which he knew was important. He had witnessed Carol Moseley Braun make this fatal error as a U.S. senator. She became distant and disconnected from her constituency during her tenure as senator because she did not return to her district to meet with people. Obama made sure this would not be his fate. In his first year as a U.S. senator, he held thirty-nine town meetings in Illinois.

Obama wanted to build relationships with his constituency; he also wanted to build relationships in Washington, DC, with both Democrats and Republicans. As a junior U.S. senator, Obama was intentional in developing relationships with veteran senators no matter their voting patterns or past political views. For instance, he visited Democrat Robert Byrd of West Virginia. Byrd was a member of the Ku Klux Klan as a young man. He sympathetically listened to Byrd as he described the sins of his youth and membership in the Klan as an albatross around his neck. Obama comforted Byrd, reminding him that if perfection is expected, everyone is destined for failure. He reminded Byrd that is why humans need God's grace and mercy to overcome their pasts.

Obama also built a relationship with Richard Lugar, a Republican senator from Indiana. As they engaged in senatorial work, the two developed a bond. Senators Obama and Lugar traveled with a congressional delegation to Russia, Ukraine, and Azerbaijan to inspect and meet with officials on weapons-storage facilities. Obama was fascinated with the events that unfolded on the trip. He and Lugar observed secret weapons sites and the dismantling of aging rockets and laboratories from the old Soviet Union's biological weapons programs. They made several of these trips—good training for the future president's foreign policy competences. Obama and Lugar published an op-ed in the *Washington Post* called, "Junkyard Dogs of War," warning against the threat of loose conventional weapons from the former Soviet Union and other Baltic countries. The connection with Lugar, who was seen as a salty conservative Republican, led to the introduction of bipartisan legislation to gain support and cooperation of other nations to tighten control of arms caches in the former Soviet Union. These caches were routinely looted and their chemicals were used to make improvised bombs in the Middle East to fuel civil wars within Africa. Their legislation helped to halt the illegal shipments of materials used in chemical, biological, and nuclear weapons.

Obama also worked on immigration reform with Mel Martinez, a Republican senator from Florida. He worked with hard right-wing Republican Tom Coburn from Oklahoma and created legislation to have greater transparency and accountability in government contracting. Developing relationships with Byrd and Lugar showed Obama's bipartisanship and penchant for reaching across the aisle to get legislation passed. He had showed this propensity his entire adult life. This had been his mode of operation as an undergraduate student, as a law school student, as an Illinois legislator, and now as a U.S. senator. As William Finnegan of *The New Yorker* explained, "He knows how to make those who disagree with his views feel comfortable" (Finnegan 2004).

Obama wanted to have a diverse office staff, but he did not see himself solely as an African American senator. He saw himself as a senator from Illinois who happened to be African American. As a U.S. senator, Obama focused on legislative efforts that impacted the state of Illinois. This included developing legislation for highway construction, infrastructure, and alternative energy. He quietly and diligently worked and soon gained the confidence of his colleagues in the Senate. He secured appointments to committees like Environment and Public Works, Foreign Relations, Veterans Affairs, Homeland Security and Government Affairs, and Health, Education, Labor, and Pensions. Obama did not rest on his laurels as a U.S. senator. During the 109th and 110th Congresses, he sponsored and cosponsored more than 570 bills. Fifteen of those bills became law after he joined the Senate in 2005 (Obama Congressional Record). His legislative effort covered a gamut of issues including energy, climate change, health care, consumer protections, congressional ethics, foreign policy, education, homeland security, and discrimination.

During this time, he avoided speaking on the hot button issue of the time, the war in Iraq. Even though he avoided making public statements about the war, he raised his profile hitting the speaking circuit. On the speaking circuit Obama began to tackle the erroneous notion that the Christian faith was monolithic in its views. This monolithic view is often promulgated by the evangelical Christians and religious right groups. He accepted an invitation to speak to a group called the Sojourners, a liberal evangelical Christian group that was opposed to the policies of the religious right. Moreover, members of this group were ardent supporters of social justice. By addressing this group, he showed there was diversity within evangelical groups within the United States. Many members of Obama's own church in Chicago, Trinity United Church of Christ, believed religious faith should correlate with a political liberation and compassion. By speaking to this group, he believed he peeled back biases embedded in the religious right's message that had dominated Christian views. He hoped by detangling the religious right's message, there might be a discovery of overlapping shared values by both religious and secular people.

Obama's first book, *Dreams of My Father*, had become a best-seller, and with the publication of his second book, *The Audacity of Hope: Thoughts on Reclaiming the American Dream*, thoughts of possibly running for president of the United States crept into his mind. In 2006 with the overwhelming media publicity and throngs of people at his book signings, he began to give serious thought to a presidential bid. As he autographed books, people encouraged him to go for it and run. He would later briefly mention he was considering a run for the presidency on *Meet the Press*. The thought of being president had crossed his mind several times.

To mount a presidential bid, he knew he had one daunting task before him. He had to convince Michelle to come onboard and support his presidential aspiration. He remembered he had promised that his U.S. Senate run would be his last foray running for public office. In 2006 during the Christmas holidays in Hawaii, the Obama family began discussing the presidency. With Michelle's blessing and the promise of a dog for his daughters if he won, the Obamas were ready to run for the White House, filing papers to run just one month later.

7

Presidential Campaign

On January 16, 2007, Obama filed papers for a presidential exploratory committee. One month later, on February 10, 2007, on a frigidly cold day at the Old State House capitol in Springfield, Illinois, Obama announced he was running for president of the United States. This space held a hallowed place in the history of state and national politics. It is the place where Abraham Lincoln began his bid for the U.S. Senate in 1858. Despite it being a bitterly cold day, approximately seventeen thousand people still came to hear his announcement and witness history. The moment was historic; 149 years after Abraham Lincoln began his campaign for public office, Barack Obama, an African American man, stepped up to commence his campaign for the highest office of the United States.

Behind the scenes prior to the announcement, controversy was brewing. Plans for the announcement speech at the Old State Capitol included an invocation by Obama's friend and Pastor of Trinity United Church, Jeremiah Wright. A few days before the event, an article in *Rolling Stone Magazine* described Pastor Wright as "a profane preacher given to an Afrocentric interpretation of the Bible reading." The quote the magazine used was taken from a ceremony almost fifteen years prior to Obama's announcement at the installation of a dean of chapel at Howard University.

Obama's aides were alarmed by the article and openly questioned whether Pastor Wright should be put onstage for the presidential announcement. They believed Pastor Wright's presence and association with the event would wreck any presidential hopes for Obama and that Hillary Clinton would use this ammunition to sink Obama's presidential campaign. David Axelrod discussed the issue with Obama. Initially, Obama resisted removing Pastor Wright from the program but reluctantly relented and called Wright. After a series of discussions between the two men about the magazine article and the possible negative impact on his budding presidential campaign, Wright withdrew from giving the invocation at the event. Obama was unaware his aides had already begun to search for someone else to pray at the announcement, and they had secured a replacement. In the wake of these confusing developments, Obama eliminated an invocation and directly made the announcement. Undoubtedly, Pastor Wright was hurt by these developments, but before the event he met with Obama and his family and led a small private prayer. During the announcement, Wright stood quietly by Obama and Michelle. The Wright controversy would creep up later in Obama's campaign. After criticism of his association with Wright persisted throughout his campaign, Obama directly addressed this issue with his Philadelphia race speech.

Another controversial issue flared on the day of Obama's presidential announcement. Tavis Smiley, a prominent African American talk show host and author, was angry because the Obama announcement was scheduled on the same day as the annual State of the Black Union Conference in Hampton, Virginia. This conference was held annually in varying locations with black leaders and scholars discussing issues affecting the African American community. The conference had become a staple in the African American community, and Obama's announcement drew attention away from this event. To compound matters, noted professor, political activist, and scholar Cornel West began to make public statements warning about the trustworthiness of Obama's campaign after Wright was removed from giving the invocation. Obama retorted his campaign was focused on inclusion and not exclusion. It was their goal to run a campaign not centered solely on race. This did not mean that they would ignore policies related to race, but ethnic issues would not be at the core of his campaign. This strategy was different from previous black presidential candidates' campaigns, where racial issues were put first on the campaign agenda.

As Obama stated in his keynote speech at the Democratic National Convention in 2004, there is not a black America or a white America. In the U.S. electorate, there are millions of voters of all ethnic groups and races: white, Latino, African American, and Asian. If he was going to win, he was going to have to appeal to all people to pull out a presidential victory and become the first African American president of the United States. He knew becoming president would be difficult to accomplish, but there were a few key contributing factors that ensured this was indeed the optimal time to make a run. Many voters had become disenchanted with the Bush administration's policies and the wars in Iraq and Afghanistan. The Bush years birthed a growing distrust of the Republican Party and tarnished the party's brand. Cornell Belcher, an Obama pollster, believed George W. Bush's ineffectiveness as president was instrumental in the rise of Barack Obama.

The electoral map was transforming. Southern States were becoming more diverse, and the religious right was losing its grip in the culture wars of the South. The Democratic Party was advancing through its efforts to increase the number of new voters. This could be an advantage for Obama's presidential bid. Also, African American elected representation in other southern states such as Virginia and North Carolina was growing fast, changing demographically, and these states' economic infrastructures were improving with high-technology jobs (Frey 2009).

Obama had shown success in suburbs and rural counties during the U.S. Senate race, and this proved his wide appeal. This was evidence he had the capacity to run well not only in African American areas but among white progressive people. It was believed that Obama could have a strong showing and even win in areas which traditionally had been mainstays of racial animosity. Mark Alexander, a professor of constitutional law at Seton Hall University, wrote a white paper about Obama's potential presidential campaign. The paper, titled "It Can Be Done," gave a positive assessment and affirmed Obama could win because of the large number of unregistered African American voters in Georgia, North Carolina, Florida, and Virginia. Getting these folks registered and out to vote would be imperative for an Obama victory. These factors made Obama's team of operatives optimistic about his chances of winning.

Though Obama was the first African American to announce a presidential bid on such a grand scale and to such wide acclaim, he was not the first African American to run for president. In 1972, Shirley Chisholm, a member of the U.S. House of Representatives from New York, made a run for president. She campaigned under the slogan "Unbought and Unbossed." A decade or so after Shirley Chisholm's presidential run, Jesse Jackson and his "rainbow coalition" made presidential bids in 1984 and 1988.

Obama's bid for the presidency was different from those of his predecessors. As with his previous senatorial campaign, Obama's presidential campaign was not designed strictly for a black politician's campaign. His campaign message was inclusive and constructed around the themes of hope and change. Jackson had built a "rainbow coalition," but Obama built a rainbow army, first in Chicago and then across the country. Obama's message was inclusive and targeted varied groups in the far reaches of the country. He connected with people. He told the stories of farmers from

---

JESSE JACKSON SR.

In November of 1983, Jesse Jackson announced his candidacy for the presidential nomination for the Democratic Party. Jackson was a veteran of the civil rights movement. He was one of the lieutenants who served and marched with Dr. Martin Luther King Jr. He was present when Dr. King was assassinated on the balcony of the Lorraine Motel in Memphis, Tennessee, on April 4, 1968. Jackson used a grassroots mobilization by attempting to build a coalition of multirace, multiethnic, and multieconomic people called the Rainbow Coalition. Jackson's presidential platform focused on tax reform, deficit reduction, and employment. At this time, Jackson's platform was considered more liberal and progressive than his Democratic Party competitors.

Jackson fared well in the Democratic primaries, but Walter Mondale ultimately won the nomination in 1984. Jackson's supporters were upset when Jackson was not chosen as Mondale's vice presidential running mate. Mondale chose Geraldine Ferraro, who became the first woman on a major party's presidential ticket. In the general presidential election, Ronald Reagan defeated Mondale by a landslide. Mondale lost both the Electoral College and the popular vote by large margins. Jackson mounted a second presidential run in 1987. During this presidential run, he did win fifteen primaries and received about 7 million votes. His primary victories were due to his campaign mobilization abilities. In 1988, Michael Dukakis won the Democratic Party nomination.

---

midwestern states. He met with miners from northeastern states. He gathered with Gulf Coast fishermen. He listened to their stories of despair and desperation. The dissatisfaction with the perceived dishonesty of the Bush presidency was a constant refrain on Obama's campaign listening tours. People were also unhappy and upset with high unemployment and extraordinarily high health care costs. Obama did not harbor any personal animus toward George W. Bush; he believed he simply disagreed on policies and what direction the country should be moving.

For Obama, a new generation of people was emerging to make America a better place, and he wanted to be the leader of this group of people. Obama believed the Bush administration was out of touch with poor people and those who needed help. He believed the majority of the Bush administration was made up of people who had no idea about people who need help in America. In addressing the Bush administration's disconnection from ordinary people, Obama stated,

> They believe in different things. They have a sense that in fact government is the problem, not the solution, and that if we dismantle government piece by piece, if we break it up in tax cuts for the wealthy and if we just make sure that we privatize Social Security and we get rid of public schools and make

sure that we don't have police on the streets, we hire private security guards and we don't have public parks and if we just break everything up, then in fact everybody's better off—that in fact we don't have obligations to each other, that we're not in it together but instead you're on your own. (Kornblut 2006).

While exploring Iowa for the presidential caucus in 2008, Obama was invited to the Tom Harkin Steak Fry to discuss his qualifications and give a stump speech. Iowa has had a tradition that if a politician wants to launch a presidential bid, he or she must come to Iowa and pal around before launching a campaign. This especially holds true if the candidate is running for the Democratic Party nomination. This speaking engagement allowed Obama to further explain his spellbinding background and interesting personal narrative. He began his speech with a description of his

---

SHIRLEY CHISHOLM

In 1968, Shirley Chisholm became the first African American woman to earn election to the U.S. House of Representative. She was also the first African American woman of a major political party to run for president of the United States in 1972. While in the U.S. House of Representatives, she worked on the Education and Labor Committee and was a founding member of the Congressional Black Caucus in 1969. Chisholm spent a portion of her childhood in Barbados with her grandmother. Chisholm graduated from Brooklyn College and later earned a master's degree in elementary education from Columbia University. Before deciding to go into politics as a career, Chisholm was a teacher and served as director of the Hamilton-Madison Child Care Center from 1953 to 1959. She also served as an educational consultant to New York City's Bureau of Child Welfare from 1959 to 1964.

In 1969, when Chisholm began the first of seven terms, she was assigned to the House Forestry Committee. She demanded reassignment because she believed this assignment would not directly assist the constituents of her district. At this time, refusing a congressional committee assignment was a daring move for white male member of Congress. It was an even more daring move for an African American, woman, and freshman member of Congress. An unrelenting Chisholm was placed on the Veterans Affairs Committee and then eventually graduated to the Education and Labor Committee. Chisholm is remembered as a champion of minority education and employment opportunities. She is also remembered as a vocal opponent of the military draft because she believed that minorities and poor men were disproportionally being sent to fight in the war in Vietnam. After serving seven terms in Congress, in 1983 Chisholm became a professor at Mount Holyoke College and was a public lecturer. During her career, she authored two books, *Unbought and Unbossed* and *The Good Fight*. Shirley Chisholm died in 2005 in Ormond Beach, Florida.

eclectic background telling the story about his parents: his mother from Kansas, his father from Kenya. He also included his maternal grandparents, who raised him. With this speech, Obama reached out to moderates. He expounded on the economy, religion, and race. Most importantly and remembering what he had learned earlier in his career, Obama listened to people even if they disagreed with him about various issues. Although Iowa had an overwhelmingly white state demographic, Obama was able to connect with many people. For Obama to gain traction in the presidential race, a strong showing in Iowa was pivotal. Only a win and not just a strong showing in Iowa would show black America that an African American man could win and become president of the United States. The more people learned about Obama and his background, the more they liked him as a presidential candidate.

For the Democratic Party presidential candidates, the Iowa caucus is the key. It is the first event, and a strong showing can help a candidate secure the Democratic Party nomination. The seven candidates on the Democratic side included Barack Obama, Hillary Clinton, John Edwards, Bill Richardson, Joe Biden, Chris Dodd, and Mike Gravel. All had various levels of elected office experience. Hillary Clinton had a sophisticated fundraising machine with an enormous network of aides and volunteers. She also had a big-gun option in her campaign organization, husband and former president Bill Clinton.

But before the Iowa caucus and New Hampshire primary, a drama between the Obama and Clinton camps emerged. The old guard of the civil rights movement and African American politicians such as John Lewis faced a dilemma between choosing between Hillary Clinton and Barack Obama. Would they choose a viable African American candidate for president or would they stick with the Clinton machine?

Andrew Young, once a close adviser to Dr. Martin Luther King Jr. and later mayor of Atlanta, a congressman, and the first African American ambassador to the United Nations during President Jimmy Carter's administration, came out in support of Hillary Clinton, citing Obama's age and perceived lack of experience, noting he should wait until 2016.

Vernon Jordan, former president of the National Urban League and civil rights attorney, also did not support Obama's presidential efforts. Jordan was a close friend and had served as an adviser to the Clintons. Though Jordan had helped raise funds for Obama's senate campaign, he threw his support behind Hillary Clinton. Privately, Jordan told Obama he would not support his run.

Fortunately for Obama, there were still living civil rights figures who admired him. John Lewis was a nineteen-year-old college student at Fisk University in Nashville, Tennessee, when he organized sit-ins at segregated lunch counters and nonviolent marches. He was the youngest of the

Big Six civil rights leaders and chairman of the Student Nonviolent Coordinating Committee (SNCC) from 1963 to 1966. During those turbulent times, Lewis participated in Freedom Rides, which challenged segregation at interstate bus terminals across the South. At age twenty-three, Lewis was the youngest organizer and a keynote speaker at the March on Washington in 1963. In 1964, Lewis coordinated the SNCC efforts to organize voter registration drives and community action programs in Mississippi. His efforts led to an orderly and peaceful march of six hundred protesters across the Edmund Pettus Bridge in Selma, Alabama, on March 7, 1965. At the end of the bridge, the protesters were met by Alabama state troopers and ordered to disperse. The encounter became violent when troopers discharged tear gas and beat protesters with night sticks. This confrontation became known as "Bloody Sunday." Lewis's skull was fractured during the incident, but he was able to escape across the bridge and back to the movement's headquarters at Brown Chapel. Before Lewis was taken to the hospital for his injury, he appeared before the television cameras asking President Lyndon B. Johnson to intervene in Alabama. The news broadcast and photographs exposing the senseless cruelty placed pressure on President Johnson's administration to pass the Voting Rights Act of 1965. Lewis's civil rights résumé was one Obama admired.

Once in Washington, Obama and Lewis quickly formed a bond, but Lewis initially endorsed Hillary Clinton for president. Lewis had a long friendship with the Clintons. During a dark period in Bill Clinton's presidency, it was Lewis who stood behind him after the Monica Lewinsky scandal. This decision to switch his endorsement was a difficult moment for Lewis. He was caught in the middle of two people he admired. Lewis had a long-standing working relationship with the Clintons but he recognized the Obama campaign was serious. It did not take long for Lewis, an eleven-term congressman, to change his mind and switch his support for Obama. During Georgia's primary, Lewis's fifth district strongly supported Obama. Lewis said, "As a U.S. representative, it is my role not to try to subdue or suppress the will of the people, but to help it prosper and grow" (Johnson, Crowley, and Mooney 2008).

Another living civil rights hero who supported Obama was Jesse Jackson. Jackson participated in the Selma to Montgomery marches with Dr. Martin Luther King Jr. and James Bevel. Dr. King was impressed with Jackson's ambition and passion and he quickly rose to the ranks within the Southern Christian Leadership Conference (SCLC). Jackson was soon given the task to establish a SCLC office in Chicago. After the death of Dr. King, Jackson began to emerge as a prominent civil rights leader; however, he clashed with Ralph Abernathy, successor to the SCLC. Three years later, Jackson broke away from SCLC and created Operation PUSH (People

United to Save Humanity, later changed to People United to Serve Humanity) (Purnick and Oreskes 1987). The goal of the organization was to move toward political action and pressure elected officials to improve economic opportunities for the poor and all races.

It was Harold Washington's victory as mayor of Chicago that gave Jackson the inspiration to run for the presidency; it was also an inspiration to Obama. In a 1983 *New York Times* article, Jackson declared:

> I seek the presidency to serve the nation at a level where I can help restore a moral tone, a redemptive spirit and a sensitivity to the poor and the dispossessed of this nation. . . . [T]his is not just one man running for the office but an attempt to inspire others—a rainbow coalition—black, white and Hispanic citizens, women, American Indians . . . the voiceless and downtrodden. . . . We Want Our Wagon Full. (Smothers 1983)

During the 1984 Democratic primaries, Jackson won 18 percent of the votes, winning South Carolina, Louisiana, and Washington, DC. In 1988, Jackson won nine states and Washington, DC. Jackson believed that the United States was far from postracial and that while he might not win the presidency, his declaration in 1984 and 1988 would plant the seeds for the idea of a black president.

The seeds grew in favor of Obama to run for the presidency, and Jackson supported his efforts. Jackson knew Obama through the Project Vote organization. Both men on occasion spoke about politics, but they were not close. Jackson was invited to speak at Saturday morning meetings at Operation PUSH. As one of the old guards from the civil rights movement, Jackson understood why John Lewis and Andrew Young were not as supportive of Obama's campaign. They were supporters of Bill and Hillary and had long, close relationships with them. Most importantly, they believed Clinton was strong enough to win because she had been in the trenches with them. Clinton had a track record with her legal defense work from Arkansas, Alabama, and Mississippi.

While Jackson supported Obama, he did not hesitate to criticize Obama's decision to not speak out on racial issues. In Jena, Louisiana, racial tensions at the high school reached a boiling point when three nooses were hung on the branches of the oak tree black students congregated under. The school's principal recommended expulsion for those involved, but the three white students were suspended for three days, with the incident described as a "prank" (Mooney 2007). Days later, six black students beat up a white student, Justin Baker, knocking him unconscious. The six black students were dubbed the Jena 6 and charged with aggravated battery and conspiracy. Because of the event, civil rights leaders, such as Al Sharpton, Jesse Jackson, and hip-hop artist Mos Def, organized a march in the small town. Obama did not participate in the activities but released a statement.

Jackson was sharply critical of Obama refusing to take an active part in the protest of the Jena 6. At a speech at Benedict College, Jackson heavily criticized Obama.

> Obama is acting like he's white. . . . [H]e needs to be bolder in his stance if he wants to make inroads in South Carolina. . . . [H]e has remarkably transcended race, however the impact of Katrina and Jena makes America's unresolved moral dilemma of race unavoidable. I think Jena is another defining moment of the issue of race and the criminal justice system. This issue requires direct and bold leadership. I commend Senator Obama for speaking out and demanding fairness on this defining issue. Any attempt to dilute my support for Senator Obama will not succeed. (Burris 2007)

Obama did not have the full support of black leaders, but proving he was a serious candidate meant appealing to a variety of voters regardless of their race or ethnicity. That is why it was so important to focus on Iowa. In September 2007, Michelle said, "If Barack doesn't win Iowa, it's just a dream" (Kornblut 2007). Obama's Iowa network was much more organized and looked less like Jackson's in 1984 or 1988. Obama supporters were upper class and college educated, and appreciated his vocal opposition to the war in Iraq.

Close to the day of the Iowa caucuses, Obama gained support from Oprah Winfrey. Winfrey, who also transcends race and is considered one of the most influential and powerful women of the twentieth century, endorsed Obama. It was the first time Winfrey had ever publicly endorsed a presidential candidate. Winfrey's influence brought out black elites in show business, finance, and academia, and her influence transformed into money through fundraisers—one at her Montecito, California, home, another in Chicago, Illinois. Winfrey's appeal also helped the Obama campaign by reaching out to ordinary people, working-class poor, lower middle class, as well as middle class. She also began campaigning in primary states. In Des Moines, Iowa, Winfrey's presence along with Obama drew over 18,500 people. She told the crowd, "I am not here to tell you what to think, I'm here to ask you to think" (Hopkins 2007). The event was considered one of the largest crowds ever, exceeding Tom Harkin's Steak Fry, which easily attracted up to 15,000 people.

On January 3, 2008, Obama won the Iowa caucus, beating Hillary Clinton and John Edwards. Iowa's 1,781 precincts reported that Obama won 38 percent of the delegates to Hillary Clinton's 29 percent. The victory was the longest, costliest, and most intensely fought in Iowa caucus history (Balz, Kombult, and Murray 2008). Party officials reported that turnout exceeded 239,000, which was far above the 124,000 who participated in the previous caucus, four years before. Obama addressed the crowd, declaring this victory "a defining moment in history."

They said this day would never come. . . . [T]hey said our sights were set too high. They said this country was too divided and to disillusioned to ever come together around a common purpose. One day, the American people will look back on the 2008 Iowa caucuses and say, "This is the moment when it all began." (Obama's Caucus Speech 2008)

While Obama lost New Hampshire to Clinton five days later, the focus was on the next primary state: South Carolina. South Carolina was going to be difficult because people were not familiar with him. Despite his national notoriety, most voters in South Carolina did not know anything about Obama, and prior to Iowa the campaign efforts in the state were minimal at best. The Clinton campaign in South Carolina had established a traditional organization with emphasis on acquiring endorsements from civic and religious leaders. The Obama campaign needed a new strategy to make South Carolina voters aware of Obama's political position and also aware that he was black. The goal in South Carolina had a two-fold purpose: to reach those African Americans who had never voted and get them registered and to emphasize a universal message that would make serious gains among white voters. It was important to get Obama's political position out to African American voters because many knew about Clinton, and she was much admired. To combat the Clinton machine, Obama volunteers repeatedly called and visited churches, barbershops, and beauty shops, handing out posters of Obama getting his hair cut in a South Carolina barbershop. This grassroots strategy was to help win the endorsement of the proprietors, who would wear an Obama button. At churches, Obama volunteers focused not on the pastor but on informal community leaders. His camp reasoned that an endorsement from respected elderly people such as church mothers and other community leaders was better than support from a pastor in South Carolina.

In Charleston and Florence, South Carolina, free gospel concerts were organized as benefits for Obama. Address or e-mail contacts were the currency needed to be admitted to the concert. By asking for e-mails, the Obama team aimed to increase its voter contact base in the state. An objective in South Carolina was to make sure that African American voters knew Obama was a black man. Initially, Obama's campaign bumper stickers and buttons did not represent this fact. Anton Gunn, a political director, and other campaign workers in South Carolina told Obama advisers it was imperative that they handed out campaign paraphernalia that showed that Obama was a black man and running for president of the United States. To appeal to the culture of the African American community, Obama's team made sure T-shirts, stickers, leaflets, and buttons were given out for free and all campaign literature featured a picture with Obama or with him and his family.

Obama's campaign relied heavily on volunteers, in particular young volunteers. Volunteers devoted to the campaign were willing to move at a moment's notice. They were formally trained in the art of grassroots community organizing and campaigning. More than three thousand volunteers pledged to spend at least six thirty-hour weeks strengthening the grassroots work. Obama's army of volunteers brought a rigor, passion, and purpose to the work of door knocking, distribution of leaflets and buttons, telephoning voters, and voter registration. Many of Obama's volunteers brought their own personal stories of their interactions with him to help bolster their comfort level with the Illinois Democrat and carry his message forth to the masses.

Many of black South Carolinians expressed concern that if Obama was elected president, he would be assassinated. This anxiety among African American voters was a growing problem, because it had the potential to deter voters. In many of these black communities, not voting for Obama was a convoluted way of protecting him as a black leader. To help ease anxieties, Obama made several trips to South Carolina, traveling to the home base of the staunchly conservative Republican state of Jim DeMint and Lindsey Graham as a means of picking up traction in the state.

By May 2007, Obama was provided with Secret Service protection and this eased some anxieties about an assassination attempt, but some still feared for his life. In June 2007, Obama traveled to Greenville, South Carolina, where more than thirty-five hundred people came to his rally. In a speech in Manning, South Carolina, November 2007, Obama addressed the anxieties many African Americans had for his safety. He attempted to ease the people's fears by assuring them that America was ready for and could handle the idea of being governed by an African American president or else he would not have mounted a campaign. Still some people were not as convinced and their fears were not erased after Obama's words. In their minds, Obama was as good as the previous generation of civil rights and political leaders, whom they had witnessed being gunned down. They compared Obama to Bobby Kennedy and John Kennedy, whose lives ended with assassinations. The fear of assassination remained pervasive among Obama supporters in South Carolina, but there was an endorsement that assured the electorate everything was okay. The magic weapon to combat the fear came from Michelle Obama. Michelle's presence assured people that despite being biracial, Obama was authentically black and though was not running an overt political campaign solely focused on black voters, he was sensitive to issues of the African American community and he was married to an African American woman.

Critics intimated that had Obama married a white woman, his chance of becoming president would be null and void because the African

Civil Rights Act of 1964

The Civil Rights Act of 1964 was the nation's premier civil rights legislation. The act outlawed discrimination on the basis of race, color, religion, sex, or national origin. The law required equal access to public places and employment and enforced desegregation of schools and the right to vote. As a result to this legislation, no longer could African Americans and other minorities be legally denied service simply based on the color of their skin. The Civil Rights of 1964 had initially been proposed by President John F. Kennedy, who met strong opposition from Southern congressmen. After Kennedy's assassination in Dallas, Texas, in 1963, Lyndon Johnson assumed the presidency. Johnson launched an intense campaign and began to lobby Congress to pass the civil rights bill. President Johnson used public speeches and private talks to advance the cause. He urged passage of the civil rights act as a lasting legacy to President Kennedy's memory. This civil rights legislation also generated significant support among liberals and moderates in the northern states.

Building on this widespread public support, he urged religious leaders throughout the nation, especially those in the southern states to use their influence to assist in the passage of the civil rights act. Johnson was a southerner who understood that racial discrimination in the United States stained the view of democracy around the world, and the public displays of violence against racial minorities was shameful and embarrassing for the United States on the international stage. Southern senators aimed to block the legislation, so they filibustered to kill its progress. Their filibuster lasted eighty-three days, the longest in Senate history. An extremely accomplished politician, Johnson thoroughly understood Congress and its complex operations. For many years, he had served as the Senate majority leader. Johnson became skillful at the art of compromise to advance the Democratic Party's legislative agenda; he used these skills to get the civil rights legislation passed in 1964. On July 2, 1964, President Johnson formally signed the Civil Rights Act of 1964 into law, using seventy-two ceremonial pens. Many dignitaries, including civil rights icons Dr. Martin Luther King Jr., Rosa Parks, and several other national civil rights leaders, attended the ceremony. In subsequent years, Congress expanded the act and passed additional civil rights legislation such as the Voting Rights Act of 1965. These acts are considered two of the crown jewels of civil rights legislation in the United States history.

American community might not have fully accepted him. The visuals mattered to this community, but Michelle represented the hopes and dreams of a picture perfect image of a successful and powerful African American family. The campaign also knew African American women were important to the campaign. Michelle represented stability. She was Obama's anchor; the mother of his children and his wife were symbols of hope for the African American community. The Obama campaign team decided to send Michelle to South Carolina to speak on Obama's behalf to assure the African American community. Michelle spoke in Orangeburg, South Carolina, on the campus of South Carolina State University, a historically black college and a pillar of student activism of the civil rights movement during the 1960s. It was known for the Orangeburg Massacre, in which South Carolina State students were protesting at a segregated bowling alley, and violent clashes erupted between the students and police. As a result of these clashes, three protesters were killed and twenty-eight protesters were injured. Michelle Obama began her speech by highlighting various women who had been instrumental in history in general and to the civil rights movement in particular:

> I had the privilege of meeting Coretta Scott King. It was an extraordinary moment for me, meeting this graceful and dignified woman, one I'll never forget. And what I remember most was that she told me not to be afraid because God was with us (Barack and me) and that she would always keep us in her prayers. And I thought, this is a woman who knows what it means to overcome. This was a woman who overcame the heat of racism as a little girl when she walked five miles to school on those rural Alabama roads, passing the doors of the whites-only school so much closer to home. This was a woman who overcame other people's doubts and ignorance by studying and succeeding and excelling past most of her classmates—black and white—earning a college degree and acceptance to a prestigious graduate school up north. As I thought about this remarkable woman, I thought about all the others who had come before her in the long journey for equality in this country—women like Sojourner Truth and Harriet Tubman. And I thought about those who had carried the torch of justice by her side— women like Rosa Parks, Fannie Lou Hamer, Dorothy Height, Shirley Chisholm, C. Delores Tucker, and Mary McLeod Bethune.

On the fear of her husband or her being fatally harmed in some way, Michelle said,

> Now I know folks talk in the barbershops and beauty salons, and I've heard some folks say, "That Barack, he seems like a nice guy, but I'm not sure America's ready for a black President." Well, all I can say is we've heard those voices before. Voices that say, "'Maybe we should wait," and "No you can't do it." "You're not ready"—"You're not experienced." Voices that focus on what might go wrong, rather than what's possible. And I understand it. I know where it comes from, this sense of doubt and fear about what the future holds. That veil of impossibility that keeps us down and keeps our children down, that keeps us waiting and hoping for a turn that may never come. . . . And I want to talk not just about fear but about love. Because I know people want to protect us and themselves from disappointment, failure. I know people are proud of us. I know that people understand that Barack is special. You don't see this kind of man often.

Michelle used an analogy to help illustrate why she supported her husband's run for president and why they should not fear his historic run. Michelle relayed she understood the community was simply attempting to protect her husband and protect themselves from being disappointed. It was better to make an effort and fail than not to make any effort at all. Michelle used an analogy to express the complications of change in the United States. She equated Obama's presidential run to the acts of the earlier civil rights movement activity and noted people had to find the courage to push for change. She also assured the crowd the world was ready for a man like her husband to become president. She implored the crowd to envision her husband as president of the United States.

Michelle's message was heartfelt and far more effective than Obama's policy messages in South Carolina. She and her husband were not going to be crippled by fear in the run for the presidency. Her speech told the voters in South Carolina it was okay to vote for Obama; more importantly, her speech assured voters he was an African American, a viable candidate, and he could win this presidential election.

On January 26, 2008, Obama won the South Carolina primary by thirty points. In a three-way race with Hillary Clinton and John Edwards, Obama captured 55 percent of the votes. With the victories in Iowa and South Carolina, civil rights veterans began to rethink their endorsements. The victories also brought new donors into the Obama campaign and helped Obama break campaign fundraising records. The $32 million raised during the month of January came at a critical time as the primaries headed to Super Tuesday, which included twenty-two states. This campaign money helped to establish a media blitz of advertising and get-out-the-vote efforts in two historically expensive states, California and New York.

The Obama campaign tapped $170 million in new contributions to rake in double the highest previous one-month total for any candidate in the election cycle (Wayne and Zeleny 2008). The money raised also helped Obama in the nomination battle with Hillary Clinton and the Clinton machine. The South Carolina victory gained Obama some significant endorsements. Ted and Caroline Kennedy endorsed Obama, and by Super Tuesday on February 5, Obama won more states, gaining fourteen delegates to tie with Hillary Clinton. As a result of this showing, he was able to raise $55 million in February; he set a record for political fundraising in one month (CNN 2008). According to CNN, the majority of money was raised online, with more than 90 percent of the donations less than $100 and more than half less than $25. During this time, the Obama campaign raised $20 million more than Hillary Clinton's campaign, a new political fundraising record in a single month. In March 2008, the Obama campaign raised more than $40 million with more than 218,000 donors giving for the first time. Voters were paying attention to the campaign. By March, the Obama campaign had raised $234 million, surpassing the Democratic Party fundraising record of $215 million that John Kerry had raised in the presidential primary in 2004 (Sinderbrand 2008). With Obama breaking campaign fundraising records and giving the Clintons an unexpectedly viable campaign competitor for the nomination, controversy arose when more video of Rev. Dr. Jeremiah Wright's sermons surfaced.

The shadow of Reverend Wright emerged again in March 2008, one year after the *Rolling Stone* article. ABC News journalist Brian Ross began digging deeper into Pastor Wright's sermons. As happened with many parishes, Pastor Wright's sermons were being sold by the church. This is largely a marketing and fundraising tool used by churches to raise money and to spread their message. On the videos, Ross found Pastor Wright's repeated denunciations of the United States. Wright's reasoning for the denunciations hinged on what he described as reading of the Gospels and the treatment of blacks in America. In one fiery sermon on the events of September 11 that would be repeatedly shown and used by Obama's political opposition, Wright mentioned,

> The government gives them the drugs, builds bigger prisons, passes a three-strike law and then wants us to sing "God Bless America." No, no, no, God damn America, that's in the Bible for killing innocent people. God damn America for as long as she acts like she is God and she is supreme. (Ross and El Buri 2008)

Initially, Obama tried to brush off the comments of Wright's sermon simply as his attempts to be a provocateur. His aides tried to clean up the matter and indicated Obama rejected the comments and the denunciation of the United States. The Clinton campaign team saw the controversial sermons of Pastor Wright as an opportunity to slow down if not wreck the momentum of the Obama campaign. The Clinton campaign began bringing these sermons to the fore, featured them in opposition ads, and discussed them on Sunday political news shows. As the Clinton team began to turn up the heat and publicize the sermons, Obama aides realized Wright's sermons could be devastating to their campaign. A statement was released distancing Obama from the sermons, but a comprehensive statement was needed to put this issue behind them.

In an attempt to move past the Pastor Wright controversy, Obama delivered a speech at the National Constitution Center, in Philadelphia on Tuesday, March 18, 2008. The speech was titled "A More Perfect Union." If the Democratic Party keynote convention speech in 2004 was the most important speech of Obama's political career, this speech in Philadelphia was a close second. An article in *Politico* captured the moment. Obama's speech conveyed several messages, the first describing the issue of race through the biographical lens of his life:

I am the son of a black man from Kenya and a white woman from Kansas. I was raised with the help of a white grandfather who survived a Depression to serve in Patton's Army during World War II and a white grandmother who worked on a bomber assembly line at Fort Leavenworth while he was overseas. I've gone to some of the best schools in America and lived in one of the world's poorest nations. I am married to a black American who carries within her the blood of slaves and slaveowners—an inheritance we pass on to our two precious daughters. I have brothers, sisters, nieces, nephews, uncles and cousins of every race and every hue, scattered across three continents, and for as long as I live, I will never forget that in no other country on Earth is my story even possible. (Obama's Speech on Race 2008)

Obama chronicles his experience living in two worlds, one white and one black. He continued his speech describing the momentum his campaign had experienced since it kicked off. He also attempted to again get voters to see he was not just an African American candidate but a candidate for all people.

In what must have been a moment of internal conflict of having to publicly denounce his former mentor and friend, Obama condemned Pastor Wright's sermons as divisive tools that could be used to divide the nation. Obama affirmed he had not heard any sermons of this kind when he attended services at the church. However, he attempted to substantiate and generate understanding of the Pastor Wright and the important work of improving the community around Trinity United Church of Christ and his dedicated leadership.

Yes. Did I strongly disagree with many of his political views? Absolutely— just as I'm sure many of you have heard remarks from your pastors, priests, or rabbis with which you strongly disagreed. . . . Given my background, my politics, and my professed values and ideals, there will no doubt be those for whom my statements of condemnation are not enough. But the truth, that isn't all that I know of the man. The man I met more than twenty years ago is a man who helped introduce me to my Christian faith, a man who spoke to me about our obligations to love one another; to care for the sick and lift up the poor. Reverend Wright is a man who served his country as a U.S. Marine; who studied and lectured at some of the finest universities and seminaries in the country, and who for over thirty years led a church that serves the community by doing God's work here on Earth. (Obama's Speech on Race 2008).

Obama continued in his speech and explained Wright's incendiary language represented a profoundly distorted view of the United States' widening racial division. Obama spoke optimistically of the world with an idea of progress and promise and the hope we could move past our arbitrary differences. In what may have been one of the most pervasive points of the speech, Obama did not outright condemn or disown Pastor Jeremiah Wright:

I can no more disown him than I can disown the black community. I can no more disown him than I can my white grandmother—a woman who helped raise me, a woman who sacrificed again and again for me, a woman who loves me as much as she loves anything in this world, but a woman who once confessed her fear of black men who passed by her on the street, and who on more than one occasion has uttered racial or ethnic stereotypes that made me cringe. (Obama's Speech on Race 2008)

By the conclusion of this speech, Obama expressed a need for unity in America. He also expressed that while the country is not perfect, we as a country must give hope for the next generation. The speech gave framework to Reverend Wright's rhetoric and placed Obama in a position to step up as the new leader of a generation willing to challenge the ways of the old civic and political leaders like Wright, Jackson, and Lewis. In addition, the speech could not have been given at a better time; Clinton and Obama were scheduled to debate soon. In addition the next set of primaries in Pennsylvania, Indiana, and North Carolina were on the horizon. The "A More Perfect Union" speech refortified, reignited, and reenergized Obama's presidential candidacy for the debate against Hillary Clinton.

April 16, 2008, Obama and Clinton debated at the National Constitutional Center. The meeting was the twenty-first time both candidates met in little more than a year. Analogous to a boxing match, both candidates began the debate jabbing and assessing their opponent but were armed with knock-out punches. They had well-formed answers to policy questions and apologies for missteps made during their campaigns. Obama apologized for his comments on small-town voters who might cling to guns, religion, or dislike toward other groups of people as a defense mechanism in hard economic times. However, he emphasized the social issues that had made it harder to deliver economic relief to those who needed it the most.

In an attempt to connect with the working class, Clinton did not waste time mentioning her grandfather was a factory worker in Scranton, Pennsylvania, and that residents in the state possessed a devotion to God and guns independent from economic conditions. Clinton also apologized for an erroneous recounting of a tarmac incident in Bosnia 1996. "I may be a lot of things but I am not dumb" (Liasson 2008). Although Obama had addressed the controversy surrounding Pastor Wright's sermons in several interviews and his speech in Philadelphia, he was hammered with questions regarding his association with Wright's critique of America. He was also pounded with questions about his connection to William Ayers, an English professor in Chicago who once belonged to the Weather Underground, a group responsible for bombings in the 1970s. Obama retorted and insisted these associations were distractions from real issues and people really did not care about them. During the debate, Clinton made several attempts to connect Obama to Ayers and his affiliation with the leftist group. In a moment of rebuke, Obama responded to Clinton noting two members of the Weather Underground had their sentences commuted by her husband, Bill Clinton, when he was president of the United States.

Clinton promised to take away $55 billion of the giveaways and subsidies that the president and Congress lavished on drug, oil, and insurance companies and give it back to middle class in the form of tax cuts. Neither candidate committed to offering the vice presidency to the other if nominated.

Both Clinton and Obama returned to their campaigning after the debate. Obama worried about his campaign's survival because polling numbers were slightly trending toward Clinton in the states of North Carolina and Indiana. He agonized over the Wright controversy and whether it was negatively affecting the campaign. He won the North Carolina primary by fourteen points and he was narrowly defeated in Indiana. He had minimized the Pastor Wright controversy and showed the resilience of his campaign.

After the North Carolina and Indiana primaries, superdelegates began to shift their support from Clinton to Obama. Clinton led with 241 to Obama's 181 superdelegates, but the Obama campaign had gained momentum, and superdelegates began to believe in Obama's candidacy. Obama closed to within one superdelegate of Clinton, picking up support of party leaders after a flurry of endorsements and narrowing the superdelegate lead for Clinton to 273 to Obama's 272 (Obama Narrows 2008). The Clinton and Obama political slugfest continued into the summer months. The Clinton campaign was now on the defense, so they began to make the argument that she was the better candidate to lead the Democratic ticket in November. She argued that she was a proven winner, having won in West Virginia, Kentucky, and South Dakota. John Edwards would drop out of the race and with Edwards's support, Obama won big in Oregon and Montana. As the convention grew nearer, 800 superdelegates attended the events associated with the convention. According to the Associated Press, when the convention opened, Obama had a slight lead in endorsements. Obama had 276 superdelegates and Clinton had 271.5 (Obama Takes the Lead). When the primaries were over and the competition between Obama and Clinton was complete, Obama emerged as the victor. Obama defeated Clinton to become the Democratic Party's nominee for president. Hillary Clinton gave a conciliatory speech supporting Obama as the nominee. For Obama, it was a matter of writing and rehearsing an acceptance speech that laid out detailed foreign, economic, and social policies. He also aimed to provide some inspiration to those who would gather and witness history. He invoked the spirit of Dr. Martin Luther King Jr. and the "I Have a Dream Speech."

And it is that promise that forty-five years ago today brought Americans from every corner of this land to stand together on a mall in Washington, before Lincoln's Memorial, and hear a young preacher from Georgia speak of his dream. The men and women who gathered there could've heard many things. They could've heard words of anger and discord. They could've been told to succumb to the fear and frustration of so many dreams deferred. But what the people heard instead—people of every creed and color, from every walk of life—is that in America, our destiny is inextricably linked. (Barack Obama's Acceptance Speech 2008)

After the Labor Day holiday of 2008, the candidates for the Democratic ticket and Republican ticket for the presidency began their general election campaigns for the presidency. Arizona senator John McCain would be the Republican nominee, and Obama's opponent for the general election. McCain chose the governor of Alaska, Sarah Palin, as his running mate. Obama chose Delaware senator Joseph Biden as his vice-presidential pick. If Obama was going to win the presidency, he would have to overcome McCain's compelling story as a war hero to do so. McCain was a decorated navy aviator and Vietnam veteran who was shot down over Hanoi in 1967. Wounded, McCain was captured by the North Vietnamese and placed in a prison camp for six years. During his time in prison, McCain was tortured, and the wounds he sustained caused lifelong disabilities.

McCain's presidential campaign focused on his experience as a senator in Washington. During his campaign, McCain and the Republican Party attempted to distance themselves from the Bush administration. In what was seen as a slight to Obama's perceived lack of experience, McCain's campaign emphasized long-term experience and the maturity necessary to be a successful president. This meant comparing his military and political experience to Obama's relatively brief tenure as a U.S. senator. In particular, McCain emphasized Obama's lack of foreign policy experience. McCain stressed the need for a president of the United States with national security knowledge during dangerous terroristic times.

For most political analysts, this would be a major criticism of Obama's candidacy. This is why Joe Biden was a logical choice as his running mate because of his many years of foreign policy experience. The Obama campaign also decided to focus on Obama's intangible talents. They showcased the need for intellect, judgment, and character to be successful in the oval office in hopes of assuring voters Obama was capable of handling the job. Also Obama's campaign platform highlighted those issues he had gathered by listening and talking with people on the campaign trail. If elected, Obama hoped to reform health care and the economy by increasing the taxes on the top incomes while providing tax cuts to the middle class. He also hoped to put in safeguards to energy and the environment. In foreign policy, he emphasized troop reduction in both wars and closing the prison at Guantanamo Bay. In contrast, the McCain campaign criticized Obama's health care reform policy and responded that his political strategies were too liberal. McCain was firmly against expanding government's role in health care. The McCain team used Republican vice presidential candidate Sarah Palin to deliver rude one-liner insults and punch lines at campaign events in an attempt to sully the Obama campaign. In one line that got much attention on conservative news channels, Palin raised questions about the radicalism of Obama through his relationship with Weatherman Underground's William Ayers. Palin expressed, "Our opponent is someone who sees America as imperfect enough to pal around with terrorists who targeted their own country" (Elperin 2008).

Obama's campaign was extremely effective. Obama had established campaign offices across the country and did not accept public subsidies, instead raising vast resources. He advertised heavily in competitive states and targeted areas where Bush won in 2004. In October 2008, several political polls showed Obama was ahead of McCain by eight points, 51 percent to 43 percent (Steinhauser 2008).

A month later and a day before the general election, Obama's grandmother, Madelyn Dunham, died of cancer. Dunham was the woman credited with helping shape Obama's character and personality. A month before her death, Obama took a break from the campaign trail and flew to Hawaii once he learned her health was declining. A day after the death of Obama's grandmother, Obama achieved the highest elected political office in the land, winning the election with 53 percent of the popular vote to McCain's 46 percent to become president of the United States. Obama won 365 electoral votes to McCain's 173 (Election Results 2008).

From the Chicago's South Side to New York's Harlem to the ancestral village of Obama's people in Kenya, the streets filled with people celebrating this historic electoral victory. Obama chose to speak to the crowd in Grant Park the night of the election. One hundred and twenty thousand people joyously sang, danced, cheered, and cried. McCain's concession speech was conciliatory. He did not shy away from the historical significance of the moment. He was gracious giving tribute to this historical moment.

As the Obama family was set to make their entrance on the stage at Grant Park, pandemonium broke out. Boisterous crowds were cheering and flag waving gave way to silence as Obama began his moving victory speech.

> If there is anyone out there who still doubts that America is a place where all things are possible, who still wonders if the dream of our founders is alive in our time, who still questions the power of our democracy, tonight is your answer.

He continued his speech, acknowledging his family and reaffirming his love for them and thanking his supporters. He also held to the promise (a puppy) he made to his daughters before making his run for the presidency. Obama provided a description on what he believed made his presidential campaign successful. He described both young people and old people working together and how so many people provided what little money they had to finance his campaign. Obama's presidential victory was historical for many reasons but also represented the hope and the heartache of a generation of African Americans who believed this day would never occur. Obama's campaign slogans, "Yes, We Can!" and "Change We Can Believe In!" became the mantra of not only his campaign but his presidency. Obama rode into the White House on the momentum of these campaign slogans. These campaign slogans hinted at instant change, but Obama would find governing slow as he muddled through his first term as president of the United States. He set his sights on legislation to reform health care in the United States.

8

Barack Obama's First Presidential Term

For many Americans, there was an air of national pride on the day Barack Hussein Obama was sworn in as the forty-fourth president of the United States. More than one million people gathered at the National Mall on one of the coldest days of the year (January 20, 2009) to witness the first African American president take the oath of office. Obama was sworn in on the Lincoln Bible used in 1861 to "faithfully execute the office of the President of the United States." He also used a second Bible, which belonged to Rev. Dr. Martin Luther King Jr. and was known as King's traveling Bible (Jackson 2013).

In his inaugural address, Obama promised to take "bold and swift" actions to restore the economy by creating jobs through public works projects, improving education, promoting alternative energy, and relying on new technology (Hulse 2009). President Obama's administration ushered in a new appreciation for public service. The view of public service had diminished after the eight years of the Bush administration. President Obama's administration emphasized transparency, civic engagement, diversity, and the opportunity for discourse through electronic town hall meetings (Bryer et al. 2010).

During his presidential campaign, Obama did not emphasize his status as an African American; however his race and his blackness was pointedly symbolic for African Americans because the inauguration events and swearing-in ceremony took place just one day after Dr. Martin Luther

King Jr.'s holiday. While the nation celebrated the historical significance of Obama's election, some members of the Republican Party were organizing to obstruct any potential success for Obama with the hope these tactics would thwart his presidency and make him a one-term president. On the night of Obama's inauguration, leading members of the Republican Party, led by Kentucky senator Mitch McConnell, held a dinner meeting and unfurled a strategy to not only win back political power, but to also obstruct President Obama's legislative agenda (Barr 2010).

While there would be ardent attempts to slow President Obama's progress, a national financial crisis loomed that needed the president's and Congress's immediate attention. The Obama administration was faced with crises from the initial moments of his presidency. The recession deepened after some of the oldest and most stable U.S. financial institutions and investment firms, such as Bear Stearns and Lehman Brothers, declared bankruptcy. President Obama and his administration had to act quickly to stabilize and resolve this massive and growing economic problem. Many wondered how a financially wealthy country like the United States could ever find itself in such financial chaos. Many of these financial problems could be attributed to very low interest rates, inflated real estate prices, and predatory lending practices, where banks granted mortgages for homes and commercial property that were not worth the amount being lent to borrowers. Investment banks bought these bad mortgages and collected the interests from them, and when these properties were foreclosed because people could not pay ballooning interest rates, financial institutions collapsed and fueled a financial downturn and economic crisis. This economic crisis was the first significant problem President Obama encountered after taking the oath of office.

Despite the downward predicament of economic problems in the United States, President Obama maintained an ambitious agenda for the country. During his 2008 presidential campaign, he promised to provide health care for all Americans, improve global climate change, remove American troops from Iraq, increase the number of troops in Afghanistan, reduce America's dependence on foreign oil, create clean energy industries, implement immigration reform, and cut taxes for the middle class. He and his administration set out to turn his campaign promises and political platform into policies. While eager to pursue his agenda, he knew the economic crisis had to take priority over his own agenda. He knew the majority of his agenda would not calm the fears of a looming financial crisis. He also knew his agenda would certainly fail if Americans were worried about the economy and an oncoming recession. Unlike most congressional Republicans, the congressional Democrats were eager to work with President Obama not only on the economy, but on his legislative agenda also. Obama proposed legislation to stimulate the economy

---

SIGNED, SEALED, AND DELIVERED

In August of 1970, Stevie Wonder released an album titled, *Signed, Sealed, and Delivered* on Tamala Records. The title song is one of Wonder's most popular songs. Wonder wrote or cowrote seven of the tracks on the album. Barack Obama called Stevie Wonder one of his "musical heroes," and Michelle Obama has called Stevie Wonder her all-time favorite artist. When Barack Obama campaigned for the presidency, this became his signature campaign song. At most campaign stops, Obama would coolly stride out to his spot on the stage and mesmerize the crowd. On the final night of the 2008 Democratic Party National Convention, Stevie Wonder performed live and sang "Signed, Sealed, and Delivered." In his reelection campaign, Obama used the song again as his signature song on the campaign trail. At the conclusion of President Obama's rallies, he usually simply left the stage and shook hands with those in the crowd. In 2012, at one campaign rally in Cincinnati, Ohio, he loosened up and swayed back and forth and clapped his hands to the beat of "Sign, Sealed, and Delivered" as he left the stage.

---

through $787 billion in new spending over the next two years. This proposed bill would increase government expenditures of the federal budget, including money to improve U.S. infrastructure by repairing roads and bridges. The bill also included money for states and social welfare programs. The practice of injecting public money into the economy during a recession to counteract decreased spending in the private sector and to stimulate the economy is a common practice in the United States. The practice had been used before and had been used by the previous administration. President Obama would utilize it as one of the strategies to get the United States out of the economic crisis. Obama and Congress used the legislative process to kick-start the U.S. economy.

On February 17, 2009, President Obama signed the American Recovery and Reinvestment Act (ARRA). The act was passed by Congress to save and create jobs and to provide temporary relief programs for those most affected by the recession. It also aimed to financially bolster public sector problems such as the country's poor infrastructure, education system, health care system, and renewable energy efforts. The goal of ARRA was to create jobs for Americans who were unemployed or underemployed. The administration's reasoning was anchored on the idea that if people who had jobs would spend money and purchase items, this would create a high demand for those items. This would, in turn, create a demand and the need for companies to provide the desired goods and services and increase their workforces. This view was too simplistic, and the crisis continued to grip the United States for almost two full years. While ARRA slowed a full-blown economic depression, the Federal Reserve channeled more money into the economy to strengthen the country's financial system. With ARRA, coupled with the work of the Federal Reserve, investors' confidence in the economy eventually began to recover. Slowly, normalcy returned to financial markets and the U.S. economy (Janda, Berry, and Goldman 2009). While the Bush administration had used a similar strategy to stabilize the economy, on this occasion Republicans criticized a parallel recovery plan under President Obama. They believed a more conservative approach was better to curtail the financial crisis. They wanted to use a market-based approach and rely on the private sector to resolve the country's financial crisis. They also wanted only limited government intervention to settle the country's economic woes.

Conservative talk show hosts and pundits erroneously claimed President Obama and his administration were moving the economy toward socialism by allowing government to own the means of production of many industries and direct the country's economy. Obama's critics reverted to a perceived inflammatory insult of calling him a socialist. This socialist ideology and name-calling resonated and became a talking point for some conservative Republicans. Not to be deterred from rebuilding the economy, the Obama administration and the federal government kept several private sector companies in the insurance industry, automobile industry, and housing industry and from financial ruin. Specifically, the federal government intervened and financially assisted General Motors, AIG, Freddie Mac, and Fannie Mae by lending them money to stay solvent.

Understanding the severity of the financial crisis and perceptions of working-class people that government officials and politicians really do not care about the working class, President Obama enacted a pay freeze for senior White House staff making more than $100,000 per year. The freeze included the White House chief of staff, national security adviser, and press secretary. Obama understood that many Americans negatively viewed politics, lobbying, and the federal legislative process. Therefore, he began to make substantial changes in the way business was conducted in the federal government. He announced a new policy on lobbyists and the lobbying process. This change prohibited anyone who worked in the White House from working as a lobbyist for at least two years after they exited their job at the White House (Montopoli, "Obama Freezes Pay," 2009). It also barred former members of presidential administrations and their employees from working for two years on issues which they previously had lobbied for. Curtailing a common practice in Washington, DC, Obama's policy also prohibited lobbyists from giving gifts of any size to members of his administration. This lobbying ban signaled the Obama administration had ripped a page from Shirley Chisholm's 1972 presidential campaign playbook by attempting to be "unbought and unbossed." Obama began to set his presidential footprint during his first hundred days in the Oval Office.

The first hundred days metric dates back to the presidency of Franklin D. Roosevelt as he laid out his agenda to improve the economy when he entered office during the Great Depression. Similar to Roosevelt's travails, much of President Obama's first hundred days was spent handling an economic crisis. Another similarity between President Roosevelt and President Obama is they both introduced new methods of reaching the American people. Both Roosevelt and Obama connected to their constituents through their period's innovative communicative technology. Roosevelt introduced weekly radio addresses. Obama produced the first weekly Saturday morning addresses by video on whitehouse.gov and YouTube. He used the Internet to connect with Americans en masse on a weekly basis. For example, Obama held the first virtual town hall meeting on the Internet in March 2009.

President Obama fielded questions from an audience assembled in the White House and from a virtual audience as well. During this online town hall meeting, conducted in the East Room of the White House, Obama answered written and video questions from the public on issues ranging from unemployment, health care, education, and the federal budget. President Obama also answered questions on the aid to the auto industry and his opposition to the legalization of marijuana (C-SPAN 2009). Obama commented, "I have to say that there was one question that was voted on ranked fairly high and that was whether legalization of marijuana would improve the economy and job creation" (Montpoli, "Obama: Legalizing," 2009).

Obama is considered one of the great presidential campaign communicators because of his creative use of technology on the campaign trail. As president of the United States, his creative use of technology continued as he reached out to people and reinforced his message to citizens. Obama's virtual town hall only cemented his reputation as a great presidential communicator as people were able to listen to him wherever and whenever they wanted through various media platforms.

President Obama used legislative measures to help women and children, who had always been a priority for him. He had been influenced by strong women throughout his life. After becoming a father, he could also see the world through the perspective of his two daughters and comprehend and acknowledge women's inequality. President Obama fully understood that women deserve equal pay for equal work in any occupation they are employed. Women voters, particularly African American women and suburban white women, were major factors in Obama's win. Therefore, it was no surprise when President Obama signed the Lilly Ledbetter Fair Pay Act, which promoted fair pay regardless of age, race, or gender.

The law was named for Lilly Ledbetter, who discovered when she was retiring that her male colleagues were earning much more than she at the

Goodyear Tire and Rubber Company plant in Gadsden, Alabama. Ledbet-ter sued, and Goodyear was found guilty of pay discrimination. However, the U.S. Supreme Court threw out the case in a 5–4 decision. The court ruled that Ledbetter should have filed her suit within 180 days of the date Goodyear first paid her less.

A few years prior, Congress attempted to pass a law that would have effectively overturned the decision during President George W. Bush's presidency. The Bush administration opposed the bill, stating it would encourage lawsuits against corporations. During President Obama's term, Congress tried again and passed the bill. A key provision in this version of the bill is the six-month clock is reset every time the worker receives a pay-check and therefore the time for a worker to make a claim is extended (Stolberg 2009). This was a victory in the fight for women's equality.

President Obama followed signing the Ledbetter Act with a bill that ensured children would receive health care. The Children's Health Insur-ance Program Reauthorization Act of 2009 (CHIPRA) provided coverage to uninsured children and improved the quality of care that all children received. The Children's Health Insurance Program (CHIP) was created in 1997. This program offers coverage to children and families who do not have affordable employer-sponsored health insurance. CHIPRA stipulated that each state must provide the resources needed to sustain and strengthen their Children's Health Insurance Program. It also directed states to enroll more of the uninsured children who already qualified for coverage (Georgetown University). Obama not only expanded existing laws to help women and children; he also renamed and reorganized some agencies within the federal government.

President Obama restructured the Office of Faith-Based and Commu-nity Initiatives, an office created under the Bush administration, and renamed this agency the White House Office of Faith-Based and Neigh-borhood Partnerships. The Bush administration had created the office to provide faith-based government grants to organizations providing social services to area communities. Obama expanded the office to form partner-ships between various federal agencies and faith-based and neighborhood organizations to advance specific goals of the administration. Among the agency's missions, the office coordinated partnerships with the president's advisory council and included a group of leaders from both faith-based and secular organizations. The advisory council also made recommenda-tions on how the federal government could more effectively partner with faith-based and neighborhood organizations.

President Obama had campaigned on ending the wars in Afghanistan and Iraq; actually ending these wars proved difficult if not impossible with-out major negative consequences for the United States. In his first year in office, he had to increase troops in Afghanistan to gain control over insurgents who had gained power in the region. By February 2009, additional troops were deployed to the war in Afghanistan. The troops deployed to the region included 8,000 marines and 4,000 army troops. Obama stated,

> This increase is necessary to stabilize a deteriorating situation in Afghanistan, which has not received the strategic attention, direction and resources it urgently requires. . . . [T]he Taliban is resurgent in Afghanistan, and al Qaeda supports the insurgency and threatens America from its safe haven along the Pakistani border. (Montpoli, "Obama Approves," 2009)

Within the first three months in office, President Obama introduced a strategy to combat the Taliban and al Qaeda threat in Afghanistan and Pakistan. The Obama plan was to "disrupt, dismantle, and defeat" al Qaeda in Pakistan and vanquish Taliban forces in Afghanistan (DeYoung 2009). With the seventeen thousand troops authorized by Obama the month before to Afghanistan, four thousand more troops would also be deployed to the region to work as trainers and advisors to the Afghan army. The addition of troops brought the total forces to more than sixty thousand troops, twice as many as non-U.S. and NATO troops (Cooper, "Putting a Stamp," 2009). Additionally, civilian officials and diplomats were deployed to improve the infrastructure and governance of the country's economy.

Along with the additional troops, Obama pledged $7.5 billion in aid for military equipment. Yet he cautioned that the additional dollars were contingent on demonstrated results to ousting al Qaeda and Taliban within the region. Obama explained,

> As President, my greatest responsibility is to protect the American people. We are not in Afghanistan to control that country or to dictate its future. We are in Afghanistan to confront a common enemy that threatens the United States, our friends and allies, and the people of Afghanistan and Pakistan who have suffered the most at the hands of violent extremists. (Rooney 2009)

President Obama and his administration had been reviewing U.S. policy in Afghanistan, and the increase in troops was made partly because of the decision to decrease the number of troops in Iraq. President Obama also kept his campaign promise by announcing plans to withdraw more troops from Iraq by 2010. His administration proposed between 35,000 to 50,000 troops would remain from the 144,000 in Iraq. Gradually, those numbers would be reduced until all forces were out of Iraq by December 31, 2011. On a trip to Cape Lejeune, Obama said,

> Let me say this a plainly as I can: By August 31, 2010, our combat mission in Iraq will end . . . by any measure, this has already been a long war and it is time to bring our troops home with the honor they have earned. (Lothian and Malveaux 2009)

There were some Democrats like House Majority Leader Nancy Pelosi who were not happy with the number of troops President Obama's proposed plan left behind. Yet, he got support from Arizona Republican senator John McCain, his opponent from the 2008 presidential election.

On February 26, 2009, President Obama submitted an expansive budget with the aim of overhauling the U.S. health care system. The budget outlined a ten-year budget proposal to pay for reforming health care, curbing global warming, expanding the government's role in education, and shifting more costs to corporations and wealthy taxpayers. President Obama proposed a two-pronged mission: to reduce the $1 trillion-plus deficit he inherited from the Bush administration to $533 billion by 2013 and make big investments in the future.

> We will each and every one of us have to compromise on certain things we care about, but which we simply cannot afford right now. That's a sacrifice we're going to have to make. . . . [W]hat I don't do is sacrifice investments that will make America stronger, more competitive and more prosperous in the 21st century. (Sahadi 2009)

Congressional Republicans criticized his first budget, which also included a $1.75 trillion deficit by the end of the fiscal year. They were quick to charge the proposal raised some taxes and would damage the economy. While President Obama concentrated on these issues on the foreign policy front, he also remained mindful of his campaign promises on the domestic front. President Obama had campaigned on making health care more accessible and affordable. He also campaigned on improving funding for medical research and the use of stem cell research to find cures and prevent diseases. He used executive orders to shift the view on stem cell research.

The Obama administration signed an executive order on March 9, 2009, reversing a Bush-era policy that limited federal tax dollars for embryonic stem cell research. The move overturned a previous executive order signed by President George W. Bush in 2001 that barred the National Institute of Health from funding research on embryonic stem cells beyond using sixty cell lines that existed at that time. Obama said,

> In recent years, when it comes to stem cell research, rather than furthering discovery, our government has forced what I believe is a false choice between sound science and moral values. . . . [I]n this case, I believe the two are not inconsistent. As a person of faith, I believe we are called to care for each other and work to ease human suffering. I believe we have been given the capacity and will pursue this research and the humanity and conscience to so responsibly. (Rovner and Gold 2009)

The executive order directed the National Institute of Health to develop revised guidelines on federal funding for embryonic stem cell research within 120 days. For administrative purposes, Obama waded into other

Bush policies by signing a memorandum ordering officials not to rely on Bush-era signing statements without first checking with Eric Holder and the attorney general's office. Obama also indicated that he would issue his own signing statements provided they were based on well-founded legal reasoning (Rooney 2009).

President Obama embarked on his first international trip in March 2009 when he traveled to London to attend the Group of 20 (G20) summit hosted by Prime Minister Gordon Brown of Britain. Global economies were paralyzed, and these global leaders needed to discuss strategies on how to stimulate world trade and regulate global financial firms. The meeting also introduced the president onto the world stage of European leaders. President Obama was not reluctant to express his views to the leaders of the world's largest economies and did not shy away from the moment. He insisted there were no great divisions between G20 nations on how to deal with the recessive global economy, but the pace of resolving the problem would have to be done sooner than later. President Obama cautioned other world leaders.

> The world has become accustomed to the United States being a voracious consumer. . . . America is going to have to look at our deficits. If there is going to be renewed growth, it can't just be the United States as the engine. Everybody has to pick up the pace. (Wintour 2009)

After President Obama's comments and the comments of G20 leaders, leaders at the summit agreed to bail out developing countries by committing to $1.1 trillion in new funding to increase the capital available to the International Monetary Fund (Lander and Sanger 2009). While in London for the G20 Summit, President Obama and the first lady also met with the Queen Elizabeth II at Buckingham Palace. During the meeting, Michelle Obama briefly placed her hand on the back of the queen. Royal etiquette indicates that "whatever you do, do not touch the queen" (Chua-Eoan 2009). However, a royal spokeswoman brushed off the criticism indicating the embrace was mutual and did not breach protocol in any way. This pseudo-controversy illustrated the intense unwarranted scrutiny not only Obama faced as president of the United States, but also the level of unwarranted scrutiny of his wife as first lady.

After the meetings in London, President Obama flew to France to meet with French President Nicolas Sarkozy and to attend the North Atlantic Treaty Organization (NATO) Summit. While in Strasbourg, France, Obama held a town hall meeting with thirty-five hundred French and German students. During the meeting, President Obama spoke about attempting to close Guantanamo Bay, a military prison holding detainees from the Iraq war and other U.S. counterintelligence operations. This was also one of his campaign promises. During this talk, he also discussed reducing nuclear stockpiles and how to combat the effects of climate change. During his conversations with world leaders, President Obama expressed the importance of making bilateral efforts to fight against extremists. He also noted more European countries needed to take part in these military efforts because the United States could not combat the extremists alone. President Obama noted in the meeting,

> I think it is important for Europe to understand that even though I'm now president and George W. Bush is no longer president, Al Qaeda is still a threat. We cannot pretend somehow that because Barack Hussein Obama got elected as president, suddenly everything is going to be O.K. It is going to be a very difficult challenge. Al Qaeda is still bent on carrying out terrorist activity. (Cooper 2009)

President Obama acknowledged France's partnership to help combat global terrorism. He also recognized President Sarkozy's effort to help the United States find a place for the 240 detainees held at Guantanamo.

> Our moral authority is derived from the fact that generations of our citizens have fought and bled to uphold the values of our nations and others. And that is why we can never sacrifice them for expedience sake. That's why I've ordered the closing of the detention center in Guantanamo Bay. (Krulak and Lehnert 2016)

During the NATO Summit, Obama received an endorsement from France and Germany for his Afghanistan strategy. This strategy aimed to balance civil and military operations and support the Afghanistan police and military. These strategic efforts were viewed as one of the best methods of reducing and removing NATO forces from the region (Cody 2009). In this pragmatic view, as Afghanistan grew stronger and more secure, eventually it would not need any assistance with security or its stability. President Obama acknowledged the need for help from European allies to implement the strategy. He said, "This was not a pledging conference but a strong down payment on the future of our mission in Afghanistan" (Obama, March 27, 2009). Although Obama requested more allied combat troops, he only received a modest commitment of three thousand mostly noncombat troops along with $600 million in financial assistance. Fully ending all military operations in the wars in Iraq and Afghanistan were two campaign promises President Obama could not accomplish by the end of his eight years in office. U.S. involvement in these two wars had become so entrenched in these country's governmental operations and economies that they would have collapsed shortly after U.S. military forces were removed.

President Obama's first hundred days in office were reassuring for many Americans after George W. Bush's eight tumultuous years as president. The first three months of his presidency was a snapshot into an administration that mirrored President Obama's pragmatic sensibilities and a vision of what was to come. Within his first hundred days, the Obama administration helped reshape the automobile industry, buttressed the American economy and kept it from collapsing, began easing tensions with Cuban president Raúl Castro, and nationalized tracts of U.S. wilderness land. President Obama then wanted to tackle other parts of his ambitious political agenda to keep his campaign promises. Specifically, he took aim at reforming the U.S. health care system.

There have been numerous presidents who attempted to create universal health care in the United States. During the Great Depression, President Franklin D. Roosevelt's first draft of federal social security legislation included funding for public health care programs. However, the American Medical Association (AMA) attacked the legislation, deriding and labeling the legislation as "compulsory health care insurance." Caving under the AMA's pressure, Roosevelt eventually removed the health care program in order for the social security legislation to pass in 1935. In 1945, President Harry Truman along with congressional leaders from both parties proposed numerous plans to protect against the rising costs of health care in the United States. President Truman wanted to create a national health insurance fund operated by the federal government. Truman would try again to get a national insurance for health care in 1949, and both attempts would fail.

During the civil rights movement of the 1950s and 1960s, the focus of various forms of universal health care emerged as public agenda items, particularly as a safeguard for the elderly through Medicare, but has remained as an unfinished public agenda item since that time. President Lyndon B. Johnson who was elected as president in 1964 swept in a new plan to shift social order through the Great Society programs, legislation aimed to eliminate poverty and racial injustice. It also set the stage for the passage of Medicare and Medicaid legislation in 1965. During the Johnson administration, liberal congressmen proposed universal health care but were met with stiff opposition, namely from Arkansas congressman and fiscal conservative Wilbur Mills, who was chair of the Ways and Means Committee. Representative Mills had been a staunch opponent of the national health care legislation and had used his power to block several attempts to pass proposed health care legislation. The legislation was designed to provide widespread health care coverage and services. Medicare provided health insurance to people who are age sixty-five and older, and Medicaid provided health insurance to people with limited income. After much wrangling and compromise with Mills, President Johnson signed the Medicare bill on July 30, 1965.

By the 1970s, health care under government programs expanded with President Richard Nixon. Under the Nixon administration, Medicare grew to offer coverage to people under age sixty-five who were severely disabled for over two years or had a chronic disease. President Nixon piggybacked President Johnson's advancement in health care by mandating more comprehensive health insurance such as an employer mandate to offer private health insurance if employees volunteered to pay 25 percent of premiums. Under the Nixon administration, the executive branch was not the only segment of the federal government to attempt to make changes to health care. The legislative branch also proposed changes to health care during this time. At the end of Nixon's presidency, there were still not any comprehensive health care laws to provide health insurance for all citizens in the United States.

Multiple policy proposals and other attempts for passing universal health care legislation were unsuccessful. During the 1990s, President Bill Clinton made another attempt to reform the health care system. Health care was a major public agenda item and First Lady Hillary Clinton was to lead the efforts for these national reforms. She was met with much resistance from special interest groups and Republican congressional leaders. The Clinton administration's proposed plan included a call for mandatory enrollment in health insurance plan with subsidies to guarantee affordability for people from all income levels. Immediately, the proposed bill faced heavy criticism from Republicans in Congress. They were successful in killing the proposed bill. The proposed bill died in the U.S. House of Representatives. President George W. Bush would also make an attempt at health care reform.

During President George W. Bush's era, a Patients' Bill of Rights was also introduced to Congress. Under the Bush administration's health care proposal, patients would receive an explicit list of rights concerning their health care. This concept was derived from ideas found in the Consumers' Bill of Rights. The Patients' Bill of Rights attempted to safeguard the quality of care of all patients by preserving the integrity of the processes used by the health care industry. Just as earlier presidential administrations faced fervent opposition, the Bush administration's proposed changes also faced opposition to reforming the U.S. health care system. As with previous presidential administrations, the America Medical Association (AMA) and now along with the pharmaceutical industry presented a united front to oppose Bush's proposed changes to provide universal health care and emergency medical care to anyone regardless of health insurance status. These interest groups also opposed coverage of preexisting conditions and patients' ability to hold medical doctors and insurance companies accountable for any and all harm done to patients. In 2002, the Patients' Bill of Rights legislation failed to pass, and the rising cost of prescription drugs remained a problem. Nevertheless, health care experienced a little success under President George W. Bush. He signed into law the Medicare

Prescription Drug Improvement and Modernization Act in 2004. This law included a prescription drug plan to lower the cost of prescriptions for elderly and disabled Americans.

After this modest success under the Bush administration, health care was paramount on Obama's legislative agenda. For President Obama, reforming and reshaping health care was personal. His mother, Ann Dunham, died of cancer on November 7, 1995. Obama retold accounts during his stops on the presidential campaign of how his mother spent the last months of her life trying to get her health insurer to pay for her treatment of uterine and ovarian cancer, which the insurer refused to cover because they ruled her cancer was a preexisting condition. To highlight his conviction of reforming health care, as part of a thirty-second campaign advertisement, Obama described his mother's death and expressed his desire to reform health care. He also spoke about this issue at campaign rallies. In 2007 in a speech given in Santa Barbara, California, Obama said,

> I remember my mother. She was 52 year old when she died of ovarian cancer, and you know what she was thinking about in the last months of her life? She wasn't thinking about getting well. She wasn't thinking about coming to terms with her own mortality. She had been diagnosed just as she was transitioning between jobs. And she wasn't sure whether insurance was going to cover the medical expenses because they might consider this a preexisting condition. I remember just being heartbroken, seeing her struggle through the paperwork and the medical bills and the insurance forms. So, I have seen what it's like when somebody you love is suffering because of a broken health care system. And it's wrong. It's not who we are as a people! (Godsey 2007)

President Obama announced his intent to work with Congress to construct a comprehensive plan for health care reform in a speech to a joint session of Congress in February 2009. By this time, the sentiments on public health care had changed. There was a positive wave of support for health care reform, in particular covering preexisting conditions, but there were still bitter battles to come. Both chambers of Congress presented bills and held meetings to develop a health care reform bill. Congressional Democrats and health care policy experts argued over whether an individual mandate would prevent healthy people from participating or people participating without contributing to the system, therefore making the system unsustainable.

There were acrimonious partisan debates over the public option health plan and public misinformation such as allegations legislation would provide for "death panels" and a big shift to socialized medicine. Republicans and conservative pundits on news networks attempted to sully health care reform, spending hundreds of millions of dollars and negatively branding the Affordable Care Act (ACA) as Obamacare.

Republicans hoped attaching President Obama's name would besmirch the bill and turn people against the proposed legislation. However, the Obama administration turned the terminology to their advantage and embraced "Obamacare." President Obama and his administration recognized that Obamacare could be a positive if America's health care system could be truly turned around (Cillizza and Blake 2012). Key provisions of the ACA or Obamacare included a ban on insurance companies refusing coverage based on a preexisting condition. They kept insurance companies from charging a different rate based on a preexisting condition or gender and repealed insurance companies' exemption from antitrust laws. The ACA established minimum standards for qualified health benefit plans and a National Healthcare Workforce Commission to be composed of fifteen individuals who would assess health care needs and make recommendations to congressional leaders. The bill also required most employers to provide coverage for their workers or pay a surtax on the workers' wages up to 8 percent, restricted abortion coverage in any insurance plans for which federal funds were used, expanded Medicaid to include more low income Americans, and provided subsidies to low- and middle-income Americans to help buy insurance. The plan also created a health insurance exchange where the public could compare policies and rates and required most Americans to carry or obtain qualifying health insurance coverage or face a fine for noncompliance.

The political process was difficult, but the Affordable Care Act passed, and Obama signed it into law March 21, 2010. There would be numerous attempts to overturn this law. In response to passage of this law, fourteen states sued to block the health care law, arguing the requirement that individuals buy health care violated the U.S. Constitution. The states listed in the lawsuit were Alabama, Colorado, Louisiana, Michigan, Nebraska, Pennsylvania, South Carolina, South Dakota, Texas, Utah, Virginia, and Washington. The case was filed by Florida's attorney general, Bill McCollum, and joined by eleven other Republican attorneys general and one Democratic attorney general. McCollum argued,

> The new law forces states to things that are practically impossible to do as a practical matter, forcing us to do it without giving any resources or money to do it. It is a question for most of us in the states of the costs to our people and to the rights and the freedoms of the individual citizens in upholding our constitutional duties as attorneys general. (Hamby and Acosta 2010)

In defense of the ACA, Democratic spokesman Hari Sevugan said, "The American people don't want any more delay, obstruction or hypocrisy on this. They want thoughtfully implemented reform so that it works for all Americans" (Hamby and Acosta 2010). The U.S. Supreme Court agreed with the Obama administration in the case *National Federation of*

Independent Business v. Sebelius, upholding the constitutionality of the law. The Supreme Court ruled the individual mandate is a tax and that Medicaid expansion required all states to expand Medicaid coverage for all. The Supreme Court further decided the creation of federal and or state health care exchanges facilitate obtaining health care insurance, and that federal financial subsidies for health care insurance met low income standards. Finally, the U.S. Supreme Court ruled that states could not deny coverage based on preexisting conditions.

States were later given the option of opting out of expanding Medicaid coverage. President Obama had accomplished what he set out to achieve and what so many prior presidents had failed to do. He had significantly reformed America's health care system. Though it was not universal health care and opponents would attempt to chip away at Obamacare throughout his presidency, he had passed his signature domestic piece of legislation.

In only his second year of his four-year term of office, there was still much work to complete on his presidential agenda. Even with this monumental legislative victory and other public agenda items ahead, President Obama continued to confront issues surrounding race, racial profiling, and the perception of a postracial society in the United States. These issues would heighten and become a part of a national conversation on race relations after the arrest of Harvard professor Henry Louis Gates.

Dr. Henry Louis "Skip" Gates Jr. was a distinguished African American historian, filmmaker, and public intellectual who was a professor of African American research at Harvard University. He had extensive knowledge of African American literature and had published extensively. Gates was born in Keyser, West Virginia, and grew up in Piedmont, Virginia. His father worked in a paper mill and his mother cleaned houses. Gates's teaching career began at Yale University, where he was jointly appointed to English and Afro-American Studies in 1979. Cornell University recruited him in 1985, where he taught until 1989. He completed a two-year teaching stay at Duke University and then was eventually recruited by Harvard University in 1991.

In July 2009, Dr. Gates returned home from a trip to China. Gates found he could not get into his house, as the front door had jammed. His driver helped him push open the front door. One of Gates's neighbors thought Gates and his driver were breaking into the house and called the police. By the time an officer arrived, Gates was in the house. The officer who responded to the call asked him to step outside. Gates refused but showed his identification, which showed his address. After showing his identification, tensions were heightened as Gates became angry. Gates asked the officer if he was being mistreated because he was black. The officer arrested Gates on a charge of disorderly conduct. The incident sparked national attention, spawning a debate about racial profiling.

With only six months under his belt as president, Obama was focused on stabilizing the economy, establishing his presence on the world stage, and passing health care reform. While race was an important issue for him, it was not an priority in his public agenda at the time of Gates's arrest. Many believed President Obama did not want to appear as if he was strictly catering to issues pertaining to black people and avoided being viewed as the president of the United States solely for black people. On the same day of Gates's arrest, President Obama was scheduled to address the centennial anniversary of the convention of the National Association of Colored People (NAACP) in New York. He was able to tie the NAACP's history with his adopted home state history. His speech also had a conservative tinge to it. This conservative tinge would occasionally be seen in several speeches during Obama's presidency.

> Because ordinary people did such extraordinary things, because they made the civil rights movement their own, even though there may not be a plaque or their names might not be in the history books—because of their efforts I made a little trip to Springfield, Illinois, a couple of years ago, where Lincoln once lived and race riots once raged, and began the journey that has led me to be here tonight as the 44th president of the United States of America.

President Obama further stated,

> Despite lingering "barriers," young black people in America should take control of their own futures. No one has written your destiny for you. Your destiny is in your hands—you cannot forget that . . . . that's what we have to teach all of our children. No excuses. No excuses. (Obama, July 19, 2009)

President Obama was asked about the incident after the news of Gates's arrest. President responded with a measured but honest tone and was drawn into a debate about race, racial profiling, and the historical practice of racism in the United States. He addressed the matter of Gates's arrest head-on at a press conference stating,

> I don't know, not having been there and not seeing all the facts, what role race played in that but I think it's fair to say, number one, any of us would be pretty angry; number two, that the Cambridge police acted stupidly in arresting somebody when there was already proof that they were in their own home, and number three, what I think we know separate and apart from this incident is that there's a long history in this country of African Americans and Latinos being stopped by law enforcement disproportionately. (McPhee and Just 2009)

If there were a perception that President Obama was avoiding addressing racial issues and that we had transitioned to a postracial society after his historic election, his statement underscored that he was aware of the myriad of issues facing African Americans and Latinos. His statement also showed that he was cognizant the issue of race remains a point of contention in the United States. For the most part, in the aftermath of the Gates arrest and President Obama's comments, most African Americans and Latinos agreed with Obama's comments. Many conservative whites did not and accused the president of supporting Gates because he was African American; they criticized President Obama for not being supportive of law enforcement. As with any White House administration entrapped in a controversial matter and a potential public relations nightmare, damage control had to be put in place to make sure opponents would not be given fodder for negative publicity.

On July 31, 2009, Obama invited Gates and the arresting police officer to the White House to have a conversation with him and Vice President Joe Biden. The meeting was dubbed "the beer summit." He hoped the meeting could serve as an example to the nation of what could be done when cooler heads prevailed in heated racial confrontations. The men talked, sipped beer, and ate peanuts and pretzels. Before the meeting, Gates and the police officer spent time getting to know each other and finding common ground while touring the White House. According to the *Washington Post*, the two men talked about their families and histories living in Cambridge (Staff Reports 2016). When the president and vice president joined the conversation, all parties were warm, cordial, frank, and quite open in their discussion. The heart of conversation focused on race and police interaction and there was not any tension among the men. After the meeting, all of them stated that they left learning something new. President Obama viewed the meeting as a teachable moment about race relations for the nation. He also wanted to bring to an end a controversy that had ballooned into a major distraction from his ambitious presidential agenda (Thompson, Thompson, and Fletcher 2009).

Of all the powers exercised by a president of the United States, the position of commander in chief offers enormous power as the highest military authority in the United States. The president also provides leadership to the entire defense system of the United States. This defense system also includes the intelligence network, which includes the Central Intelligence Agency (CIA), National Security Council (NSC), National Security Agency (NSA), and the Federal Bureau of Investigation (FBI). During President Obama's first term in office, he exercised his power as commander-in-chief when he authorized deadly force on Somali pirates to save personnel on the *Maersk Alabama*, deployed the coast guard to participate in the rescue and cleanup following the British Petroleum (BP) Deepwater Horizon explosion off the Gulf of Mexico, reduced the number of troops from Iraq, and increased the number of troops to Afghanistan. The most extraordinary deployment President Obama authorized during his first term of office was still yet to come. He authorized a raid on the compound that led to the killing of Osama bin Laden.

Osama bin Laden was the founder and leader of al Qaeda, a militant Sunni Islamist organization founded in 1988. This group is an extremist group designated as a terrorist cell by the United Nations Security Council, the North Atlantic Treaty Organization, the European Union, the United States, United Kingdom, Russia, India, and other countries. Al Qaeda has backed attacks on civilians and military targets in a variety of countries, including the 1998 bombings of U.S. embassies in Nairobi, Kenya, and Dar es Salaam, Tanzania. The most horrific attacks by al Qaeda occurred on September 11, 2001. These terrorist attacks consisted of violent and deadly strikes on the World Trade Center in New York, the Pentagon in Washington, DC, and United Airlines Flight 93. This was the first time since Pearl Harbor that a major attack occurred on U.S. soil. After these terrorist acts, Osama bin Laden eluded the U.S. military and intelligence for ten years. He frustrated the Bush administration with his ability to elude capture and continue to communicate with followers of the organization through video and audio communications.

One of the campaign promises Obama made was an earnest pledge to seek and kill Osama bin Laden for his role in the acts of terrorism on September 11. Obama swore, "We will crush al-Qaeda. That has to be our biggest national security priority" (CNN 2008). On May 2, 2011, President Obama made good on his campaign promise when the al Qaeda leader was killed by U.S. Special Forces during an early morning raid in Abbottabad, Pakistan. In an interview with CBS's news show *60 Minutes*, Obama said,

> the decision is always tough every time I send men and women into a war theatre. This was a very difficult decision, in part because the evidence that we had was not absolutely conclusive. This was circumstantial evidence that he was gonna be there. Obviously it entailed enormous risk to the guys that I sent in there. But ultimately I had so much confidence in the capacity of our guys to carry out the mission that I felt that the risks were outweighed by the potential benefit of us finally getting our man. (Kroft 2011)

Accounts of the details of the raid showed the president did not take this decision lightly nor was it made without input from his senior advisers and officials. The decision to send Special Forces was heavily debated among senior staff. The decision was confirmed when U.S. intelligence personnel tracked and identified Osama bin Laden's most trusted courier in late 2010. Within months of intelligence information and surveillance, President Obama's national security team concluded that Osama bin Laden was hiding on the third floor of a heavily guarded compound near Abbottabad, Pakistan. When surveillance showed a tall man resembling Osama bin Laden walking through the compound's courtyard, Obama discussed the decision to infiltrate the compound with his national security team. Some members of his team wanted more intelligence and more time to do more surveillance, however, Obama believed it was reasonable to think bin Laden was hiding in the compound. If they did not take action at that moment, bin Laden would slip away again and they would have missed a great opportunity to capture or kill him. President Obama understood if this mission failed and American lives were lost, there would be significant blowback in the United States, and it might ruin good relations with the Pakistani government. President Obama attended the annual correspondents' dinner and told jokes at this event. Obama was jovial, laughing and smiling throughout the event; no one knew he had given orders and the raid on bin Laden's compound would be carried out later that night.

Once the raid began, President Obama and his security team watched the raid on live video feed. Under the cover of darkness, four U.S. helicopters landed in the compound and discharged members of the Navy SEAL team. There was much anxiety among the members of the national security team while the raid was being carried out. This anxiety grew as one of the aircraft sustained damage as it landed near the compound. Nevertheless, the Navy SEAL team killed a guard on the first floor, shot one of Osama bin Laden's sons on the second floor, and then a team member shot Osama bin Laden. The entire military operation took a total of forty minutes. The president's team recognized the gravity of this raid and what it meant to many people in American society. President Obama indicated no one on his security team watching the operation cheered or "high-fived" each other; there was absolute silence before and after the operation. The pursuit of Osama bin Laden was over. Despite President Obama's perceived lack of foreign policy experience prior to taking office, he planted himself firmly among foreign leaders with goodwill and in some cases use of military force.

Obama supported a coalition of European and Arab governments in military action against Muammar Gaddafi of Libya. Gaddafi's totalitarian regime had ruled for forty-two years until a coup ended his reign in 2011, when he was overthrown. Minister Louis Farrakhan, the leader of the Nation of Islam, condemned President Obama over the bombing and killing of Muammar Gaddafi and for causing instability in the region. Gaddafi's autocratic leadership was bolstered by the country's oil wealth. After many years of economic sanctions for allegedly sponsoring terrorism, Libya and Gaddafi began attempting to rebuild relations with Western countries. In an effort to rebuild these relations, Gaddafi agreed to relinquish the country's nuclear weapons. Gaddafi renounced his support for terrorist groups and surrendered his pursuit of nuclear weapons. He also shifted toward domestic policies that featured privatization and international investments.

Sanctions on Libya were gradually lifted, but when the revolt occurred in 2011, Western nations supported forces carrying out the coup. After the

Louis Farrakhan and the Million Man March

Minister Louis Farrakhan is the leader of the Nation of Islam. He is the descendant of immigrant parents. His mother was from Barbados and his father was from Jamaica. At the time of birth, his name was Louis Eugene Wolcott. When he became the leader of the Boston Temple, he was known as Louis X. As a young man, he attended Winston-Salem State University; a historically black college located in Winston-Salem, North Carolina, but he did not graduate. He converted and joined the Nation of Islam after hearing Elijah Muhammad preach in Chicago. After Malcolm X severed his relationship with the Nation of Islam and his subsequent death, Farrakhan became the minister at Mosque No. 7 in Harlem, New York. After Elijah Muhammad's death, he designated his son, Warith Muhammad, to replace him in his leadership role, which he did for a short period. Farrakhan assumed leadership of the Nation of Islam within three years after the death of Elijah Muhammad. Libyan colonel Muammar Gaddafi provided $5 million to the Nation of Islam for economic development of poor African American communities. Prior to the 1984 presidential election, the Nation of Islam had a tradition of not participating in electoral politics in the United States. In 1984, Farrakhan endorsed Jesse Jackson, breaking this tradition.

On October 16, 1995, the Nation of Islam sponsored the Million Man March. Farrakhan called the event a holy day of atonement and reconciliation. The march aimed to reconcile man's spiritual being and redirect the black man's focus on developing their communities. It also aimed to empower black men through the Spirit of God to effectively use funds and the power of the vote to rebuild black communities in the United States. Though the march was a monumental success, there arose a dispute about the actual number of men who attended the march. This controversy withstanding, even conservative leaders embraced the key ideals of the march: self-dignity, family values, social responsibility, community responsibility, and capitalism. In January 2018, a photograph surfaced that showed Obama and Farrakhan smiling and standing next to each other at an event. Farrakhan had been invited to speak at the weekly Congressional Black Caucus lunch in 2005. Askia Muhammad, the photographer, withheld the photo from public view until after Barack Obama had completed his two terms as President of the United States.

uprising, Gaddafi was caught and killed. President Obama addressed the situation in Libya in the White House Rose Garden after video was shown of Gaddafi's bloody dead body. President Obama said, "One of the world's longest-serving dictators is no more" (Youngman 2011). He also stated, "The Libyans had won their revolution" and "the dark shadow of tyranny has been lifted." President Obama later acknowledged miscalculations in Libya as one of the biggest regrets of his presidency. "Probably failing to plan for the day after what I think was the right thing to do in intervening in Libya" (Tiereny 2016). After Gaddafi's death, Libya tumbled into chaos as militias took over and fights occurred among rival governments all claiming power. President Obama noted that one the worst mistakes of his presidency was an underestimation of tribal differences and the lack of planning for the aftermath of a post–Muammar Gadaffi Libya.

After influencing Libya, President Obama also effected developments in Egypt. He urged Egyptian President Hosni Mubarak to step down as president of his country. Mubarak's dictatorship ended after a thirty-year rule of Egypt. President Obama also tightened sanctions on Iran to deter Iran's pursuit of nuclear weapons and strengthen the country's nuclear weapons program. President Obama signed the Comprehensive Iran Sanctions, Accountability, and Divestment Act of 2010 to squeeze the economy of Iran in hopes they would drop their nuclear weapons program. The sanctions targeted both Iran and those countries doing business with Iran. The act punished firms and individuals who aided Iran in selling oil. The Obama administration coordinated with Japan, South Korea, and China to shift their oil purchases away from Iran.

Obama nominated and obtained confirmation for two seats on the U.S. Supreme Court. Sonia Sotomayor became the first Latinx woman on the court in 2009. A year later, President Obama gained another appointment to the high court with the appointment of Elena Kagan in 2010. Justice Sotomayor and Justice Kagan became the third and fourth women respectively appointed to the Court. They replaced David Souter and John Paul Stevens. In 2015, a third seat came open with the death of Antonin Scalia in 2015, but a Republican-led Congress with control of both chambers refused to have a hearing for President Obama's nominee Merrick Garland, a judge on the U.S. Court of Appeals in the Washington, DC, circuit.

Despite President Obama's many successes, the implementation of his presidential agenda, and the perception of a bedlam in White House after George W. Bush's two terms as president, there were frustrating failures. While Obamacare was passed during a time when the Democrats had a majority in both the U.S. House of Representatives and the U.S. Senate, the 2010 midterm elections brought on what President Obama deemed a "shellacking" as the Democratic Party lost control of the House of Representatives. By 2010, Republicans gained control of the House of Representatives and proceeded to obstruct most if not all legislation President Obama had in sight. Republican leaders were going to make sure they held true to the promise to obstruct President Obama's legislation and do their best to make him a one-term president. President Obama managed some victories but could not escape an obstructionist Congress and the weight of a backlash of racism and poor race relations in America.

As President Obama's first term in office concluded, he and his administration still had high hopes after accomplishing a win for health care provision for 13 million people and a financial stimulus bill to help ease the nation out of a recession. He supported same-sex marriage and gays in the military, reduced military troops in Iraq, and ended the Bush administration's hawkish rhetoric about bombing Iran. President Obama also signed the Dodd-Frank Wall Street Reform and Consumer Protection Act of 2010, which strengthened regulations on the financial sector by tightening capital requirements on large banks. He also gave the Food and Drug Administration (FDA) the power to regulate tobacco by signing the Family Smoking Prevention and Tobacco Control Act of 2009. This law mandates that tobacco manufacturers disclose all ingredients in tobacco products. Moreover, this law also requires that tobacco companies obtain FDA approval for new tobacco products and magnifies the size and prominence of warning labels on cigarettes. President Obama also expanded regulations on food safety when he signed the Food Safety Modernization Act of 2011. The act increased the budget of the FDA by $1.4 billion, expanded its responsibilities to increase food inspections and to exact food recalls, and reviewed current food safety practices of countries sending products into the United States. With several victories under his belt, President Obama braced himself for an uphill battle for his second term with a Republican-led Congress keyed on not allowing his administration move ahead with his agenda. They continually attempted to obstruct most if not all of his initiatives and introduced bills to overturn and chip away at his signature legislative accomplishment, the Affordable Care Act or Obamacare.

9

Barack Obama's Second Presidential Term

The second term of any presidency usually comes with harsh realities. A second-term president also usually does not experience a honeymoon with Congress. The second terms of some presidents of the United States have been marred in some form of major controversies or scandals. President Ronald Reagan experienced the Iran-Contra scandal during his second term. President Bill Clinton had an affair with an intern (Monica Lewinsky) and was eventually impeached but not removed from office. President Richard Nixon was forced to resign as a result of the Watergate scandal.

President Obama entered his second term riding high with his most substantial achievement of the Affordable Care Act (Obamacare) under his belt. Obama was the third president of the United States from the Democratic Party history to be elected twice with a majority of the popular vote each time. Unlike other second-term presidents, Obama's popular vote totals decreased in his second election. In the 2008 presidential election, Obama won 69.5 million votes. However in the 2012 presidential election, he won 65.9 million votes, losing 3.6 million votes. President Obama's reduced popular vote totals were due to some whites losing confidence in his administration and in turn voting for Republican Party presidential candidate Mitt Romney. The African American electorate remained loyal to President Obama, overwhelmingly voting for him in

2008 and 2012. He and his team saw an opportunity with Latinx voters, replacing those white voters who abandoned him with Latinx voters.

Much like President Obama's 2008 presidential campaign, his 2012 campaign was well organized with a technology-driven voter mobilization. During President Obama's second term, the Republicans controlled both chambers of Congress. They had a 234–204 majority in the U.S. House of Representatives. The also had control of the U.S. Senate, with a 55–45 advantage. With Republicans controlling both chambers of Congress, partisan polarization made it very difficult for President Obama to overcome legislative obstacles and pass anything through Congress. President Obama remained hopeful that his administration could accomplish more than he had during his first term. In his second-term inaugural speech, Obama laid the plans for his second term.

> It is now our generation's task to carry on what those pioneers began. For our journey is not complete until our wives, our mothers and daughters can earn a living equal to their efforts. Our journey is not complete until our gay brothers and sisters are treated like anyone else under the law for if we are truly created equal, then surely the love we commit to one another must be equal as well. Our journey is not complete until we find a better way to welcome the striving, hopeful immigrants who still see America as a land of opportunity, until bright young students and engineers are enlisted in our workforce rather than expelled from our country. Our journey is not complete until all our children, from the streets of Detroit to the hills of Appalachia, to the quiet lanes of Newtown, know that they are cared for and cherished and always safe from harm. (Obama, January 21, 2013)

President Obama followed his first-term accomplishments by continuing on some of his previous presidential items while turning his attention to other issues. During his second term, he focused on equal pay, gay rights, immigration reform, upgraded gun control, and clean energy. The Obama administration aimed to aggressively move toward passing and implementing these progressive policies. President Obama was able avoid the obstructionist efforts of Congress by utilizing executive orders to accomplish his legislative objectives during his second term. During President Obama's second term, Republicans enjoyed a comfortable majority in the House of Representatives and the Senate. These members of Congress had no intentions of compromising with or entertaining any bipartisanship with his administration. Still, the president looked for opportunities to work with Congress and to implement some of his presidential initiatives like reforming the nation's gun laws. There was hope that reforming gun laws would transpire after a mass shooting occurred at Sandy Hook Elementary School in Newtown, Connecticut, in December 2012.

At Sandy Hook Elementary, twenty children and six adults were killed by a young assailant. In the aftermath of these tragic events, President

Obama turned to Congress and called for stronger gun laws. President Obama endorsed universal background checks on gun purchases, banning assault weapons, and limiting the amount of ammunition magazines (Sink and Lillis 2013). These proposed gun control initiatives ended in defeat in the U.S. Senate by a margin of 52–46 (Gillin 2017). Congressional Republicans had no interest in supporting any gun reform proposals. While these gun reforms fell on congressional deaf ears, several mass shootings occurred during the Obama presidency: at a movie theater in Aurora, Colorado, in 2012; at a navy shipyard in Washington, DC, in 2013; in Isla Vista, California, near the University of California in 2014; at Emanuel Methodist Episcopal Church in Charleston, South Carolina, in 2015; and at the Pulse Night Club in Orlando, Florida, in 2016.

Obstruction was the name of the game to hinder and impede President Obama's agenda. The U.S. House Republicans repeatedly voted to repeal the Affordable Care Act (Obamacare), knowing the U.S. Senate would not take up the measure or Obama would veto the bill. Republicans also refused to confirm President Obama's nominees for various positions. The Senate blocked Obama's judicial nominees to the federal bench and to executive branch cabinet positions. After negotiations and outright threats from Senate Democrats, Republicans relented and allowed the nomination of Thomas Perez as secretary of labor to come forth. The nomination was confirmed on a straight party line vote. This was the first time a nominee was confirmed without a single vote from the opposition party.

In February 2013, President Obama delivered the State of the Union to a joint session of Congress and unveiled more presidential agenda items he wanted to accomplish. In his speech, President Obama vowed to push for economic policies to help the middle class, increase the minimum wage, and withdraw 34,000 troops from Afghanistan, and he restated from his inaugural address the need for better gun control policies, gay rights, and immigration reform. Though the national economy was showing moderate signs of recovery, there was still a fiscal impasse gripping the country's economy (Obama, February 13, 2013). Republican congressional leaders temporarily put aside their obstructionist efforts to keep the country from falling off a fiscal cliff and losing the gains of the economic recovery that had been taking place. President Obama and congressional leaders endured tough negotiations to avert plunging the economy into turmoil. The potential economic turmoil was the result of a compromise deal the political parties had previously agreed upon and was set to be enacted on January 1, 2013. This compromise deal consisted of $500 billion or more in tax increases and across-the-board spending cuts scheduled to take effect after January 1 for the fiscal year 2013 (Calmes 2012). If this deal had not gone into effect, the economy of the United States would possibly have plunged into peril.

During Obama's second term, he called for comprehensive immigration reform, but his record on immigration was mixed. After Congress failed to pass a bipartisan bill to reform immigration, he issued an executive order authorizing Deferred Action for Childhood Arrivals (DACA). Thousands of young undocumented immigrants who were brought to the United States as young children were allowed to stay in the country. Provisions under DACA gave more than 800,000 young undocumented immigrants known as "Dreamers" the opportunity to obtain temporary work permits and protection from deportation (Shoichet, Cullinane, and Kopan 2017). More than 2.8 million undocumented immigrants were deported over his two terms as President. In 2014, Obama unveiled a set of sweeping executive actions meant to build on DACA, expanding the pool of program beneficiaries to nearly 5 million undocumented immigrants (Sakuma 2017). Twenty-five states challenged these executive actions, and the case went to the U.S. Supreme Court. The Supreme Court rendered a decision that kept President Obama's executive actions on immigration and prevented the president from offering legal status to millions of undocumented immigrants. President Obama expressed his disappointment at the Court's ruling and the failure of Congress to pass comprehensive immigration reform.

In February 2013, President Obama gave the state of the union address. In this address, he stuck with many of the same themes that had become the cornerstone of his presidential agenda. In social policy, President Obama renewed his call for comprehensive immigration reform. Within this call for reform, he wanted to create a path to citizenship for immigrants now residing in the United States illegally. He also made a call for gun legislation that banned assault weapons and high-capacity magazines as well as closing loopholes in background checks. He stated he would focus on using executive orders to reaffirm his commitment to battle the effects of climate change by moving the United States toward using more natural gas and renewable energy sources and increasing efficiency in the energy sector.

The 2013 state of the union also focused on the economy. President Obama emphasized restoring manufacturing jobs. Among other initiatives, he proposed reforms that would lower the corporate tax rate and make the research and development tax credit permanent and provide incentives for manufacturers and others who invested in the U.S. economy. He also called for a new minimum tax on offshore earnings. Other high points mentioned in this address were the call for a new partnership between the federal government and the states to provide access to high-quality education for preschool children. President Obama provided insight on the crucial role of community colleges in providing marketable skills and higher wages. He also renewed his call for a Paycheck Fairness

Act to close the gap between men and women and also recommended an increase in the minimum wage from $7.25 to $9.00 per hour (Obama, February 12, 2013).

Six months after the state of the union, he renewed his focus on battling climate change. At a speech at Georgetown University, President Obama unveiled his goals. He released a plan designed to reduce greenhouse gas emissions from cars, trucks, factories, and power plants. He called for a reduction of carbon pollution by using more clean energy like wind and solar power. He wanted to phase out dependence on fossil fuels; the federal government would take the lead in clean energy, take the lead on fighting extreme weather events, push for energy efficiency, and promote clean energy on a global scale. He called for a partnership with communities seeking help to prepare for droughts and floods, reduce the risk of wildfires, protect wetlands, and erect natural storm barriers. In 2015, nearly two hundred countries signed the Paris Climate Accord by agreeing to adopt environmentally friendly practices in order to keep global temperatures from rising. In 2017, the Trump administration withdrew the United States from the agreement.

Healthcare.gov launched in October 2013, but the troubled rollout of the program's website almost derailed the implementation of Obamacare. Part of the problem stemmed from the government awarding $600 million in private contracts to construct the website. Millions of people had enrolled in the program, but it was plagued by problems. Many of the problems began well before the website's less than stellar debut on October 1, 2013, with the employees charged with handling those private contracts failing to oversee and manage those companies. President Obama made attempts to calm fears and alleviate frustrations of the U.S. public. He held a news conference in the Rose Garden and did not make any excuses for the bumbling of the rollout. "Nobody's madder than me about the website not working as well as it should, which means it is going to get fixed." He also stated, "You can bypass the website and apply by phone or in person. . . . So don't let problems with the website deter you from signing up or signing your family up or showing your friends how to sign up, because it is worth it. It will save you money" (Whitman 2015). Republicans continued to root for the failure of President Obama's signature law and attempted to undermine the Affordable Care Act and used members of their party to attack the law (Cohen 2013). They made several attempts to overturn the law.

Senate Minority Leader Mitch McConnell mockingly tweeted that when a visit to the Obamacare website made a trip to the Department of Motor Vehicles seem pleasant, "it's time for the President to consider delaying this rushed effort" (Payne 2013). On the Sunday morning political talk show *Face the Nation*, McConnell stated, "Only God knows how much money they have spent on this. . . . You know the government simply isn't going to be able to get this job done correctly" (Schieffer 2013). The Congressional Budget Office expected 7 million people to enroll by April 1, 2013 (Banthin and Masi n.d.). By October 2013, more than 250,000 people had registered for health care insurance through the government. By 2015, an estimated 10 to 12 million people had enrolled.

In 2016, Republican Party candidate Donald J. Trump ran for president on repealing and replacing the health care law and Obamacare. It has proven difficult to repeal the law. In 2015, the U.S. Supreme Court upheld the constitutionality of the health care law in a 6–3 decision in *King vs. Burwell*. Republicans underestimated the popularity of the law over time. By 2014, sentiments about the health care law had changed, with much of the country supporting the new law. In 2018, the Trump administration made changes to the signup process. Some saw this as an effort to upend the law. They slashed the open enrollment period and cut the advertising promoting the program. The Trump administration also reduced support for assistance for those having problems with enrollment. In 2017, the Republicans attempted to repeal the health care law. It was a deeply unpopular bill called the American Health Care Act. The measure failed to pass the U.S. Senate. By 2018, Americans when polled listed health care as one of the top issues of concern.

In 2014, President Obama signed an executive order raising the minimum wage for federal contractors from $7.25 per hour to $10.10 per hour. In a ceremony at the White House flanked by workers, Obama stated the wage hike would make a difference. A Quinnipiac University poll revealed 71 percent of Americans, of which more than half were Republicans, favored raising the minimum wage (National Employment Law Project 2015). The hike for federal contractors went into effect on January 1, 2015, and applied to contracts and expiring contracts.

In 2015, President Obama's approval rating hit an all-time low of 40 percent according to a NBC News-*Wall Street Journal* poll. President Obama's low approval ratings were probably due to the American public's disdain for government and politicians. Although the economy had improved, the U.S. public seemed to be upset with the lingering effects of the recession and the handling of foreign policy, and many thought the country was on the wrong track. President Obama's approval rating was poor, but Congress's approval was even worse, hovering around 14 percent. In addition, Americans held congressional Republicans in lower regard with a 54 percent unfavorable rating; congressional Democrats' rate was just marginally above President Obama at 46 percent unfavorable (America's Fed Up 2014). With this rating dip, President Obama continued to press on toward implementing his agenda.

In 2014, he approved a plan to allow unaccompanied minors to apply for refugee status in the United States. He cited an ongoing refugee problem as the rationale for opening the country's borders to children from the Central American countries of Guatemala, Honduras, and El Salvador. Many of these children were escaping violence. In 2013, he directed his administration to explore restoring diplomatic relations with Cuba. Cuba and the United States had been enemies for nearly fifty years. Obama authorized John Kerry to review Cuba's status as a state sponsor of terrorism. They also aimed to ease travel restrictions and increase the commerce between the two countries. The United States also opened a U.S. embassy in Cuba. After eighteen months of secret negotiations, President Obama and Cuban president Raul Castro brokered a deal that call for a release of U.S. and Cuban prisoners from each side and the lifting of a U.S. embargo that had been imposed on Cuba for about fifty-five years. For twenty-four years, the United Nations had condemned the embargo.

President Obama and his administration made progress in advancing equality and justice for all Americans. One group who immensely benefitted from Obama's efforts in equality were lesbian, gay, bisexual, and transgender (LGBT) Americans. Overcoming years of impasse creating legislation associated with hate crimes, President Obama worked with Congress to pass and sign into law the Matthew Shepard and James Byrd Jr. Hate Crimes Prevention Act into law in October 2009 and extended the coverage of federal hate crimes law to include attacks based on the victim's actual or perceived sexual orientation or gender identity. In a monumental move, Obama advocated for same-sex domestic partner benefits. This cleared the way for the State Department to extend the full range of legally available benefits and allowances to same-sex domestic partners of members of the Foreign Service sent to serve abroad. After the State Department's new policy took effect, the Office of Personnel Management (OPM) expanded its federal benefits for federal employees and their same-sex partners. This advancement allowed same-sex domestic partners to apply for long-term care insurance.

In December 2010, President Obama signed bipartisan legislation to repeal Don't Ask, Don't Tell. Gays, lesbians, and bisexual Americans were allowed to serve openly in the military without fear of being dismissed. In February 2011, the President Obama and U.S. Attorney General Eric Holder announced that the Department of Justice would no longer defend the Defense of Marriage Act's provision that defined marriage as only between a man and woman. This policy decision would be challenged in court, and ultimately the U.S. Supreme Court's held the Defense of Marriage Act was unconstitutional. After the *United States v. Windsor* decision, in which the Supreme Court struck down Section 3 of the Defense of

Marriage Act as unconstitutional, President Obama directed administrators to review federal statutes and regulations to ensure the decision was promptly and efficiently implemented to recognize the rights of same-sex couples in the United States. In 2015 after the U.S. Supreme Court issued a decision in *Obergefell v. Hodges*, the Social Security Administration began to recognize all same-sex marriages for purposes of determining entitlement to Social Security benefits or eligibility for Supplemental Security Income.

In July 2015, President Obama became the first president of the United States to address the African Union. The African Union is an intergovernmental organization formed to promote unity and solidarity in all fifty-five countries of Africa. The African Union was established in 2001 in Ethiopia and replaced the Organization of African Unity that operated from 1963 to 2002. It was part of a five-day, two-nation tour of east Africa. Obama's keynote address was at the African Union headquarters in Mandela Hall in Addis Ababa, Ethiopia. During his address, the president criticized some African leaders and their quest to hold on to power even after their presidential terms ended. His address was interrupted several times with thunderous applause. Obama stated, "Africa's democratic progress is also at risk when leaders refuse to step aside when their terms end. Now, let be honest with you, I don't understand this" (Obama, July 28, 2015).

Obama also addressed corruption and the mistreatment of women in African countries. This echoed sentiments of the speech he had given earlier in the week Nairobi, Kenya. Obama's visit to Africa was different from his first visit in 2009. Many nations in Africa had built relationships with China. Chinese investments have help to eliminate some of the stereotypes such as Africa being overrun by poverty and war. China has also invested in many African nations, which has made them less inclined to take policy direction from the United States and other Western powers. President Obama also addressed ending the culture of corruption in some countries in Africa, which is preventing these countries from reaching their full economic potential.

In March 7, 2015, President Obama went to Selma, Alabama, to commemorate the fiftieth anniversary of the Selma to Montgomery March and the passage of the Voting Rights Act of 1965. More than 100,000 people showed up to participate in the festivities. President Obama, President George W. Bush, and President Bill Clinton were there to remember the tragic events known as "Bloody Sunday" on the Edmund Pettus Bridge. In 1965 during the apex of the modern civil rights movement, activists organized a march from Selma to Montgomery, the state capital. The marchers wanted to bring attention to African American being denied the right to vote and to participate in electoral process. On March 7, 1965, some six hundred people assembled at a downtown church, prayed, and began to walk slowly and solemnly through the streets of Selma. When they

---

VOTING RIGHTS ACT OF 1965 AND BLOODY SUNDAY

While the Civil Rights Act of 1964 made provisions that assisted in removing impediments keeping African Americans from voting in southern states, white resistance was prevalent in southern state governments. In states such as Alabama, most of the black population was prevented from voting. In Dallas County, Alabama, fewer than four hundred of the fifteen thousand eligible black voters were registered to vote. President Lyndon B. Johnson initially refused to send federal troops to Alabama to protect workers who came to Alabama to help register voters. President Johnson's view would change when violence erupted in Dallas and Perry Counties in Alabama. When Jimmie Lee Jackson was killed while trying to protect his mother from being beaten by an Alabama state trooper in Perry County, national attention was cast on the dire situation in Alabama. The Southern Christian Leadership Conference announced a mass march from Selma to Montgomery, which was scheduled to take place on March 7, 1965. When the marchers approached the Edmund Pettus Bridge, state troopers teargassed and beat the marchers with clubs. Images of these tragic events were captured by the media and were broadcast to the rest of the world. Dr. Martin Luther King Jr. and other civil rights leaders scheduled a second march a few days later. President Johnson urged the leaders to call off the march, and a federal judge issued an injunction preventing it. On the march, Dr. King and approximately fifteen hundred protesters marched to the edge of the bridge but turned around. Dr. King did not want to violate a court injunction or get on the wrong side of President Johnson, whom he knew he needed to secure voting rights legislation.

When James Reeb, a white Unitarian minister from Boston, Massachusetts, who came to Selma to support the cause was murdered by whites, President Johnson pressed forward and announced that he would sign voting rights legislation in a televised address to Congress on March 15, 1965. Finally on March 21, 1965, Dr. Martin Luther King Jr. led thousands of nonviolent demonstrators to the steps of the capitol in Montgomery after a five day, fifty-four-mile march from Selma. Each year in Selma, Alabama, there is a celebration of Bloody Sunday. Congress passed the Voting Rights Act of 1965 on August 6, 1965. The act outlawed the educational requirement to be able to vote. The legislation also gave the attorney general of the United States the authority to have the federal registrars enroll voters. As a result of the Voting Rights Act of 1965, black voter registration in southern states rose dramatically.

---

approached the Edmund Pettus Bridge, the marchers were met by Alabama state troopers swinging nightsticks, clubs, and whips to break up a civil rights voting march. Five months after this incident, President Lyndon B. Johnson signed the Voting Rights Act of 1965. The act protected African Americans' right to vote, which had been granted in 1870 by the Fifteenth Amendment but had not been followed in some states.

President Obama opened his speech reminding the audience of Rev. Dr. Martin Luther King Jr. and of Addie Mae Collins, Cynthia Wesley, Carole

Robertson, and Denise McNair, the four girls who died in the 16th Street Baptist Church bombing in 1963. Obama exclaimed the civil rights battles of the past were clashes to determine the true meaning of America and its ideals. He then acknowledged the civil rights leaders and civil rights foot soldiers of the past who endeavored to make the country more inclusive and just. He also noted that the events that transpired on the bridge could not be analyzed in isolation but were a part of a long history of the struggle for freedom.

> In one afternoon fifty years ago, so much of our turbulent history, the stain of slavery and anguish of civil war; the yoke of segregation and tyranny of Jim Crow; the death of four little girls in Birmingham, and the dream of a Baptist preacher met on this bridge. It was not a clash of armies, but a clash of wills; a contest to determine the meaning of America. And because of men and women like John Lewis, Joseph Lowery, Hosea Williams, Amelia Boynton, Diane Nash, Ralph Abernathy, C.T. Vivian, Andrew Young, Fred Shuttlesworth, Dr. King, and so many more, the idea of a just America, a fair America, an inclusive America, a generous America that idea ultimately triumphed. As is true across the landscape of American history, we cannot examine this moment in isolation. The march on Selma was part of a broader campaign that spanned generations; the leaders that day part of a long line of heroes. They saw that idea made real in Selma, Alabama. They saw it made real in America. (Obama, March 7, 2015)

President Obama then acknowledged what the events that took place on Edmund Pettus Bridge and the subsequent march from Selma to Montgomery did for the African American community. He also understood this as a shining moment in paving the way to open doors for other minority communities. He also understood that the events on the Edmund Pettus Bridge were key to him becoming the first African American president of the United States.

> Because of campaigns like this, a Voting Rights Act was passed. Political, economic, and social barriers came down, and the change these men and women wrought is visible here today in the presence of African-Americans who run boardrooms, who sit on the bench, who serve in elected office from small towns to big cities; from the Congressional Black Caucus to the Oval Office. (Obama, March 7, 2015)

Because of what they did, the doors of opportunity swung open not just for African-Americans, but for every American. Women marched through those doors. Latinos marched through those doors. Asian Americans, gay Americans, and Americans with disabilities came through those doors. Their endeavors gave the entire South the chance to rise again, not by reasserting the past, but by transcending the past. President Obama also used the historical events and the anniversary of the Voting Rights Act of 1965 to connect it to contemporary issues and injustices facing America.

He urged people to use their imaginations to search for solutions because change depends on individuals exacting change. Reminiscent of his speech at the Democratic National Convention in 2004, he called on Americans to look past race and recognize change is needed.

> This is work for all Americans, and not just some. Not just whites. Not just blacks. If we want to honor the courage of those who marched that day, then all of us are called to possess their moral imagination. All of us will need to feel, as they did, the fierce urgency of now. All of us need to recognize, as they did, that change depends on our actions, our attitudes, the things we teach our children. And if we make such effort, no matter how hard it may seem, laws can be passed, and consciences can be stirred, and consensus can be built. (Obama, March 7, 2015)

He then noted what could be accomplished if people stuck together. He believed that trust between police and the African American community could improve if just policies were created. He also addressed the injustice prevalent in the U.S. criminal justice system, in particular overcrowded prisons and unfair sentencing. He suggested that it needed to fixed because it is a main contributor to breaking up families and poverty.

> With such effort, we can make sure our criminal justice system serves all and not just some. Together, we can raise the level of mutual trust that policing is built on the idea that police officers are members of the communities they risk their lives to protect, and citizens in Ferguson and New York and Cleveland just want the same thing young people here marched for—the protection of the law. Together, we can address unfair sentencing, and overcrowded prisons, and the stunted circumstances that rob too many boys of the chance to become men, and rob the nation of too many men who could be good dads, and workers, and neighbors. With effort, we can roll back poverty and the roadblocks to opportunity. Americans don't accept a free ride for anyone, nor do we believe in equality of outcomes. But we do expect equal opportunity, and if we really mean it, if we're willing to sacrifice for it, then we can make sure every child gets an education suitable to this new century, one that expands imaginations and lifts their sights and gives them skills. We can make sure every person willing to work has the dignity of a job, and a fair wage, and a real voice, and sturdier rungs on that ladder into the middle class. (Obama, March 7, 2015)

President Obama noted the efforts to roll back voting statutes such as the federal government monitoring elections and creation of voting districts that either weaken or strengthen a political party's hold on districts. He affirmed that voting is the bedrock of a functioning democracy and again acknowledged that the events and the efforts were the product of sacrifice of those willing to put their lives on the line for the right to vote.

> And with effort, we can protect the foundation stone of our democracy for which so many marched across this bridge and that is the right to vote.

Right now, in 2015, fifty years after Selma, there are laws across this country designed to make it harder for people to vote. As we speak, more of such laws are being proposed. Meanwhile, the Voting Rights Act, the culmination of so much blood and sweat and tears, the product of so much sacrifice in the face of wanton violence, stands weakened, its future subject to partisan rancor. (Obama, March 7, 2015)

Three months after this speech, President Obama would face another tragic racial event with the mass killing of African Americans in a Charleston, South Carolina, church. On June 17, 2015, Dylann Roof, a white man, killed nine African American churchgoers while they prayed and had Bible study at Emanuel African Methodist Episcopal Church in downtown Charleston, South Carolina. Reverend Clementa Pinckney, a South Carolina state legislator, who was also the pastor of the church, was one of those killed in this shooting. The gunman was later found in North Carolina and extradited to South Carolina. The shooter was charged with several crimes, including a hate crime. This church had historic roots in slave resistance, which may have been the reason it was targeted. In 1833, the historic church was investigated for its involvement with a planned slave revolt in Charleston. Denmark Vesey, one of the church's founders, was hanged for organizing a slave uprising. Dylann Roof confessed to police and admitted the act of violence was influenced by the race of the congregants. He also had been photographed with symbols of white supremacy on his clothing, and his car had a Confederate States of America license plate on it. The shooter's roommates stated that Roof was "into segregation" and "wanted to start a race war." As he shot the victims in the church, Roof reportedly yelled, "You rape our women, and you're taking over our country" (Mosendz 2015). President Obama spoke to the nation about these tragic events. "Michelle and I know several members of Emanuel AME Church. We knew their pastor, Reverend Clementa Pinckney, who, along with eight others, gathered in prayer and fellowship and was murdered last night." President Obama continued, "And to say our thoughts and prayers are with them and their families, and their community doesn't say enough to convey the heartache and the sadness and the anger that we feel" (Time Staff 2015). President Obama utilized tradition well observed in the African American church by concluding Pinckney's eulogy with the hymn, "Amazing Grace."

By the conclusion of President Obama's second term in 2016, a CNN and Opinion Research Corporations (ORC) poll found that the majority of Americans, 54 percent, believed that race relations between blacks and whites had worsened under President Obama. These numbers included 57 percent of whites and 40 percent of African Americans (Agiesta 2016). In the same poll, whites and blacks differed on the equal treatment between black people and white people. About three-quarters of blacks and one-half of whites felt the criminal justice system favored whites. With the election of Barack Obama, polling numbers on problems with race relations ticked upward, with many whites seeing race problems as a serious problem. With the death of Supreme Court Justice Antonin Scalia in February 2016, President Obama should have gotten the opportunity to nominate another justice to the U.S. Supreme Court. President Obama quickly named Merrick Garland to fill the vacancy on the Court. Garland had been serving as the chief judge on the U.S. Court of Appeals for the District of Columbia Circuit. Garland was considered a moderate and on the short list of nominees for an appointment to the court. Under most circumstances, Garland would have been easily confirmed. He had been widely praised by Republicans in the past, but when President Obama named him as his choice for the court, they moved to obstruct the move.

U.S. Senator Mitch McConnell from Kentucky declared that any of President Obama's Supreme Court appointments or nominees put forth would be null and void. McConnell stated the next Supreme Court justice should be chosen by the next president after the election the following year. McConnell would later brag, "One of my proudest moments was when I looked Barack Obama in the eye and I said, Mr. President, you will not fill the Supreme Court vacancy" (Elving 2018). McConnell was joined by other members of the Senate Judiciary Committee stating they would not consent to any President Obama's nominees for the U.S. Supreme Court. In the end, the Republicans did not hold any kind of hearing for Garland's nomination. A federal lawsuit was filed to force McConnell to hold a vote on Garland. The lawsuit was thrown out because a judge stated an ordinary voter had no standing to sue. Democrats fumed about this blatant disrespect of the president and the Republicans circumventing the U.S. Constitution. With Republicans controlling both chambers of the legislative branch, Democrats were left with very little power to get President Obama's nomination confirmed.

10

After the Presidency and Presidential Legacy

On November 8, 2016, the Republican ticket of Donald Trump and Indiana Governor Mike Pence defeated the Democratic Party ticket of former secretary of state Hillary Clinton and Virginia senator Tim Kaine. Hillary Clinton received about 3 million more popular votes than Trump. However, Trump won the electoral college, winning thirty states and crucial victories in swing states such as Florida, Iowa, Michigan, and Ohio. Trump became only the fifth person to win and become president without having won the popular vote. He is also the first person to become president without any experience in public service. Most media outlets and political polls did not believe Trump could pull out a victory and were astonished at his victory. After Clinton's stunning failed presidential bid and one of the most divisive elections in history, Obama attempted to heal a divided nation. On November 9, 2016, President Obama spoke to the nation from the Rose Garden of the White House. He discussed the peaceful transition of power, speaking with the president-elect, and uniting the country after the election. He also reminded citizens that the office of the president and the country's future are bigger than one individual.

> I had a chance to talk to President-elect Trump last night—about 3:30 in the morning, I think it was—to congratulate him on winning the election. And I had a chance to invite him to come to the White House tomorrow to talk

about making sure that there is a successful transition between our Presidencies.

Now, it is no secret that the President-elect and I have some pretty significant differences. But remember, 8 years ago, President Bush and I had some pretty significant differences. But President Bush's team could not have been more professional or more gracious in making sure we had a smooth transition so that we could hit the ground running. And one thing you realize quickly in this job is that the Presidency—and the Vice Presidency—is bigger than any of us. (Transcript 2016)

During this speech after the election, President Obama also reminded the country that the true purpose of government is to help its people.

I also told my team today to keep their heads up, because the remarkable work that they have done day in, day out—often without a lot of fanfare, often with a lot of attention—work in agencies, work in obscure areas of policy that make Government run better and make it more responsive and make it more efficient and make it more service friendly so that it's actually helping more people, that remarkable work has left the next President with a stronger, better country than the one that existed 8 years ago. (Ibid.)

He reaffirmed the mission of his administration and its core value to assist U.S. families who are attempting to make a decent living. He also addressed the nature of politics and elections in the United States. He stressed his faith in democracy and his belief that this faith has been a major contributor in the success of the country. He urged the country to put this bitter battle behind them and move forward in making the country a better place.

So win or lose in this election that was always our mission. That was our mission from day one. And everyone on my team should be extraordinarily proud of everything that they have done, and so should all the Americans that I've had a chance to meet all across this country who do the hard work of building on that progress every single day: teachers in schools; doctors in ER clinics; small businesses putting their all into starting something up, making sure they're treating their employees well; all the important work that's done by moms and dads and families and congregations in every State—the work of perfecting this Union. That's the way politics works sometimes. We try really hard to persuade people that we're right. And then, people vote. And then, if we lose, we learn from our mistakes, we do some reflection, we lick our wounds, we brush ourselves off, we get back in the arena. We go at it. We try even harder the next time. (Ibid.)

President Obama also emphasized that faith was an essential part of democracy and the United States has advanced because it promoted freedom. He reminded the audience at the country's founding, civil rights were not extended to everyone, but were later expanded and became more inclusive.

He pointed this expansion of laws to include all citizens as progress in the United States' development.

> The point, though, is that we all go forward, with a presumption of good faith in our fellow citizens, because that presumption of good faith is essential to a vibrant and functioning democracy. That's how this country has moved forward for 240 years. It's how we've pushed boundaries and promoted freedom around the world. That's how we've expanded the rights of our founding to reach all of our citizens. It's how we have come this far. (Ibid.)

As President Obama prepared to leave the oval office, he left a letter to President-elect Donald J. Trump. This has become an honored tradition of presidents. President Bill Clinton left a letter for George W. Bush. President George W. Bush left a letter for Barack Obama. President Obama followed the tradition of leaving a letter to his successor on inauguration day 2017. In the letter, Obama urged the new president to honor the traditions and institutions of the country. He also reflected on of his tenure as president of the United States and reminded the new president of the inequities in the United States and how the America's status in the world is important because it is a beacon of democracy. He also reminded the new president to reserve time for his family and friends. The letter attempted to make President-elect Trump aware of the gravity of the job and the responsibility of being a leader of the nation.

> *Dear Mr. President,*
>
> *Congratulations on a remarkable run. Millions have placed their hopes in you, and all of us regardless of party, should hope for expanded prosperity and security during your tenure. This is a unique office, without a clear blueprint for success, so I don't know that any advice from me will be particularly helpful. Still, let me offer a few reflections from the past eight years.*
>
> *First, we've both been blessed, in different ways, with great fortune. Not everyone is so lucky. It's up to us to do everything we can (to) build more ladders of success for every child and family that's willing to work hard.*
>
> *Second, American leadership in this world is really indispensable. It's up to us, through action and example, to sustain the international order that's expanded steadily since the end of the Cold War, and upon which our own wealth and safety depend.*
>
> *Third, we are just temporary occupants of this office. That makes us guardians of those democratic institutions and traditions—like rule of law, separation of powers, equal protection and civil liberties—that our forebears fought and bled for. Regardless of the*

push and pull of daily politics, it's up to us to leave those instruments of our democracy at least as strong as we found them.

And finally, take time, in the rush of events and responsibilities, for friends and family. They'll get you through the inevitable rough patches.

Michelle and I wish you and Melania the very best as you embark on this great adventure, and know that we stand ready to help in any ways which we can.

Good luck and Godspeed,

BO

Former U.S. presidents have chosen many different paths after they have served in the highest elected office in the land. Some like Bill Clinton and

---

BARACK OBAMA PRESIDENTIAL PORTRAIT

On February 12, 2018, the presidential portrait of Barack Obama was unveiled at the National Portrait Gallery in Washington, DC. This gallery is home to the only complete collection of presidential portraits. Congress created the National Portrait Gallery in 1962, and it opened in 1968. The National Portrait Gallery has been commissioning portraits of American presidents since the administration of President George H. W. Bush.

President Obama's portrait was painted by artist Kehinde Wiley. Also on this day Michelle Obama's portrait was also unveiled. Her portrait was painted by Amy Sherald. Both artists were the first African Americans commissioned to paint official portraits of the first couple for the National Portrait Gallery. Both of these artists has an extraordinary and vivid depictions of African American life. Wiley, who painted Barack Obama's portrait, is noted for his distinct way of featuring young African American men in a collection called the street cast, where these young men are featured in striking scenes and poses that replicated classic depictions of western artwork. Wiley gained a following in the early 2000s for these life-size paintings. Wiley's work challenges the stereotypes of African American men, so it is not coincidental Barack Obama chose Wiley as the artist for his portrait.

President Obama's portrait is a little over seven feet tall. In the portrait Obama is dressed in a dark suit, with a white open-collar shirt seated in a thronelike chair. Obama's face in the portrait does not show emotions, and he appears quite composed. President Obama sits leaning forward with his elbows on his knees, arms crossed, as if he is intensely paying attention to those viewing the portrait. The Obama figure in the portrait is cast in front of symbolic flowers: African blue lilies that represent Kenya, his father's birthplace; jasmine, which represents Hawaii; and chrysanthemums, the official flower of Chicago, his adopted hometown and where Obama's political career began.

Jimmy Carter have been actively engaged in their foundations and causes dear to them. Other presidents like George H. W. Bush and George W. Bush have kept a lower profile. On January 20, 2017, Barack Obama returned to private life following the inauguration of Donald J. Trump as the forty-fifth president of the United States. After Obama left office, he kept a low profile at least for a while. The Obamas chose to stay in the Washington, DC, area so their daughter Sasha could complete high school and graduate from Sidwell Friends High School while Malia completed a gap year before beginning her college career at Harvard University.

Most of former president Obama's time has been spent engaged in activities such as speaking engagements, overseeing his presidential library, delivering stump speeches for Democratic Party candidates, charity work, and expanding the global range of the Obama Foundation. Immediately after leaving office, the Obamas vacationed in Palm Springs, the British Virgin Islands, and French Polynesia. On his vacation in the British Virgin Islands with Richard Branson, billionaire and Virgin Group founder, Obama talked about the restrictions placed on him as president; he revealed to Branson that he had not been surfing in a while. Branson challenged Obama to a kitesurfing competition. Obama claimed to have won the competition. Obama's postpresidency life did not just consist of vacations and golfing. In his return to ordinary citizenry, he had to participate and fulfill democratic duties just as all other citizens would. Obama was served with a notice of jury duty in November 2017. Although he was not selected for a jury and was dismissed before noon, he provided citizens a sterling but simple example of fulfilling one's civic duty.

In 2017, Penguin Random House signed Barack and Michelle Obama book contracts. Top publishers engaged in a bidding war to secure the rights to the package deal of the former President and First Lady. The Obama's book deal was reportedly worth over $65 million for the rights to memoirs by both Obamas. Penguin Random House plans to donate one million printed books in the Obama Family's name to First Books and then provide electronic versions of the books through Open eBooks. First Books is a non-profit that distributes books to disadvantaged children. The Obamas planned to donate a significant portion of their author proceeds to charity, including their own charity. Barack Obama has a proven track record as an author. His previous three books have been on the best-seller list and sold over four million copies. *Dreams of My Father, The Audacity of Hope*, and a children's book title, *Of Thee I Sing*, were all published by Crown Publishing, an imprint of Random House. Michelle Obama also published a healthy guide to eating titled *American Grown* with Crown Publishing. Barack Obama's publishing deal greatly exceeds publishing deals for former U.S. presidents. Bill Clinton reportedly received $15 million for his memoir, *My Life*, and George W. Bush received about

$10 million for his memoir, *Decision Points.* Clinton and Bush's memoirs sold more than a million copies. Many believe that Obama's memoirs could be the most valuable presidential memoirs ever published. Obama kept extensive notes in a journal while he was president, and his book will reflect on his time during the White House years. Michelle Obama's memoir was released in November 2018 and quickly became the best-selling book of the year. Also in 2018, the Obamas signed a deal with Netflix, for which they will produce television shows and films. The deal will give the Obamas an international television platform during his postpresidency. They created Higher Ground Productions to produce television shows.

Obama has been wading into domestic and international politics since leaving office. This involvement has come mainly in the form of endorsements. In May 2017, Barack Obama recorded a message for the people of France. He endorsed Emmanuel Macron, a centrist candidate who was running for president of France. Macron was up against Marine Le Pen, who was a far-right candidate. La Pen had harshly criticized the European Union and had vowed to pull France out of NATO. She had also garnered the endorsement of President Donald Trump. In the video, Obama wore a charcoal gray suit and a silver tie with an U.S. lapel pin.

> The French election is very important to the future of France and the values that we care so much about. Because the success of France matters to the world. I have admired the campaign of Emmanuel Macron has run. He stood up for liberal values, he put forward a vision for the important role that France plays in Europe and around the world. And he is committed to a better future for the French people. He appeals to people's hopes and not their fears. I am not planning to get involved in many elections now that I don't have to run for office again, but the French election is very important to the future of France and to the values that we care so much about. (Tatum 2017)

Barack Obama ended the video message endorsing Macron with the phrase, "Qui on peut!" or "Yes we can!" Shortly after the message aired, the French people began an online petition to persuade Obama to run for the French presidency. It not common for U.S. presidents to publicly endorse candidates in foreign elections; they typically support them privately. Considering the wave of populism that pushed Donald Trump into the White House, Obama spoke out to prevent La Pen, who had been called the Donald Trump of France, from achieving victory in the French presidential elections.

Obama was not only involved in elections internationally; he has been involved in elections in the United States as well. In October 2016, Obama endorsed a slate of Democratic Party House of Representative candidates. Obama taped political advertisements and robocalls for several candidates in the hopes that the Democratic Party would flip seats in Congress. In California, Obama endorsed Ami Bera, Michael Eggman, Salud Carbajal, and Doug Applegate. In Nevada, Obama endorsed Jacky Rosen and Ruben Kihuen. In Arizona, Obama endorsed Tom O'Halleran. In Colorado, Obama backed Morgan Carroll. In Iowa, he endorsed Monica Vernon and Jim Mowrer. In Nebraska, he endorsed Brad Ashford, and in Kansas, he endorsed Jay Sidie. He also has provided endorsements for Cheri Bustos in Illinois, Angie Craig in Minnesota, and Suzanna Shkreli in Michigan. In Florida, Obama recommended Stephanie Murphy, Val Demings, and Joe Garcia. In Virginia, Obama backed LuAnn Bennett and Jane Dittmar. In Pennsylvania, the former president favored Steve Sanarsiero and Christina Hartman. In New York, Obama supported Tom Suozzi, Sean Patrick Maloney, Zephyr Teachout, and Colleen Deacon. In New Jersey, he supported Josh Gottheimer. In Maine, Obama endorsed Emily Cain and Carol Shea-Porter. Lastly, he endorsed Annie Kuster in New Hampshire.

During the Democratic Party primaries in 2016, Obama did not endorse either candidate, Bernie Sanders or Hillary Clinton. He waited until the end of the primary process and then endorsed the party's nominee. Obama did signal through an editorial in the *New York Times* that he "would not campaign for, vote for or support a candidate, even in my own party, who does not support common-sense gun reform" (Shear 2016). Many interpreted this as a silent endorsement of Hillary Clinton. Obama's and Clinton's ideologies were in line on gun control.

As members of the U.S. Senate, Obama and Clinton voted against the Protection of Lawful Commerce in Arms Act, although it was later signed into law. Bernie Sanders also voted for immunity from prosecution for gun sellers in 2005; this view did not line up with Obama's ideology on gun control. Sanders also voted against the Brady Bill five times. The Brady Bill mandated background checks for those who buy guns. Sanders defended his stance by justifying the love of hunting in Vermont. He later distributed a 2008 Clinton presidential campaign advertisement hitting Obama on gun control via Twitter. The advertisement attempted to paint Obama as flip-flopper on guns and recycled a line from an Obama speech where he accused "people in rural places and small towns of being bitter people who cling to guns." The tweet ended with the tagline, "What does Barack Obama really believe?" (Ferris 2016). After the dust settled from the Democratic Party primaries, Obama waded into the 2016 presidential race by endorsing and campaigning for his former secretary of state and 2008 Democratic presidential primary rival, Hillary Clinton, in the general election.

Among the roles Obama saw for himself after leaving the presidency was developing and cultivating candidates for the Democratic Party. There was not much diversity in the Democratic Party's roster of candidates, and the party found themselves looking for a clear leader after Obama's presidency ended. The Democratic Party messaging and strength had built on the charisma and appeal of Obama. Former secretary of labor Thomas Perez and Minnesota Representative Keith Ellison looked to take over the helm of the leadership of the Democratic Party. Both men represented two strong factions of the party. Perez represented the labor union wing of the party, while Ellison represented the racial minority and liberal factions of the party. Both Barack Obama and Joe Biden had been critical of the Democratic Party after the 2016 presidential election, noting it had become too elitist and the party's messaging to rural white people had been lost. Obama acknowledged that he had not been able to transfer his energy and duplicate the strategies he used during his presidential victories in 2008 and 2012 to the overall party.

Obama believed a new and bold strategy should be used. He believed that every race should have a strong Democratic Party candidate and followed this belief with action. He was assertive and endorsed numerous candidates in congressional and state races. Eighty-seven of his candidates won, although most of the winners were incumbents. Few of the challengers Obama endorsed won their races. The national Democratic Party's leadership targeted thirty-two state legislative seats held by Republicans in the key battleground states of Florida, Michigan, North Carolina, Ohio, Pennsylvania, and Wisconsin. They won only eight of those seats. Although not as successful as he would have liked, Obama pushed this aggressive strategy of challenging every race to the Democratic Party's national leadership. As Obama left office, he left some wisdom for the Democratic Party. In an interview on National Public Radio in December 2016, Obama asserted,

> One of the big suggestions that I have for Democrats as I leave, and something that I have some ideas about, is how we can do more of that ground-up building? What I am interested is developing a whole new generation of talent. For example, we know that the Republicans, funded through organizations like the Koch brothers, have been systematic at building from the ground up and communicating to state legislators and financing school board races and public utility commission races. I am a proud Democrat, but I think that we have a bias toward national issues and international issues and as a consequence I think we have ceded too much territory. I take some responsibility for that. (Inskeep 2016)

This strategy seemed have taken hold because the Democratic Party consistently flipped U.S. congressional seats and some state legislature seats in conservative states. The Democratic Party's strategy was to run viable candidates in all races and not cede any race by challenging in state and national elections. The Democrats flipped two seats in Connecticut, New Hampshire, Wisconsin, and Florida in 2018. The Democratic Party was able to flip a seat in the U.S. Congress when Doug Jones defeated Roy Moore in a special election after Jeff Sessions became the attorney general of the United States. This was the first member of the Democratic Party to win a statewide election in Alabama since 2008. The 2018 midterm elections saw the Democratic Party take control of the U.S. House of Representatives while the Republicans made small gains in the U.S. Senate.

After his time as president of the United States, Barack and Michelle Obama began the planning of his presidential library and museum. Several locations were vying for the opportunity to have Barack Obama's presidential library and museum located in their city. Columbia University in New York, the University of Hawaii in Honolulu, and University of Illinois at Chicago competed for the coveted right to handle the former president's archival holdings and be the location choice for the Obama's presidential library. Obama had a strong personal connection to the University of Chicago. He had served as a constitutional law professor at the university, his wife had been an administrator at the university's medical center, and she grew up on the South Side of Chicago. It would be no surprise it was chosen as the place to hold Obama's archival materials. "All the strands of my life came together in Chicago. That's where I really became a man. That's where I met my wife. That's where my children were born" (Glanton, Bowean, and Gregory 2015).

The Anderson Economic Group and the University of Chicago believed the presidential library would bring thirty-three hundred jobs to the South Side of Chicago and about eight hundred thousand visitors a year with an estimation that four hundred thousand of these visitors would be tourists (Staff Writer 2014). The university estimated the presidential library would bring about forty new businesses and restaurants and about nineteen hundred new jobs to the South Side. The Obama Library would be an economic boom, bringing in about $200 million annually (Manier 2015). After Chicago was chosen as the library's site, Chicago residents tried to influence and pinpoint the exact location the library would be placed. Jackson Park and Washington Park, two of Chicago's parklands, were proposed sites. Friends of the Park emerged as an opposition group who sought to block usage of park land for the Obama presidential library. According to a *Chicago Tribune* poll, a majority of the city's residents were supportive of using parklands for the presidential library. Another group of young activists attempted to press the former president to choose some other site if the University of Chicago did not restore its adult trauma care at its medical center. The lack of the trauma unit at the medical center had been a source of contention between the University of Chicago and the predominately African American neighborhood that surrounds it. The University of Chicago pushed back on this argument, noting the services it provided such as a pediatric trauma center and a neonatal trauma center. The opposition group responded by stating the University of Chicago is not a cash-strapped university and should not be rewarded for adverse behavior. Some believed the conflation of the presidential library and the trauma center made the opposition group out of step with the widespread enthusiasm for the Obama's presidential library being located in Chicago. After much discussion and deliberation, the University of Chicago and Jackson Park in Chicago, Illinois, was chosen as the site of Obama's presidential Library.

Martin Nesbitt, the chair of the Obama Foundation, was tasked with overseeing the planning and construction of the library's facilities. Tod Williams and Billie Tsien created the architectural designed for the library and its campus. The architectural team's previous designs included the Reva and David Logan Center for the Arts at the University of Chicago and the Barnes Foundation museum in Philadelphia. Like the other thirteen presidential libraries, the Obama presidential library was financed through private funding. The design of the presidential library and museum consists of three buildings that include exhibition space, public spaces, offices, and education meeting rooms. They also hope to have a city branch of the library located in the facilities also.

The blueprints for the library have a sprawling campus with the museum located at the northern end of a plaza. The total size of the center is estimated to range from 200,000 to 225,000 square feet on a 500-acre lakefront area (Madhani 2017). The library is expected to be completed by 2021. The University of Chicago stated the library would bring numerous jobs to the area. The William J. Clinton Presidential Library and Museum drove $1 billion in real estate investment in downtown Little Rock, Arkansas. The George W. Bush Presidential Center on the Southern Methodist University campus was projected to inject $50 million annually into the local economy of Dallas, Texas. Obama hopes his library will be the hub of the community and a place to train young people for future leadership roles. He also hopes it will become a place where performing artist will come and find creative inspiration to create work and teach people about film, music, and other creative arts.

In his postpresidency, Barack Obama has received several awards and recognitions. In 2017, Barack Obama was awarded the Profiles in Courage Award at the John F. Kennedy Library in Boston, Massachusetts. The award was presented by John Kennedy's daughter, Caroline Kennedy. Also in 2017, Obama was awarded the German Media Prize in Baden-Baden, Germany. He also held several meetings with some of the heads of state of the United States' traditional allies. Obama met with German chancellor Angela Merkel at an event on democracy and global responsibility in Berlin, Germany.

Obama also met Canada's Prime Minister Justin Trudeau during a visit to address the Montreal Chamber of Commerce in Montreal, Quebec, Canada. Obama and Prince Harry watched the wheelchair basketball match during the Invictus Games in Toronto, Canada, in 2017. The Obama Foundation later tweeted that the two leaders discussed "their shared commitment to developing the next generation of leaders" (Vale 2017). The former president delivered the keynote address at the Green Economy Summit in Cordoba, Argentina, in 2017. Obama made a plea for the world to use science to overcome climate change. Obama warned, "We cannot condemn our children and their children to a future they cannot repair" (Barnett 2017).

In 2017, all of the living former presidents of the United States gathered for the first round of the Presidents Cup. Former U.S. presidents Barack Obama, George W. Bush, and Bill Clinton appeared together during the first round at Liberty National Golf Club in Jersey City, New Jersey. All five former presidents also appeared at a concert to raise money for hurricane victims in Texas, Virgin Islands, Florida, and Puerto Rico. President Donald J. Trump did not appear in person but provided a video greeting that played during the benefit. In 2018, there were a few subsequent gatherings of the former presidents at the funerals of Arizona senator John McCain, former first lady Barbara Bush, and former president George H. W. Bush. McCain requested that Obama give the eulogy at his funeral.

Several foundations and wealthy individuals made repeat contributions of more than $1 million each. Among the many goals of the Obama Foundation's aim is to help young people become digitally engaged and connect. Obama hoped to influence and encourage young people to be more civic minded. He hoped to train others to advance human progress. He hoped to bring more civility to the public discourse after a divisive 2016 presidential election.

> One of the things we're going to be spending time on, through the Foundation is finding ways in which we can study this phenomenon of social media and the internet to see if there are ways we can bring people different perspectives to start having a more civil debate and listen to each other more carefully. (Owen 2018)

Obama during his postpresidency has been an ambassador of sorts. He traveled to Japan, Australia, New Zealand, and Singapore but he remains a domestic statesman. In February 2018, there was a mass shooting at Marjory Stoneman Douglas High School in Parkland, Florida. A month later, Barack and Michelle Obama sent a handwritten note of encouragement and to express how they were inspired by the students' acts of courage during and in the aftermath of this tragedy.

We wanted to let you know how inspired we have been by the resilience, resolve, and the solidarity that you all have shown in the wake of this unspeakable tragedy. Not only have you supported and comforted each other, buy you have helped awaken the conscience of the nation, and challenged decision makers to make safety of our children the country's top priority. Throughout history, young people like you have led the way in making America better. There may be setbacks; you may feel sometimes like progress is too slow in coming. But we have no doubt you are going to make an enormous difference in the days and years to come, and we will be there for you. (Bacon 2018)

Obama accepted an honorary membership to the Beverly Country Club. The country club has a championship history. It has a reputation as being one of a few country clubs that is inclusive in their membership, accepting its first African American member in 1997. The country club has a people in its membership from all races and ethnicities as members. It even has a cross-section of people of different genders, faiths, and political parties. The membership also includes Nobel Prize laureate recipients such as Eugene Fama and Richard Thaler, who are professors at the University of Chicago. Other notable members of the country club include Illinois politicians such as the state Speaker of the House, Michael Madigan.

The country club is conveniently located not far away from the Obama Presidential Library. By being an honorary member, Obama is allowed to play without having to pay an initiation fee or dues. He will be charged only when he brings guest to the country club. Obama is reportedly a member of several country clubs in the Washington, DC, area where several professional golf tournaments have been hosted. He hopes to have a public golf course next to the Obama Presidential Library when it opens. Those who have played golf with Barack Obama note that he talks plenty of trash while playing.

In 2008, Barack Obama's election as the first African American president of the United States was misjudged as the beginning of a post-racial America. Some believed it was penance for America's original sin of slavery and the scar of segregation. It was not! In 2014, President Obama told a group of young black activists that change was "hard and incremental" (Sheer and Stack 2016). Many in the nation, including President Obama, underestimated the significance of race on his presidency. His legitimacy was questioned. His legislative agenda was obstructed. There have been attempts to undo his accomplishments as president. Yet, his presidency is an example of grace, dignity, and professionalism. His two terms as president of the United States were free of scandal.

In 2016, Michelle Obama was asked to give an address at the Democratic Party's national convention in Philadelphia, Pennsylvania. One of the most memorable lines from her speech was, "When someone is cruel

---

President Obama's Tan Suit Controversy

On August 28, 2014, President Barack Obama wore a tan suit to a press conference and this caused a faux controversy. Political pundits on conservative cable news networks created hysteria about President Obama wearing a tan suit instead of the traditional black, gray, or navy blue suit. Republican politicians and hypocritical conservative pundits stated President Obama's tan suit was not presidential, forgetting there are several photo images of President Ronald Reagan sporting a tan suit.

U.S. House of Representative member Peter King from New York stated that Obama wearing a tan suit meant that he did not care about national security threats. Others complained it was not the fact he was wearing a tan suit; he was wearing a tan suit while discussing crucial issues of foreign policy about ISIS in Iraq and Syria with the press. They claim that it was a somber occasion and a president's fashion should match the tenor of the moment. More than four thousand people tweeted about the president's unusual tan suit during the opening minutes of the press conference. Some tweets condemned the president's fashion choice while others supported it. "The Obama Tan Suit Controversy" was much ado about nothing.

---

or acts like a bully, you don't stoop to their level. When they go low, we go high!" (Staff 2016). On her book tour for her memoir, she revealed this sentence was actually her husband's and is a lesson they have passed on to their daughters. This motto is indicative of how Barack Obama lives his life.

At an event at the James Baker Center at Rice University, Obama stated, "If you had to choose any time and any place to be born for all the problems, you would choose America." Obama also stated, "Politics based on a nationalism that's not pride in country but hatred for somebody on the other side of the border. And you start getting the kind of politics that does not allow for compromise, because it is based on passions and emotions" (Goldberg 2018). In 2018, a survey from the Pew Research Center found that 44 percent of Americans believed Obama was the best or second best president of their lifetime, while 33 percent named Bill Clinton and 32 percent came out in support of Ronald Reagan. In December 2018, a Gallup poll in *Time Magazine* named Michelle Obama as the most admired woman, followed by Oprah Winfrey. Barack Obama came in first place for most admired person for the eleventh consecutive year (Sinclair 2018). President Barack Obama's legacy has proven to rest on a familiar phrase: "Hope and Change" in order to form a more perfect union.

Why Barack Obama Matters

This chapter explores the cultural and historical significance of the Obama presidency and the people, political processes, and public policies that shaped his legacy. Barack Obama's significance extends well beyond his role as the first African American to lead the United States. He's demonstrated himself to be a balanced, prolific, and well-rounded individual with diverse accomplishments from his membership in the U.S. Senate to his two terms as President of the United States to accepting the Nobel Peace Prize. Many individuals helped to lay the groundwork for Obama's pioneering presidential run and invaluable contributions; the following highlights Barack Obama's impact within the broader historical context.

JOHN LEWIS'S ENDORSEMENT OF BARACK OBAMA

John Lewis is a civil rights icon. He is also a Democratic congressman of the Fifth Congressional District in the state of Georgia. Lewis became nationally known after his prominent role in the civil rights movement. He is originally from Pike County, Alabama, and was born the son of share-croppers on February 21, 1940. As an adolescent, he was inspired by the happenings surrounding the Montgomery Bus Boycott and inspirational speeches of Reverend Dr. Martin Luther King Jr. that he heard over the radio newscasts. Lewis was also one of the student leaders at the "Bloody Sunday March" from Selma to Montgomery for African American voting rights and a featured speaker before Dr. Martin Luther King's famous "I Have A Dream" speech on the steps of the Lincoln Memorial during the march on Washington, DC, in 1963. Lewis has remained at the vanguard of the civil rights movement ever since. As a college student at Fisk University in Nashville, Tennessee, he organized sit-ins at segregated lunch counters and nonviolent marches. He was the chair of the Student Nonviolent Coordinating Committee from 1963 to 1966. During those turbulent times, Lewis organized sit-ins at segregated lunch counters and participated in Freedom Rides, which challenged segregation at interstate bus terminals across the South. At twenty-three, Lewis was the youngest organizer and the keynote speaker at the 1963 March on Washington and led protesters across the Edmund Pettus Bridge in Selma, Alabama, for voting rights in 1965.

Initially, John Lewis endorsed Hillary Clinton for president in October 2007. At the time of this public endorsement he stated, "As our former Secretary of State, Senator from New York, and first Lady of the United States, Hillary Clinton is the most qualified person to be President of the United States." In February 2008, Lewis reversed course and endorsed Barack Obama for the presidency. In response to John Lewis's endorsement, Barack Obama stated, "John Lewis is an American hero and a giant of the civil rights movement, and I am deeply honored to have his support."

BARACK OBAMA THE FIRST UNITED STATES PRESIDENT TO VISIT A FEDERAL PRISON

As a part of his call for prison reform in the United States, Barack Obama became the first sitting U.S. president to visit a federal prison in July 2016. President Obama visited the El Reno Federal Correctional Institution in Oklahoma. El Reno is a prison complex that includes sections of buildings that are separated by large green prison yards and barbed wire fences. While at the El Reno prison, Obama visited a nine-by-ten foot cell and examined its bunk beds and marveled at the tiny space allotted for three full-grown men. President Obama also met with six inmates convicted for drug offenses. Also in July 2016, President Obama commuted the federal prison sentences of forty-six nonviolent drug offenders, fourteen of whom were serving life terms in prison. As president of the United States, Obama made the case for shortening or eliminating mandatory minimum sentences for some offenders. He also spoke out against solitary confinement. In 2012, the Sentencing Project reported 5.8 million people were not allowed to vote because of their felon status. African American men had higher imprisonment rates across all age demographics. Also, African American women's imprisonment rates were twice those of white women.

OBAMA'S CAMEO APPEARANCE ON *SATURDAY NIGHT LIVE*, 2007

On November 3, 2007, Barack Obama made a cameo during the cold opening sketch of the comedy show *Saturday Night Live*. Obama delivered the opening line for the show, "Live from New York, it's *Saturday Night!*" Obama's appearance on *Saturday Night Live* solidified his status as a popular culture icon and was a boon to his presidential candidacy with young people. Obama appeared in the opening sketch at a Halloween party thrown by actors playing Bill and Hillary Clinton. Also in the scene were other Democratic candidates played as actors. Everyone was in costume, including Barack, who wore an Obama mask. As the scene progressed, Obama then ripped the mask off to reveal his real face. The audience roared with applause at this unveiling as Obama delivered the lines, "I have nothing to hide. I enjoy being myself. I'm not going to change who I am just because it is Halloween." Obama's live appearance was a ratings hit for the show.

AFRICAN AMERICAN NOBEL PEACE PRIZE WINNERS

The first Nobel Prizes were awarded in 1901. It was not until 1950 that a black person was a recipient. Dr. Ralph J. Bunche was the first black man to receive the distinguished prize for his work as a United Nations mediator. Bunche's leadership led to the Arab-Israeli armistice agreement in 1949. In 2009, President Barack Obama received the Nobel Peace Prize. This was for his extraordinary efforts to strengthen international diplomacy and cooperation between peoples. With the Nobel Prize for peace, the committee attached special importance to his vision of and work for a world without nuclear weapons. When Obama was awarded the prize, they noted President Obama had created a new climate in international politics. The committee pointed to Obama's use of multilateral diplomacy and of the United Nations in resolving international conflicts. His vision of a world free from nuclear arms powerfully stimulated disarmament and arms control negotiations. Prior to Obama receiving this award, other blacks had received a Nobel Prize for Peace. Those Nobel Peace Prize recipients included Albert John Luthuli in 1960, Martin Luther King Jr. in 1964, Bishop Desmond Tutu in 1984, Nelson Mandela in 1993, Kofi Annan in 2001, Wangari Maathai in 2004, Ellen Johnson Sirleaf and Leymah Gbowee in 2011, and Denis Mukwege in 2018. Of the preceding list of Nobel Peace Prize winners, only three have been from the United States: Ralph Bunche, Martin Luther King Jr., and Barack Obama.

AFRICAN AMERICAN PRESIDENTIAL CANDIDATES, 1970s–1990s

Since the 1970s several African Americans launched campaigns for the presidency; however, none of these garnered enough delegates to seriously challenge their prospective parties' nomination candidates. Among these African American candidates to seek the presidency were Shirley Chisholm in 1972, Jesse Jackson in 1984, 1988, and 1992, Alan Keyes in 1996 and 2000, and Carol Moseley Braun and Al Sharpton in 2004. While most of the previous presidential candidates have been affiliated with the Democratic Party, Alan Keyes is affiliated with the Republican Party.

Prior to the election of Obama, most presidential campaigns by African Americans were not taken seriously by the political mainstream and were largely viewed as symbolic. Their campaigns were largely centered on race and race relations, which usually translated to less support from whites. Shirley Chisholm's presidential run in 1972 was groundbreaking for many reasons. Chisholm had been the first African American woman elected to the House of Representatives in 1968. For the most part, a majority of past African American political candidates have been overtly race conscious. Chisholm represented this overtly race conscious generation of politicians, and she along with a dozen other African American lawmakers formed the Congressional Black Caucus (CBC) in 1971. She was also a charter member of the National Organization for Women (NOW). Chisholm's campaign platform was centered on opposition to the Vietnam War and assistance for the downtrodden and poor. Though Chisholm was instrumental in the founding of both the CBC and NOW, neither group endorsed her candidacy. NOW did not endorse Chisholm because it believed that her chances of winning the party's nomination were bleak and even quoted Chisholm as saying that she was not a serious candidate; also some members in the organization wanted to remain politically neutral. One would think that she certainly would have gotten the endorsement of the black caucus; however, some members were quite negative about her presidential run. On the surface it seems that the reason for the hostility toward Chisholm's campaign was a combination of sexism combined with her short tenure in office and the prevailing notion that is underscored in the African American community that "one must pay their dues" before grasping the reins of leadership. Chisholm received only 5 percent of the vote in the Democratic primaries.

In 1984, Jesse Jackson failed to get the endorsement of the CBC largely because many believed that Jackson had not paid his dues; moreover, he had no viable chance of winning the party's nomination and did not warrant their endorsement. While Jackson's presidential runs in 1984 and 1988 were largely viewed as symbolic, they did empower a number of

African American Democrats and increased the number of African American delegates in the party. Obama faced the same "pay your dues" criticisms from the African American old guard when he announced his run for president. Both Chisholm and Jackson operated on overtly race conscious philosophies during their presidential runs; however, some black candidates, most notably Alan Keyes, did not subscribe to an overtly race conscious philosophy by specifically targeting black voters.

Keyes made runs for public office in Maryland in 1988 and 1992 and lost both bids. In 1996, he centered his presidential campaign on the cornerstone of pro-life issues and an abortion ban, which was his attempt to force the abortion issue on the public's agenda. In 2004, the Republican Party drafted Keyes to run for the U.S. Senate from Illinois even though he had never lived in the state. Keyes was drafted after the Republican nominee withdrew from the race because of an impending scandal and Keyes was soundly defeated by then State Senator Barack Obama. In 1996, 2000, and 2008 ultraconservative Republican Alan Keyes launched presidential bids but did not receive much attention from the African American community nor did he receive earnest attention from political analysts or the electorate as a serious candidate in his runs for president.

AFRICAN AMERICAN PRESIDENTIAL CANDIDATES, 2000S

In 2004, two African Americans sought the Democratic Party's nomination for the presidency, Carol Moseley Braun and Al Sharpton. Sharpton had roots in the black civil rights movement, having served as a youth director of Operation Breadbasket. Sharpton is a social activist and operates on the overtly race conscious philosophy and the 1950s and 1960s civil rights movement model of public demonstrations in pushing for civil and social change. Carol Moseley Braun also sought the presidency after serving in the Illinois legislature for ten years prior to her 1998 U.S. Senate victory. Neither of these African American contenders for the presidency campaigns gained any real traction or national attention. Sharpton did win twenty-seven delegates but failed to win key areas with large majority African American populations, South Carolina and Washington, DC. Moseley Braun's campaign was never really viable because she failed to secure the financial backing needed to mount a serious run for the presidency.

In 2008, Cynthia McKinney also announced her bid for the presidency. McKinney had been the youngest African American woman from Georgia elected to the U.S. House of Representatives in 1992, 1994, and 1996; however, she lost her seat in 2002. She regained her seat in 2004 but lost it again in 2006. Once a member of the Democratic Party, McKinney ran for the presidency as a candidate of the Green Party in 2008. McKinney is from a royal pedigree of African American politics and certainly African American politics in Georgia; she is the daughter of former state representative Billy McKinney. Like most of her Democratic presidential predecessors, she embraced an overtly race conscious stand. Her campaign was overshadowed as the African American community and country was swept away by the rising tide of Barack Obama. McKinney's candidacy for president was largely ignored by the mainstream.

COLIN POWELL AND THE BRADLEY/WILDER EFFECT

The first African American in the White House could have been Colin Powell if he had decided to launch a presidential bid. Mainstream America had a favorable opinion of Powell, and he had received support from Republicans, Democrats, and Independents; however, in the end Powell's wife, Alma Powell, feared an assassination attempt on Powell and for his overall general welfare, and thus convinced him not to run. We cannot know if Powell could have actually won the presidency or would have suffered what is now known as the "Bradley Effect."

The Bradley Effect is named after former Los Angeles mayor Tom Bradley, an African American who ran for California governor in 1982. Exit polls showed Bradley, the Democratic nominee, leading by a wide margin, and many thought it would be an early election night and an easy victory for Bradley. But to the amazement of the political pundits, Bradley lost to the Republican nominee George Deukmejian because the exit polls were inaccurate. The theory of the "effect" was that polling was wrong because some voters did not want to appear bigoted and therefore stated that they would vote or had voted for Bradley even though they had not. It has been a common practice for pollsters to survey voters after they have voted, and the general public will usually oblige pollsters with accurate information, but in the case of the Bradley campaign, voters did not honestly indicate whom they voted for, which skewed the results.

The Bradley Effect as it is known is also called the "Wilder Effect" named after L. Douglas Wilder, who was elected governor of Virginia in 1989. Although Wilder won, the margin of victory was closer than the preelection and exit polls indicated and this was attributed to fact that Wilder is an African American and the general public provided inaccurate information to pollsters. Certainly there was not much evidence of the "Bradley-Wilder Effect" in the 2008 presidential election. The Obama and Biden ticket took 365 electoral votes compared to the McCain and Palin ticket's 162 electoral votes. In fact some argue that it was the opposite of the Bradley-Wilder Effect, where many whites stated that they were not going to vote for Obama but actually did, pushing Obama to victory. This is being referred to as the "Obama Effect." Wilder, who later served as the mayor of the City of Richmond, has maintained that the "effect" is in fact dead.

ATTENDANCE AT PRESIDENT BARACK OBAMA'S INAUGURATIONS

In 2009, the District of Columbia officially estimated the crowd that attended Barack Obama's first inauguration at 1.8 million people. The numbers overshadowed 1.2 million, the previous record, set by President Lyndon B. Johnson's inauguration in 1965. Since the Million Man March in 1995, the National Park Service has been prohibited from making crowd estimates because of its low estimation of the crowd size of that event. At the first inauguration, Pastor Rick Warren delivered the invocation for the ceremony and singer Aretha Franklin sang a stirring rendition of "My Country, 'Tis of Thee." President Obama's second inauguration took place on Monday, January 21, 2013. There was an estimated crowd of 1 million attending the ceremony. The second inauguration fell on the Martin Luther King Jr. holiday, so events were scaled down compared to Obama's first inauguration. In 2017, a controversy arose when Sean Spicer, White House press secretary, erroneously claim that President Donald Trump had the largest inaugural crowd ever. In a hastily called press conference, Spicer stated, "This was the largest audience to ever witness an inauguration, period, both in person and around the globe."

U.S. ATTORNEY GENERAL ERIC H. HOLDER

Eric Holder served as the attorney general in the administration of President Barack Obama from 2009 to 2015. Holder was the first African American to serve in this position. Prior to becoming attorney general, Holder served as a judge in the Superior Court of the District of Columbia as the U.S. Attorney for the District of Columbia. Holder was born in the Bronx, New York, and his adolescent life was spent in Queens, New York. He graduated with a bachelor of arts degree in American History from Columbia University. He also graduated from Columbia University's law school and then worked for the National Association for the Advancement of Colored People's legal defense fund. President Bill Clinton nominated Holder as a Deputy Attorney General under Attorney General Janet Reno. Holder was unanimously confirmed by the Senate. Before he became Attorney General, he worked as an attorney at Covington and Burling in Washington, DC. In 2008, President Obama announced Holder's nomination for attorney general of the United States. He was formally nominated in January 2009 and confirmed in February 2009.

During Holder's tenure, he defended the use of drone strikes and raids in fighting terrorism, garnered cooperation to fight against terrorism, protected voting rights found in the Voting Rights Act of 1965, and supported courses of action that led to legalization of same-sex marriage. In 2014, *Time* magazine named Holder to its list of one hundred most influential people. Including his tenure as attorney general, Holder has served in government for more than thirty years, having been appointed to various positions requiring U.S. Senate confirmation by Presidents Barack Obama, Bill Clinton, and Ronald Reagan.

NATIONAL MUSEUM OF AFRICAN AMERICAN CULTURE AND HISTORY

On September 24, 2016, President Barack Obama was present to formally open the National Museum of African American Culture and History in Washington, DC, the first national museum of African American history. Black veterans of the Civil War first proposed an African American museum in 1915. Subsequently, Congressman John Lewis fought for fifteen years by proposing legislation to build the museum, and each year the legislation was not funded. It was not until 2003 that Congress approved appropriations to fund construction; President George W. Bush signed the bill. It took four years to build the museum, located in Washington, DC, on the National Mall. The building was designed by British architect David Adjaye.

The National Museum of African American Culture and History contains 36,000 items that range from trade goods used to buy enslaved people from Africa to a segregated railway car from the 1920s, a red Cadillac convertible belonging to musical pioneer Chuck Berry, and the casket of fourteen-year-old Emmett Till who was lynched for allegedly whistling at a white woman. Speaking at the opening ceremony, President Obama urged African Americans to "come here and see the power of your own agency. The very fact of this day does not prove that America is perfect, but it does validate the ideas of our founding that this country born of change, of revolution, of we the people, that this country can get better."

BIRTH CERTIFICATE CONTROVERSY AND BIRTHERISM

During Barack Obama's historic run for the U.S. presidency, some individuals falsely asserted that Obama was not born in the United States and thus was ineligible to run for president as required by the U.S. Constitution. Conspiracy theorists who subscribe to the Obama birtherism fabrication stated that Obama was born in Kenya, instead of his home state of Hawaii. These falsehoods expanded to also encompass Obama's religious affiliation. While many believe Donald J. Trump began these false controversies about the citizenship and religious affiliation of Barack Obama, the controversy actually began when Obama was running for Illinois State Senate in 2004. Donald Trump's public political career was, in part, built on this lie.

In response to the rumors swirling around Obama's citizenship, on June 12, 2008, Obama's campaign released an image of his official birth certificate in an attempt to fight the falsehoods that were being hurled and combat the lies that had been used to smear him during his presidential campaign. This lie continued to be pushed by conspiracy theorists and Donald J. Trump, and his lawyer, Michael Cohen, began to publicly question the legitimacy of Obama's birth certificate and his citizenship. As president, Obama did address this controversy a few times. In 2010, at the National Prayer Breakfast, Obama stated, "Surely you can question my policies without questioning my faith. Or for that matter my citizenship." On the night of the correspondents' dinner in 2011, President Obama singled out Trump and took revenge for Trump's involvement in the birther campaign by making several jokes about Trump. The gags were good, and while Trump stoically acknowledged the jokes, President Obama had humiliated him. Some believed as a result of the jokes hurled at him during this event, Trump may have decided to run for president in 2016. On the next day after the correspondents' dinner, President Obama announced the Navy SEAL's forces had killed Osama bin Laden.

SUPERDELEGATES

The process of becoming president of the United States is not easy. Our form of government favors a two-party system (Republicans and Democrats) that work to choose candidates who can win the nomination and the presidency. The fight for the presidential nomination begins with state party caucuses and primaries, in which delegates to the parties' national convention are chosen. Those delegates are committed to voting for a particular candidate at the convention.

A caucus is a meeting of political party members in each local community who gather to discuss the candidates. They then vote for the candidate of party preference or choose delegates who will be sent to the state and national conventions. Caucuses can be time consuming with low participation rates. Only registered voters can participate in a caucus, and they are limited to the specific political party. Recently, there has been a surge in caucus participation. Bernie Sanders, senator from Vermont, did well in the 2016 primaries with states that use caucuses (i.e., Washington, Utah, Kansas, Idaho, Alaska, Hawaii, Colorado, Maine, New Hampshire, Missouri, Nebraska, Minnesota, Nevada, and Iowa). His supporters were enthusiastic and likely took the time necessary for a caucus to succeed. States with the caucus process tend to be northern and western states with a white population.

Primaries are the most direct way of choosing presidential candidates and delegates statewide. Primaries can be either open or closed depending on the rules the state party organization adopts. In open primaries, any registered voter may vote regardless of political affiliation. In closed primaries, only registered voters affiliated with the party organization can participate. Primaries and caucuses vary from state to state in the times at which they are conducted. Traditionally, the Iowa caucus and the New Hampshire primary are the first contest for presidential candidates. These two events get an enormous amount of media attention for the delegates and the potential presidential candidates. The Iowa caucus is held on February 1 the year of the presidential election. The New Hampshire primary follows on the second Monday in March. Democrats send elected state officials, governors, and elected members of Congress to the national convention. These delegates are known as superdelegates and are able to vote as free agents. This means these delegates have not pledged to vote for one particular candidate.

Republicans do not have superdelegates; however, they have voiced a need to have them at the 2016 convention to offset the vote of Donald J. Trump. Distribution of delegates to candidates varies based on the parties' primary rules. Democrats use proportional representation, in which the candidates get the percentage of delegates equal to the percentage of primary vote they win. For Republicans, each state can choose from proportional representation to winner-take-all, which means the candidate with the most votes gets the delegates even if the win is not an absolute majority win.

In 2018, due to pressures from the Bernie Sanders' supporters, the Democratic Party changed its rules on superdelegates. Beginning with the 2020 nomination process, presidential candidates will no longer be able to count superdelegates if they want to win the party's nomination on the first ballot of voting at the convention. This will make it impossible for superdelegates to change the outcome of the pledged delegates.

SUPER TUESDAY

"Super Tuesday" refers to the greatest number of presidential primaries and caucuses held across the country. Super Tuesday does not have a set date from each presidential cycle, and the timing in which specific states participate varies greatly depending on the primary. For example, in 2008, twenty-five states (Alabama, Alaska, American Samoa, Arkansas, Arizona, California, Colorado, Connecticut, Delaware, Georgia, Idaho, Illinois, Kansas, Massachusetts, Minnesota, Montana, Missouri, New Jersey, New Mexico, New York, North Dakota, Oklahoma, Tennessee, Utah, and West Virginia) held their contests on the same day, February 5. In contrast, only ten states (Alaska, Georgia, Idaho, Massachusetts, North Dakota, Ohio, Oklahoma, Tennessee, Vermont, and Virginia) held their contests on March 6, 2012.

Super Tuesday began in 1980, with Alabama, Florida, and Georgia holding their primaries on the same day. However, it was not until 1988 when "Super Tuesday" became notable, when Democrats attempted to end a long absence in the presidency by concentrating eleven southern primaries on one date. The hope was to moderate southern Democrats who would choose an electable nominee. The vote split along racial lines and allowed Michael Dukakis, governor of Massachusetts, to secure the presidential nomination. In turn, Democrats would have to wait another four years before winning the presidency as George H. W. Bush beat Dukakis in the general election. In 2008, Hillary Clinton and Obama emerged from Super Tuesday declaring victory. Clinton won Massachusetts, New Jersey, New Mexico, California, Arizona, American Samoa, New York, Oklahoma, and Tennessee. Obama won Alabama, Alaska, Colorado, Connecticut, Delaware, Georgia, Idaho, Illinois, Kansas, Minnesota, Missouri, North Dakota, and Utah. While Clinton beat Obama with popular vote (8,081,748 to 7,987,247), Obama won the number of delegates (847 to 834). In 2012, President Obama ran uncontested in most of the states for the Democratic presidential nomination, capturing enough delegates to become the party's nominee.

TEAM OF RIVALS: THE POLITICAL GENIUS OF ABRAHAM LINCOLN

Doris Kearns Goodwin's 2005 book, *Team of Rivals: The Political Genius of Abraham Lincoln*, won the Pulitzer Prize. This 944-page book discusses President Abraham Lincoln's strategy of using his political rivals in his presidential cabinet after the 1860 election. Three of the individuals Lincoln selected to his cabinet ran against him in 1860. The book discusses Lincoln's life as the U.S. president and his assassination in 1865. Barack Obama stated Goodwin's book was one of his favorite reads. When Obama was elected to the presidency in 2008, he used this same model in selecting his cabinet. Obama made overtures to his political rivals. In

---

JOSEPH R. BIDEN

Joseph "Joe" Biden served as vice president under President Barack Obama. Prior to being vice president, he served in the U.S. Senate from 1973 to 2017. He is a member of the Democratic Party. Biden served as the former chairman of the Foreign Relations Committee. Biden ran for president in 1998 and 2008 but did not fare well in the Democratic primaries and withdrew from both presidential races. On November 4, 2008, Biden was elected vice president of the United States as Obama's running mate. He was appointed chairman of Obama's transition team. In October 2010, Obama asked Biden to stay on as his vice president as he mounted a reelection campaign for the 2012 election.

In November of 2012, Obama was elected to a second term. Many believed Biden would run for president in 2016. Ahead of the 2016 campaign, he was deeply conflicted and mourning the death of his son Beau, who died of brain cancer. Joe Biden ultimately announced that he would not run for the presidency. Biden was presented with the Presidential Medal of Freedom with Distinction in 2017. After his vice presidency, Biden was named the Benjamin Franklin Presidential Practice professor, and the University of Delaware named its school of public policy after him in 2018. In 2019, Biden announced his third run for the President of United States.

---

interviews with the press, Obama proclaimed he did not just want people who always agreed with him working with him. Obama notably selected Joe Biden as his vice presidential running mate and Hillary Rodham Clinton as his secretary of state. Both had launched bids for the Democratic Party nomination in 2008. Obama and Clinton had a bitter fight for the nomination during the primaries, with Obama finally securing enough votes for the nomination on June 3, 2008.

Critics of Obama's use of Lincoln's rival's model argue that Obama chose truly only one authentic rival (Hillary Clinton) to serve in his cabinet while Abraham Lincoln chose several: Edward Bates as attorney general, Salmon Chase as secretary of the treasury, and William H. Seward as secretary of state. In 2012, Goodwin's book was adopted for a movie titled *Lincoln*, directed by Steven Spielberg and starring Daniel Day-Lewis as Abraham Lincoln.

THE AFFORDABLE CARE ACT (OBAMACARE)

On March 10, 2010, President Barack Obama signed the Affordable Care Act into law. This was the biggest expansion of health care since Medicaid and Medicare were enacted in the 1960s. Although some members of the Republican Party began referring the bill as "Obamacare" as a pejorative when Obama began to tout health care reform. Initially, Obama rejected having his name associated with the reform but then he embraced the title of this bill. Obama noted at a public event, "I kind of like the term, 'Obamacare' because I do care. That's why I passed the bill." The Affordable Care Act had been an idea that had been put forth by both the Democratic and Republican Parties and the majority of the health care industry for many years.

Obamacare was modeled after the health care law that was implemented in Massachusetts under Republican governor Mitt Romney. Obama chose to take on health care reform because of the rising cost of health care that was leading to many uninsured Americans filing for bankruptcies and price discrimination based on gender and health status. It was also common practice for insurance companies to deny coverage to individuals with preexisting conditions. Most of the bill's provisions were phased into law in 2014 with other provisions to be phased in by 2020. The Congressional Republicans made many attempts to repeal and replace the Affordable Care Act and pass their own version of health care law. One such bill was called the American Health Care Act. To date, none of the repeal and replace attempts have passed; however many changes have been made to make obtaining suitable and affordable health care more difficult under the administration of President Donald J. Trump. Despite its nonpartisan attempt to provide universal health care for all Americans, Congressional Republicans have used the Affordable Care Act as a divisive and partisan political issue over time.

Timeline

1959

Barack Obama Sr., a Kenyan student, is awarded a scholarship to the University of Hawaii.

1961

Barack Obama Sr. marries Ann Dunham. Dunham is already pregnant with Barack Obama.

1963

Barack Obama Sr. wins a scholarship to Harvard University for graduate study. He leaves behind Ann Dunham and his young son. Dunham files for divorce from Obama Sr.

1965

Barack Obama Sr. completes his master's degree at Harvard and goes back to Kenya.

1967

Ann Dunham marries Lolo Soetoro, and when Barack Obama is six, the family moves to Jakarta, Indonesia.

1969

Lolo Soetoro, Barack Obama's stepfather, is promoted in the U.S. oil company in which he is employed.

1970

Barack Obama's sister, Maya Soetoro, is born. Dunham wishes to return to the United States and raise her children.

1971

When Barack Obama is ten years old, his mother sends him back to live with his grandparents in Hawaii. Barack gets a scholarship to Punahou, a prestigious prep school in Honolulu, Hawaii.

1972

Ann Dunham leaves Indonesia and returns to Hawaii. She begins work on a master's degree in anthropology at the University of Hawaii.

1975

While in high school, Barack Obama joins the basketball team and becomes a leader in his class.

1979

Barack Obama begins his first semester at Occidental College, Los Angeles. He becomes friends with several African American students but does not feel connected with them. At the end of his sophomore year, he transfers to Columbia University.

1980

Ann Dunham files for divorce from her second husband, Lolo Soetoro.

1982

Barack Obama's father is killed in an automobile accident. Barack Obama decides to pursue a career as a community organizer to confront the issues of race and poverty in Chicago.

1988

Barack Obama is 26 years old. Before going to law school, he decides to visit the homeland of his father and meets his father's family for the first time.

Obama begins his studies at Harvard Law School. At the end of his first year, a top law firm hires him. He meets a young lawyer, Michelle Robinson, and they later start dating.

1990

Barack Obama becomes the first African American president of the *Harvard Law Review*.

1991

Barack Obama graduates from Harvard with a juris doctor, magna cum laude.

Obama begins writing an autobiography, *Dreams from My Father*.

1992

Barack Obama marries Michelle LaVaughn Robinson on October 3.

1995

Dreams from My Father, a memoir of the life of Barack Obama, is published on July 18.

Ann Dunham, Barack Obama's mother, dies of ovarian cancer on November 7.

Obama announces his run for the Illinois State Senate on September 19.

1996
Barack Obama runs for the Illinois State Senate. He wins the Democratic nomination and is elected to the Illinois State Senate.

1998
Malia Ann Obama, Barack and Michelle's daughter, is born on July 4. Barack is reelected to the Illinois State Senate.

1999
Barack Obama runs for U.S. Congress and is defeated by Bobby Rush. Obama returns to his work in the Illinois State Senate.

2001
Natasha Obama, Barack and Michelle's second daughter, is born on June 10.

2002
Barack Obama is reelected to the Illinois State Senate.

2003
In January, Barack Obama officially enters the race for the U.S. Senate.

2004
Barack Obama wins the Illinois Democratic primary with 53 percent of the vote. In the general election for the U.S. Senate, Obama faces Republican Jack Ryan.

Obama is chosen to deliver the keynote address at the National Democratic Convention in Boston, Massachusetts. This becomes a defining moment of Obama's political career and brings him national and international recognition.

In November, Obama is elected to the U.S. Senate. He wins with 70 percent of the vote to Alan Keyes's 27 percent. Obama becomes the nation's fifth African American U.S. senator.

2005
Barack Obama is sworn in as a U.S. senator on January 4.

Obama's first bill is passed. The bill is cosponsored by Republican Tom Coburn. The bill allows citizens to go online and see how their tax dollars are being spent.

2006
On October 22, Illinois senator Barack Obama appears on *Meet the Press* and says he is considering running for president.

Obama's book, *The Audacity of Hope: Thoughts on Reclaiming the American Dream*, is published.

2007

On January 16, Barack Obama announces that he has filed papers for a presidential exploratory committee.

On February 10, Obama formally announces that he is running for president at the Old State House capitol in Springfield, Illinois.

Secret Service starts guarding Obama on May 3. This is the earliest the Secret Service has ever begun guarding a candidate.

On September 12, Obama outlines a plan for withdrawing troops from Iraq by 2008.

On December 8, Oprah Winfrey joins Barack Obama on the campaign trail for a series of rallies in Des Moines, Iowa.

2008

On January 3, Barack Obama wins the Iowa Democratic caucus, beating John Edwards and Hillary Clinton. Five days later, Obama loses New Hampshire's Democratic primary.

On January 26, Obama secures an overwhelming majority of the vote of African Americans to win the South Carolina primary by thirty points.

Twenty-two states and American Samoa hold nominating primaries on Super Tuesday, February 5. Obama wins more states, but Hillary Clinton wins more popular votes and gains a few more delegates.

On February 27, Georgia Democrat, U.S. House of Representatives member, and civil rights icon John Lewis officially reverses his endorsement for Hillary Clinton and supports Obama.

On March 18, at the National Constitutional Center in Philadelphia, Obama gives a speech titled "A More Perfect Union" on race in America and condemns his former pastor's controversial sermons.

On April 16, Barack Obama and Hillary Clinton debate at the National Constitutional Center in Philadelphia.

On May 6, Obama wins a landslide victory in the North Carolina primary and has a narrow defeat in Indiana.

Obama takes the lead in the superdelegate count on May 11. Hillary Clinton once led Obama by nearly 100 superdelegates.

On May 13, Obama loses the West Virginia primary by forty-one points.

On May 20, Obama loses the Kentucky primary by 250,000 votes but wins big in Oregon's contest the same day.

The Democratic primary season ends on June 3. Clinton wins in South Dakota. Obama wins Montana.

Barack Obama defeats Hillary Clinton to become the Democratic Party's nominee for president.

Madelyn Dunham, Barack Obama's grandmother, dies of cancer, one day before the presidential election.

In November, Barack Obama wins the presidential election and becomes the first African American elected as president of the United States.

2009

On January 20, Barack Obama is inaugurated as forty-fourth president of the United States.

Obama is awarded the Nobel Peace Prize on October 9.

President Obama enacts a pay freeze for senior White House staff making more than $100,000 per year. He announces stricter guidelines to raise the ethical standards and practices of the White House.

President Obama signs his first bill into law. The Lilly Ledbetter Fair Pay Act promotes fair pay regardless of age, race, or gender.

President Obama announces that companies receiving large federal bailout funds through Troubled Assets Relief Program (TARP) must cap top executive pay at $500,000.

President Obama signs into law the Children's Health Insurance Program Reauthorization Act of 2009.

President Obama travels to Springfield, Illinois, to celebrate the 200th anniversary of the birth of Abraham Lincoln and speaks at the Lincoln Bicentennial Celebration.

President Obama signs into law the $787 billion Recovery and Reinvestment Act in Denver, Colorado.

President Obama approves a deployment of 17,000 additional troops to Afghanistan.

President Obama overturns rules and policies limiting federal money used for embryonic stem cell research.

On March 12, President Obama renews economic sanctions against Iran, first imposed by the U.S. government in 1995.

President Obama holds an online town hall meeting at the White House, the first U.S. president to do so, on March 26.

President Obama is the first president to host a White House Seder for the second night of Passover on April 9.

On April 13, President Obama signs a presidential memorandum eliminating limits on Cuban-American visits and items sent to the island.

President Obama signs the Edward M. "Ted" Kennedy Serve America Act into law on April 21.

On April 27, President Obama addresses the National Academy of Sciences and announces an increase to the budget for research and development and the budgets of the National Science Foundation and the National Institute of Science and Technology to reduce carbon pollution.

On April 29, President Obama holds a news conference to discuss the first 100 days of his presidency.

On May 19, President Obama announces plans to create new automobile fuel efficiency standards requiring cars as well as light trucks to get more miles per gallon of gas.

On May 26, President Obama nominates Sonia Sotomayor to replace retiring Justice David Souter to the U.S. Supreme Court. Sotomayor is confirmed in August 2009, becoming the first Latina appointed to the court.

President Obama signs a memorandum on June 17 extending certain benefits to federal employees involved in same sex partnerships.

The removal of combat troops from major cities in Iraq begins on June 27.

President Obama holds an online town hall meeting to discuss health care reform on July 1.

President Obama gives a speech at the 100th anniversary of the National Association for the Advancement of Colored People (NAACP) in New York City on July 16.

President Obama gives the eulogy at the funeral of Edward Moore "Ted" Kennedy on August 23. Three of the four living former U.S. presidents attend the funeral.

President Obama appears on *The Late Show with David Letterman* on September 21. This is his second talk show appearance since becoming president.

President Obama addresses the Climate Change Summit at the United Nations General Assembly in New York and is also a guest speaker at the Clinton Global initiative on September 22.

President Obama chairs the United Nations Security Council summit on nuclear disarmament on September 23.

On October 30, President Obama signs an executive order lifting a twenty-two-year travel ban on travel to the United States by people with HIV.

President Obama signs an executive order establishing the Council of Veterans Employment on November 2.

On November 10, President Obama gives a eulogy at a Fort Hood ceremony honoring those who were killed in a mass shooting.

2010

President Obama commits $1 billion to help Haiti recover from a devastating earthquake. He solicits help from former president Bill Clinton and former president George W. Bush on January 14.

President Obama participates in community service activities to honor civil rights leader Rev. Dr. Martin Luther King Jr. on January 18.

On January 21, President Obama announces the "Volcker Rule" and other banking regulatory reforms that restrict banks from making speculative investments that do not benefit customers.

President Obama delivers the first State of the Union Address to a joint session of Congress on January 27.

President Obama announces his proposal for the fiscal year 2011 federal budget on February 1.

President Obama and First Lady Obama host a concert of music from the civil rights movement era at the White House to commemorate Black History Month.

President Obama holds an urban economy summit with Al Sharpton of the Social Action Network, Marc Morial of the National Urban League, and Benjamin Jealous of the NAACP in the Oval Office on February 10.

President Obama announces $8.3 billion in federal loan guarantees to help Southern Company build two nuclear reactors in Burke County, Georgia.

On March 1, President Obama announces that $900 million in grants would be given to underperforming schools in America if they adhere to the reform model.

The Patient Protection and Affordable Care Act (Obamacare) passes on March 23.

President Obama signs the Health Care and Education Reconciliation Act of 2010 at Northern Virginia Community College on March 30.

On March 31, President Obama announces approval of oil and gas exploration in the eastern Gulf of Mexico and off the coast of Virginia and ends the moratorium on drilling off the East Coast of the United States.

President Obama and Russian president Dmitry Medvedev sign a Strategic Arms Reduction Treaty on April 8. It reduces stockpiles of nuclear weapons in both countries.

On April 15, President Obama proposes adding $6 billion to NASA's budget over the next five years to aid in deep space exploration.

On April 15, President Obama orders the Department of Health and Human Services to write regulations that prevent hospitals that receive

Medicaid and Medicare funding from denying visitation privileges on the basis of race, color, national origin, sexual orientation, gender identity, or disability.

President Obama and Vice President Biden meet with family members of West Virginia miners killed in a mine explosion. President Obama delivers the eulogy at a memorial service on April 25.

On April 28, President Obama speaks on the urgent need to pass Wall Street reform at Quincy, Illinois.

President Obama, First Lady Michelle Obama, and Vice President Biden attend the funeral of civil rights leader Dorothy Height at the National Cathedral on April 29.

President Obama appoints Elena Kagan as his nominee for the U.S. Supreme Court. She is confirmed on May 10 and sworn in on August 8.

President Obama signs the Daniel Pearl Freedom of the Press Act in the Oval Office on May 17.

On June 10, President Obama meets with family members of causalities due to the BP Deepwater Horizon explosion and later goes to the Gulf Coast to see the efforts to cap the oil spill.

President Obama and Vice President Biden speak at a memorial service for Senator Robert C. Byrd on July 2.

President Obama travels to Kansas City, Missouri, and visits Smith Electric plant, which had gotten $32 million to build all-electric trucks.

President Obama signs the Dodd-Frank Wall Street Reform and Consumer Protection Act on July 21.

President Obama sponsors an Iftar dinner celebrating Islam's holy month of Ramadan on August 13.

President Obama announces an end to the combat mission in Iraq with a speech from the Oval Office on August 31.

President Obama signs the Small Business Jobs and Credit Act into law on September 27.

President Obama and Second Lady Dr. Jill Biden conduct the White House Summit of Community Colleges. President Obama also signs Rosa's Law, which changes references in federal statues from "mental retardation" to "intellectual disability."

The Democratic Party gets trounced in midterm elections.

President Obama proposes a two-year pay freeze for federal employees.

President Obama grants nine presidential pardons. These are the first pardons of his presidency.

President Obama signs the Healthy, Hunger-Free Kids Act of 2010 into law on December 13.

President Obama signs the Tax Relief, Unemployment Insurance Reauthorization and Job Creation Act of 2010 on December 17.

President Obama signs the Don't Ask, Don't Tell Repeal Act 2010 on December 22.

On December 29, the compromise tax plan is passed, extending the tax cuts initiated by George W. Bush.

2011

On January 12, President Obama delivers remarks at a memorial service for the six victims of the shooting in Tucson, Arizona.

On January 25, President Obama delivers the State of the Union Address to a joint session of Congress.

President Obama submits a spending request for the 2012 federal budget.

On March 2, President Obama presents the National Medal of Arts and the National Humanities Medal to awardees in the White House.

On March 2, President Obama signs a short term budget extension bill to fund the federal government.

President Obama ends his two-year ban on military trials for detainees held at Guantanamo Bay with Executive Order 13567 on March 8.

President Obama and the First Lady host the first Conference on Bullying Prevention at the White House on March 10.

President Obama orders military air strikes against Libya on March 19.

On March 28, President Obama delivers a speech explaining the military strike in Libya at the National Defense University.

President Obama announces his bid for reelection on April 4.

Osama bin Laden is killed in a U.S. military raid in Pakistan on May 2.

On May 10, President Obama delivers a speech in El Paso, Texas, on immigration reform.

On May 29, President Obama visits Joplin, Missouri, in response to tornado destruction.

President Obama visits Puerto Rico on June 14, the first such trip by a sitting U.S. president since John F. Kennedy.

On June 22, President Obama announces his plan to withdraw 33,000 U.S. troops from Afghanistan by summer 2012.

President Obama signs into law the Budget Control Act of 2011 on August 2.

President Obama embarks on a three-day, five-city bus tour to host town hall meetings to discuss the economy and jobs during August 15–17.

On August 18, President Obama calls for Syrian President Bashar al-Assad to step down and issues an executive order prohibiting certain financial transactions with Syria.

President Obama speaks to a joint session of Congress on September 8. He presents the American Jobs Act and his plan to create jobs and revive the economy.

On October 13, President Obama and the First Lady host their fifth state dinner at the White House to honor South Korean president Lee Myung-bak.

President Obama speaks at the dedication ceremony for the Rev. Dr. Martin Luther King Jr. Memorial in Washington, DC, on October 16.

President Obama gives remarks on the death of Libyan leader Colonel Gaddafi on October 20.

On November 28, President Obama hosts a White House summit for leaders of the European Union to discuss the European sovereign debt crisis.

2012

President Obama praises lawmakers after the House of Representatives votes to pass fiscal cliff measure on January 2.

President Obama rejects a proposed extension of the Keystone Pipeline on January 18.

President Obama delivers the State of the Union Address before a joint session of Congress on January 24.

President Obama meets with former president George H. W. Bush and his son, former governor Jeb Bush, at the White House on January 27.

President Obama speaks at the National Prayer Breakfast on February 2.

President Obama signs the No Budget, No Pay Act into law on February 4.

President Obama signs an executive order aimed at freezing the assets of Iranian government and financial institutions on February 6.

President Obama announces his plan to establish the National Network for Manufacturing Innovation on March 9.

President Obama signs the Stop Trading on Congressional Knowledge Act into law on April 4.

President Obama makes an unannounced visit to Afghanistan on May 1.

President Obama presents the Presidential Medal of Freedom to Israeli president Shimon Peres on June 13.

On June 15, President Obama explains his Executive Order on Immigration ending deportations of young undocumented immigrants.

President Obama addresses the nation after health care reform, and the Patient Protection and Affordable Care Act (Obamacare) is upheld by the Supreme Court on June 28.

President Obama speaks at the National Urban League Convention in New Orleans, Louisiana, on July 25.

President Obama delivers a speech at the Democratic National Convention in Charlotte, North Carolina, on September 6.

President Obama speaks to the United Nations General Assembly on September 25.

President Obama participates in the first 2012 presidential debate against Republican challenger Mitt Romney in Denver, Colorado, on October 3.

President Obama becomes the first sitting president to vote early on October 25.

Barack Obama is reelected to a second term as U.S. president, defeating Mitt Romney on November 6.

President Obama meets with labor leaders for input on deficit reduction on November 13.

President Obama visits New York City on November 15 to see the devastation by Hurricane Sandy.

President Obama meets with Mitt Romney for lunch at the White House on November 29.

President Obama and First Lady Obama host a White House celebration on the sixth day of Hanukkah on December 13.

On December 16, President Obama speaks at an interfaith vigil for the victims of the Sandy Hook Elementary school shooting.

President Obama is selected as *Time* magazine's Person of the Year on December 19.

President Obama signs into law a five-year extension of the Foreign Intelligence Surveillance Act of December 30.

2013

Barack Obama begins his second term as U.S. president on January 20.

President Obama holds a roundtable discussion and delivers an address in Minneapolis outlining his gun control campaign on February 4.

On February 12, President Obama delivers the State of the Union Address and announces a drawdown of 34,000 troops from Afghanistan.

President Obama visits Ramallah in the West Bank and holds a news conference with Palestinian Authority president Mahmoud Abbas on March 21.

President Obama presents his proposed 2014 federal budget to Congress on April 11.

On April 18, President Obama speaks at a prayer service for the victims of the Boston Marathon bombing.

President Obama and the First Lady attend the opening of the George W. Bush Presidential Library on April 23.

President Obama delivers a speech on counterterrorism policy at the National Defense University on May 23.

President Obama announces the Climate Action Plan to cut carbon pollution and discusses the impact of climate change on June 15.

President Obama meets with senators John McCain and Charles Schumer to discuss immigration reform on July 11.

President Obama appears with Jay Leno on the *Tonight Show* on August 7.

On August 27, President Obama meets with mayors of eighteen major U.S. cities to discuss reducing youth violence.

President Obama delivers remarks at the Lincoln Memorial commemorating the fiftieth anniversary of the March on Washington on August 28.

On the twelfth anniversary of the event, President Obama attends a September 11 Observance Ceremony at Pentagon Memorial.

President Obama addresses the United Nations General Assembly on September 24.

President Obama meets with the House Democratic caucus on October 9.

President Obama meets with the Senate Democratic caucus on October 10.

President Obama visits the Walter Reed National Military Medical Center in Bethesda, Maryland, on November 5.

President Obama signs the Streamlining Claims Processing for Federal Contractor Employees Act, HIV Organ Policy Act, and Veterans' Compensation Cost of Living Adjustment Act of 2013 into law on November 21.

President Obama joins other world leaders at a memorial service for Nelson Mandela in Johannesburg, South Africa, on December 10.

The Continuing Appropriations Act is signed into law containing a continuing resolution ending the U.S. government shutdown and the debt-ceiling crisis.

2014

President Obama signs a $1.1 trillion spending bill on January 7.

President Obama delivers the State of the Union Address before a joint session of Congress on January 28.

President Obama and the First Lady attend the annual National Prayer Day on February 6.

President Obama signs the Agriculture Act of 2014 at Michigan State University on February 7.

President Obama proposes the 2015 federal budget on March 4.

On March 6, President Obama announces financial sanctions against Russia for stealing assets and money from Ukraine.

President Obama attends the annual White House Correspondent's Dinner on May 3.

President Obama makes an unannounced trip to Afghanistan to visit troops on May 25.

President Obama joins other world leaders in France to commemorate the seventieth anniversary of the Battle of Normandy on June 6.

President Obama meets with members of the Congressional Hispanic caucus on July 16.

President Obama visits the Walter Reed National Military Medical Center in Bethesda, Maryland, on July 29.

President Obama delivers a statement on violence in Ferguson, Missouri, on August 15.

On September 10, President Obama delivers a speech outlining his plan to fight the Islamic State.

President Obama signs the Continuing Appropriations Resolutions into law on September 19.

President Obama addresses the United Nations General Assembly and bilateral meetings on September 24.

On October 14, President Obama meets with twenty foreign chiefs of defense to discuss strategies and coalition efforts against the Islamic State.

On November 7, President Obama announces additional troops will be sent to Iraq to train Iraqi and Kurdish armed forces.

President Obama nominates Loretta Lynch for attorney general. She is confirmed on February 25, 2015.

On December 17, President Obama meets with Archbishop Joseph Kurtz, president of the U.S. Conference of Catholic Bishops. He later meets with the members of the National Security Council.

On December 17, President Obama announces that the United States is to restore relations with Cuba.

On January 7, President Obama delivers remarks about the terrorist attacks in Paris, France.

President Obama participates in a service day honoring Rev. Dr. Martin Luther Jr. at the Boys and Girls Club in Washington, DC, on January 19.

President Obama delivers the State of the Union Address on January 20.

President Obama releases a proposal for the 2016 federal budget on January 23.

President Obama signs the Clay Hunt Suicide Prevention for American Veterans Act into law on February 12.

President Obama delivers remarks at the Cybersecurity and Consumer Fraud Summit in San Francisco, California, on February 13.

President Obama delivers remarks at the White House Summit on Countering Violent Extremism on February 19.

President Obama delivers remarks at the National Governors Association on February 23.

President Obama participates in a video conference with European leaders on global security on March 2.

President Obama signs the Department of Homeland Security Appropriation Act into law on March 3.

On March 9, President Obama signs Executive Order 13692, which blocks the property and suspends entry of certain persons from Venezuela.

President Obama signs the Medicare Access and CHIP Reauthorization Act of 2015 into law on April 16.

President Obama delivers remarks to top teachers from all fifty states and the National Teacher of the Year on April 29.

President Obama signs the Energy Efficiency Improvement Act into law on April 30.

President Obama delivers remarks at the National Peace Officers' Memorial Service on May 15.

President Obama lays a wreath at the Tomb of the Unknown Soldier and delivers the Memorial Day Service on May 25.

On June 26, President Obama gives a eulogy in Charleston, South Carolina, following the Charleston shooting at Emanuel African Methodist Episcopal.

President Obama visits the Rev. Dr. Martin King Jr. Memorial with Brazilian president Dilma Rouseff on June 29.

President Obama delivers remarks on the twenty-fifth anniversary of the Americans with Disabilities Act on July 20.

President Obama gives an address at the 116th National Convention of the Veterans of Foreign Wars in Pittsburgh, Pennsylvania, on July 21.

President Obama visits Nairobi, Kenya, his father's homeland, from July 23 to 24.

President Obama delivers remarks at the Young African Leaders Initiative on August 3.

President Obama gives remarks to commemorate the fiftieth anniversary of the Voting Rights Act on August 6.

On August 5, President Obama delivers remarks on the nuclear deal reached with Iran.

President Obama delivers remarks at the National Clean Energy Summit in Las Vegas, Nevada, on August 24.

On August 27, President Obama visits New Orleans to commemorate the ten-year anniversary of Hurricane Katrina.

On September 1, President Obama becomes the first sitting president to visit the Arctic Circle.

President Obama welcomes Pope Francis to the White House on September 23.

On October 9, President Obama meets with families of victims of the Umpqua Community College shooting.

President Obama delivers remarks on criminal justice reform at Rutgers University on November 2.

On December 18, President Obama meets with families of the victims of the San Bernardino shooting.

2016

On January 5, President Obama announces an executive order on gun control that requires that those purchasing guns undergo background checks.

President Obama gives his final State of the Union Address on January 12.

On January 16, President Obama signs an executive order lifting some of the economic sanctions on Iran.

President Obama addresses the Illinois General Assembly in the state capitol in Springfield, Illinois, on February 10.

President Obama issues a statement on the death Antonin Scalia, associate justice of the U.S. Supreme Court, on February 13.

On March 16, President Obama announces Merrick Garland as his replacement for Antonin Scalia on the U.S. Supreme Court.

President Obama travels to Cuba and becomes the first president to do so since Calvin Coolidge in 1928. He meets with Cuban president Raul Castro and gives an address to the Cuban citizens from March 22 to 23.

President Obama attends the White House Correspondents' Dinner on April 30.

On May 23, President Obama announces the full lifting of the arms embargo against Vietnam.

On June 16, President Obama travels to Orlando, Florida, to meet with the victims of the mass shooting at the Pulse Night Club.

President Obama gives an address at the Parliament of Canada in Ottawa on June 29.

President Obama speaks at the Democratic National Convention in Philadelphia, Pennsylvania, on July 27.

President Obama dedicates the Smithsonian National Museum of African American History and Culture on the National Mall on September 24.

Republican nominee Donald J. Trump wins the presidential election on November 8.

On November 9, President Obama calls to congratulate Donald Trump on his victory.

President Obama makes his final international trip, to Greece, from November 15 to 16.

On November 26, President Obama releases a statement on the death of former Cuban president Fidel Castro.

On December 14, President Obama signs the 21st Century Cures Act, expanding medical research.

President Obama holds his final press conference of 2016 on December 16.

2017

President Obama visits lawmakers on Capitol Hill on January 4 to urge them to keep the Patient Protection and Affordable Care Act (Obamacare).

President Obama signs an executive order to end exemptions for Cubans who arrive in the United States without visas. He awards Vice President Joe Biden with the Presidential Medal of Freedom on January 12.

President Obama holds the final press conference of his presidency on January 18.

On January 19, President Obama grants 330 commutations to nonviolent drug offenders, the most granted by any president on one day.

Barack Obama leaves office after two terms as president of the United States on January 20. Donald J. Trump is inaugurated as the forty-fifth president of the United States.

Obama enters his postpresidency life on January 21.

Obama vacations and learns to kitesurf on a private island with billionaire Richard Branson in February.

Obama announces plans for his presidential library on May 3.

Obama receives the John F. Kennedy Profile in Courage Award on May 7.

Obama gives a speech to the Montreal Chamber of Commerce in Montreal, Canada, on June 6.

Barack and Michelle take their oldest daughter, Malia, to Harvard University on August 21.

Barack Obama accompanies fellow ex-presidents George W. Bush and Bill Clinton to the kickoff of the Presidents Cup golf tournament at the Liberty National Golf Club in New Jersey on September 28.

On October 2, Obama issues a statement in response to the mass shooting in Las Vegas, the deadliest in modern U.S. history.

2018

Barack Obama delivers the eulogy at Sen. John McCain's funeral in Washington, DC, on September 1.

Obama gives a speech to students at the University of Illinois on September 7.

Former president Obama and former vice president Joe Biden cause a stir when they visit Dog Tag Bakery in Georgetown on July 30.

The Obama Foundation gathers two hundred young leaders in Johannesburg, South Africa, to study the legacy of Nelson Mandela on July 17.

On May 21, Barack and Michelle Obama announce they have signed a development deal to produce films with Netflix.

Obama delivers the keynote address at an event hosted by the Bill and Melinda Gates Foundation in New York City on September 20.

Obama surprises six hundred attendees when he joins his former vice president at a fundraiser for the Beau Biden Foundation for the Protection of Children in Wilmington, Delaware, on September 25.

Obama issues a statement on the Harvey Weinstein sexual assault controversy on October 10.

Obama travels to reunite with former vice president Joe Biden, Dr. Jill Biden, and Prince Harry at the Invictus Games in Toronto, Canada, on September 29.

Barack Obama surprises Michelle Obama while on her book tour with a guest appearance and flowers on November 18.

Obama releases his Best of List of 2018 on December 28.

2019

Barack Obama speaks to young men at an event hosted by My Brother's Keeper in Oakland, California, on February 21.

Obama goes to the Duke University versus University of North Carolina basketball game on February 22. He wears a black bomber jacket with the number 44 on the sleeve, and it becomes a trending topic on Twitter.

Obama gives a speech in Calgary, Canada, at the Scotiabank Saddledome on March 5.

Obama speaks at Qualtrics X4 Summit in Salt Lake City, Utah, on March 6; other featured speakers are Oprah Winfrey and Richard Branson.

Obama tweets for International Women's day on March 8: "On International Women's Day, I'm reflecting on the future we all want for our daughters: one where they can live out their aspirations without limits. And I'm celebrating some of the women who are building that future for all of us today."

PRIMARY DOCUMENTS

Barack Obama's Presidential Election Victory Speech (November 4, 2008)

In the 2008 presidential election, Americans got the opportunity to vote in the first presidential general election featuring an African American candidate representing one of the two major political parties in the United States. On November 4, 2008, Democratic Party presidential nominee Senator Barack Obama defeated Republican nominee Senator John McCain. Barack Obama became the first African American to win the White House. Millions of voters across the United States cast ballots in record numbers. On the night of the election and after John McCain conceded the presidential race, President-elect Obama, along with his wife and daughters, attended an election night rally at Ulysses S. Grant Park in Chicago, Illinois, where he gave an election night speech. After the speech, Vice President–elect Joe Biden joined Obama on the platform at Grant Park. National and international media outlets were dominated with news of Barack Obama's historic victory.

Hello, Chicago.

If there is anyone out there who still doubts that America is a place where all things are possible, who still wonders if the dream of our founders is alive in our time, who still questions the power of our democracy, tonight is your answer.

It's the answer told by lines that stretched around schools and churches in numbers this nation has never seen, by people who waited three hours and four hours, many for the first time in their lives, because they believed that this time must be different, that their voices could be that difference.

It's the answer spoken by young and old, rich and poor, Democrat and Republican, black, white, Hispanic, Asian, Native American, gay, straight, disabled and not disabled. Americans who sent a message to the world that we have never been just a collection of individuals or a collection of red states and blue states.

We are, and always will be, the United States of America.

It's the answer that led those who've been told for so long by so many to be cynical and fearful and doubtful about what we can achieve to put their hands on the arc of history and bend it once more toward the hope of a better day. It's been a long time coming, but tonight, because of what we did on this date in this election at this defining moment, change has come to America.

A little bit earlier this evening, I received an extraordinarily gracious call from Sen. McCain. Sen. McCain fought long and hard in this campaign. And he's fought even longer and harder for the country that he loves. He has endured sacrifices for America that most of us cannot begin to imagine. We are better off for the service rendered by this brave and selfless leader.

I congratulate him; I congratulate Governor Palin for all that they've achieved. And I look forward to working with them to renew this nation's promise in the months ahead. I want to thank my partner in this journey, a man who campaigned from his heart, and spoke for the men and women he grew up with on the streets of Scranton and rode with on the train home to Delaware, the vice president–elect of the United States, Joe Biden.

And I would not be standing here tonight without the unyielding support of my best friend for the last 16 years the rock of our family, the love of my life, the nation's next first lady Michelle Obama.

Sasha and Malia, I love you both more than you can imagine. And you have earned the new puppy that's coming with us to the new White House.

And while she's no longer with us, I know my grandmother's watching, along with the family that made me who I am. I miss them tonight. I know that my debt to them is beyond measure.

To my sister Maya, my sister Alma, all my other brothers and sisters, thank you so much for all the support that you've given me. I am grateful to them.

And to my campaign manager, David Plouffe, the unsung hero of this campaign, who built the best—the best political campaign, I think, in the history of the United States of America.

To my chief strategist David Axelrod who's been a partner with me every step of the way.

To the best campaign team ever assembled in the history of politics— you made this happen, and I am forever grateful for what you've sacrificed to get it done. But above all, I will never forget who this victory truly belongs to. It belongs to you. It belongs to you. I was never the likeliest candidate for this office. We didn't start with much money or many endorsements. Our campaign was not hatched in the halls of Washington. It began in the backyards of Des Moines and the living rooms of Concord and the front porches of Charleston. It was built by working men and women who dug into what little savings they had to give $5 and $10 and $20 to the cause.

It grew strength from the young people who rejected the myth of their generation's apathy who left their homes and their families for jobs that offered little pay and less sleep. It drew strength from the not-so-young people who braved the bitter cold and scorching heat to knock on doors of perfect strangers, and from the millions of Americans who volunteered and organized and proved that more than two centuries later, a government of the people, by the people, and for the people has not perished from the earth.

This is your victory. And I know you didn't do this just to win an election. And I know you didn't do it for me. You did it because you understand the enormity of the task that lies ahead. For even as we celebrate tonight, we know the challenges that tomorrow will bring are the greatest of our lifetime—two wars, a planet in peril, the worst financial crisis in a century.

Even as we stand here tonight, we know there are brave Americans waking up in the deserts of Iraq and the mountains of Afghanistan to risk their lives for us. There are mothers and fathers who will lie awake after the children fall asleep and wonder how they'll make the mortgage or pay their doctors' bills or save enough for their child's college education. There's new energy to harness, new jobs to be created, new schools to build, and threats to meet, alliances to repair.

The road ahead will be long. Our climb will be steep. We may not get there in one year or even in one term. But, America, I have never been more hopeful than I am tonight that we will get there. I promise you, we as a people will get there.

There will be setbacks and false starts. There are many who won't agree with every decision or policy I make as president. And we know the government can't solve every problem.

But I will always be honest with you about the challenges we face. I will listen to you, especially when we disagree. And, above all, I will ask you to join in the work of remaking this nation, the only way it's been done in America for 221 years—block by block, brick by brick, calloused hand by calloused hand.

What began 21 months ago in the depths of winter cannot end on this autumn night. This victory alone is not the change we seek. It is only the chance for us to make that change. And that cannot happen if we go back to the way things were. It can't happen without you, without a new spirit of service, a new spirit of sacrifice.

So let us summon a new spirit of patriotism, of responsibility, where each of us resolves to pitch in and work harder and look after not only ourselves but each other. Let us remember that, if this financial crisis taught us anything, it's that we cannot have a thriving Wall Street while Main Street suffers. In this country, we rise or fall as one nation, as one people. Let's resist the temptation to fall back on the same partisanship and pettiness and immaturity that has poisoned our politics for so long.

Let's remember that it was a man from this state who first carried the banner of the Republican Party to the White House, a party founded on the values of self-reliance and individual liberty and national unity. Those are values that we all share. And while the Democratic Party has won a great victory tonight, we do so with a measure of humility and determination to heal the divides that have held back our progress.

As Lincoln said to a nation far more divided than ours, we are not enemies but friends. Though passion may have strained, it must not break our bonds of affection. And to those Americans whose support I have yet to earn, I may not have won your vote tonight, but I hear your voices. I need your help. And I will be your president, too. And to all those watching tonight from beyond our shores, from parliaments and palaces, to those who are huddled around radios in the forgotten corners of the world, our stories are singular, but our destiny is shared, and a new dawn of American leadership is at hand.

To those—to those who would tear the world down: We will defeat you. To those who seek peace and security: We support you. And to all those who have wondered if America's beacon still burns as bright: Tonight we proved once more that the true strength of our nation comes not from the might of our arms or the scale of our wealth, but from the enduring power of our ideals: democracy, liberty, opportunity, and unyielding hope. That's the true genius of America: that America can change. Our union can be perfected. What we've already achieved gives us hope for what we can and must achieve tomorrow.

This election had many firsts and many stories that will be told for generations. But one that's on my mind tonight's about a woman who cast her ballot in Atlanta. She's a lot like the millions of others who stood in line to make their voice heard in this election except for one thing: Ann Nixon Cooper is 106 years old.

She was born just a generation past slavery; a time when there were no cars on the road or planes in the sky; when someone like her couldn't vote for two reasons—because she was a woman and because of the color of her skin. And tonight, I think about all that she's seen throughout her century in America—the heartache and the hope; the struggle and the progress; the times we were told that we can't, and the people who pressed on with that American creed: Yes, we can.

At a time when women's voices were silenced and their hopes dismissed, she lived to see them stand up and speak out and reach for the ballot. Yes, we can.

When there was despair in the dust bowl and depression across the land, she saw a nation conquer fear itself with a New Deal, new jobs, a new sense of common purpose. Yes, we can.

When the bombs fell on our harbor and tyranny threatened the world, she was there to witness a generation rise to greatness and a democracy was saved. Yes, we can.

She was there for the buses in Montgomery, the hoses in Birmingham, a bridge in Selma, and a preacher from Atlanta who told a people that "We shall overcome." Yes, we can.

A man touched down on the moon, a wall came down in Berlin, a world was connected by our own science and imagination. And this year, in this election, she touched her finger to a screen, and cast her vote, because after 106 years in America, through the best of times and the darkest of hours, she knows how America can change. Yes, we can.

America, we have come so far. We have seen so much. But there is so much more to do. So tonight, let us ask ourselves—if our children should live to see the next century; if my daughters should be so lucky to live as long as Ann Nixon Cooper, what change will they see? What progress will we have made?

This is our chance to answer that call. This is our moment. This is our time, to put our people back to work and open doors of opportunity for our kids; to restore prosperity and promote the cause of peace; to reclaim the American dream and reaffirm that fundamental truth, that, out of many, we are one; that while we breathe, we hope. And where we are met with cynicism and doubts and those who tell us that we can't, we will respond with that timeless creed that sums up the spirit of a people: Yes, we can.

Thank you. God bless you. And may God bless the United States of America.

Source: Barack Obama. "Address in Chicago Accepting Election as the Forty-fourth President of the United States," November 4, 2008.

Barack Obama's First Presidential Inaugural Address (January 20, 2009)

Each inaugural ceremony in the United States marks the peaceful transfer of power. Inaugural ceremonies symbolize a time of hope, reflection, and celebration. Barack Obama was inaugurated as president of the United States on Monday, January 20, 2009. Inauguration day temperatures were below freezing in Washington, DC. Even with the freezing temperatures, an estimated 1.8 million people flooded onto the National Mall to view President Barack Obama take the oath of office to become the nation's first African American president. At the ceremony, Pastor Rick Warren delivered a prayer and singer Aretha Franklin sang "My Country, "Tis of Thee." U.S. Supreme Court Chief Justice John Roberts administered the oath of office, but made a small mistake. This forced the oath of office to be administered again the next day. President Barack Obama's first inaugural speech lasted twenty minutes.

My fellow citizens:

I stand here today humbled by the task before us, grateful for the trust you have bestowed, mindful of the sacrifices borne by our ancestors. I thank President Bush for his service to our nation, as well as the generosity and cooperation he has shown throughout this transition.

Forty-four Americans have now taken the presidential oath. The words have been spoken during rising tides of prosperity and the still waters of peace. Yet, every so often the oath is taken amidst gathering clouds and raging storms. At these moments, America has carried on not simply because of the skill or vision of those in high office, but because We the People have remained faithful to the ideals of our forbearers, and true to our founding documents.

So it has been. So it must be with this generation of Americans.

That we are in the midst of crisis is now well understood. Our nation is at war, against a far-reaching network of violence and hatred. Our economy is badly weakened, a consequence of greed and irresponsibility on the part of some, but also our collective failure to make hard choices and prepare the nation for a new age. Homes have been lost; jobs shed; businesses shuttered. Our health care is too costly; our schools fail too many; and each day brings further evidence that the ways we use energy strengthen our adversaries and threaten our planet.

These are the indicators of crisis, subject to data and statistics. Less measurable but no less profound is a sapping of confidence across our land—a nagging fear that America's decline is inevitable, and that the next generation must lower its sights.

Today I say to you that the challenges we face are real. They are serious and they are many. They will not be met easily or in a short span of time. But know this, America—they will be met.

On this day, we gather because we have chosen hope over fear, unity of purpose over conflict and discord.

On this day, we come to proclaim an end to the petty grievances and false promises, the recriminations and worn out dogmas, that for far too long have strangled our politics.

We remain a young nation, but in the words of Scripture, the time has come to set aside childish things. The time has come to reaffirm our enduring spirit; to choose our better history; to carry forward that precious gift, that noble idea, passed on from generation to generation: the God-given promise that all are equal, all are free, and all deserve a chance to pursue their full measure of happiness.

In reaffirming the greatness of our nation, we understand that greatness is never a given. It must be earned. Our journey has never been one of short-cuts or settling for less. It has not been the path for the fainthearted—for those who prefer leisure over work, or seek only the pleasures of riches and fame. Rather, it has been the risk-takers, the doers, the makers of things—some celebrated but more often men and women obscure in their labor, who have carried us up the long, rugged path towards prosperity and freedom.

For us, they packed up their few worldly possessions and traveled across oceans in search of a new life.

For us, they toiled in sweatshops and settled the West; endured the lash of the whip and plowed the hard earth.

For us, they fought and died, in places like Concord and Gettysburg; Normandy and Khe Sahn.

Time and again these men and women struggled and sacrificed and worked till their hands were raw so that we might live a better life. They saw America as bigger than the sum of our individual ambitions; greater than all the differences of birth or wealth or faction.

This is the journey we continue today. We remain the most prosperous, powerful nation on Earth. Our workers are no less productive than when this crisis began. Our minds are no less inventive, our goods and services no less needed than they were last week or last month or last year. Our capacity remains undiminished. But our time of standing pat, of protecting narrow interests and putting off unpleasant decisions—that time has surely passed. Starting today, we must pick ourselves up, dust ourselves off, and begin again the work of remaking America.

For everywhere we look, there is work to be done. The state of the economy calls for action, bold and swift, and we will act—not only to create new jobs, but to lay a new foundation for growth. We will build the roads and bridges, the electric grids and digital lines that feed our commerce and bind us together. We will restore science to its rightful place, and wield technology's wonders to raise health 'care's quality and lower its cost. We will harness the sun and the winds and the soil to fuel our cars and run our factories. And we will transform our schools and colleges and universities to meet the demands of a new age. All this we can do. And all this we will do.

Now, there are some who question the scale of our ambitions—who suggest that our system cannot tolerate too many big plans. Their memories are short. For they have forgotten what this country has already done; what free men and women can achieve when imagination is joined to common purpose, and necessity to courage.

What the cynics fail to understand is that the ground has shifted beneath them—that the stale political arguments that have consumed us for so long no longer apply. The question we ask today is not whether our government is too big or too small, but whether it works—whether it helps families find jobs at a decent wage, care they can afford, a retirement that is dignified. Where the answer is yes, we intend to move forward. Where the answer is no, programs will end. And those of us who manage the public's dollars will be held to account—to spend wisely, reform bad habits, and do our business in the light of day—because only then can we restore the vital trust between a people and their government.

Nor is the question before us whether the market is a force for good or ill. Its power to generate wealth and expand freedom is unmatched, but this crisis has reminded us that without a watchful eye, the market can spin out of control—and that a nation cannot prosper long when it favors only the prosperous. The success of our economy has always depended not just on the size of our Gross Domestic Product, but on the reach of our prosperity; on the ability to extend opportunity to every willing heart—not out of charity, but because it is the surest route to our common good.

As for our common defense, we reject as false the choice between our safety and our ideals. Our Founding Fathers, faced with perils we can scarcely imagine, drafted a charter to assure the rule of law and the rights of man, a charter expanded by the blood of generations. Those ideals still light the world, and we will not give them up for 'expedience's sake. And so to all other peoples and governments who are watching today, from the grandest capitals to the small village where my father was born: know that America is a friend of each nation and every man, woman, and child who seeks a future of peace and dignity, and we are ready to lead once more.

Recall that earlier generations faced down fascism and communism not just with missiles and tanks, but with the sturdy alliances and enduring convictions. They understood that our power alone cannot protect us, nor does it entitle us to do as we please. Instead, they knew that our power grows through its prudent use; our security emanates from the justness of our cause, the force of our example, the tempering qualities of humility and restraint.

We are the keepers of this legacy. Guided by these principles once more, we can meet those new threats that demand even greater effort—even greater cooperation and understanding between nations. We will begin to responsibly leave Iraq to its people, and forge a hard-earned peace in Afghanistan. With old friends and former foes, we'll work tirelessly to lessen the nuclear threat, and roll back the specter of a warming planet. We will not apologize for our way of life, nor will we waver in its defense, and for those who seek to advance their aims by inducing terror and slaughtering innocents, we say to you now that our spirit is stronger and cannot be broken; you cannot outlast us, and we will defeat you.

For we know that our patchwork heritage is a strength, not a weakness. We are a nation of Christians and Muslims, Jews and Hindus—and non-believers. We are shaped by every language and culture, drawn from every end of this Earth; and because we have tasted the bitter swill of civil war and segregation, and emerged from that dark chapter stronger and more united, we cannot help but believe that the old hatreds shall someday pass; that the lines of tribe shall soon dissolve; that as the world grows smaller, our common humanity shall reveal itself; and that America must play its role in ushering in a new era of peace.

To the Muslim world, we seek a new way forward, based on mutual interest and mutual respect. To those leaders around the globe who seek to sow conflict, or blame their society's ills on the West—know that your people will judge you on what you can build, not what you destroy. To those who cling to power through corruption and deceit and the silencing of dissent, know that you are on the wrong side of history; but that we will extend a hand if you are willing to unclench your fist.

To the people of poor nations, we pledge to work alongside you to make your farms flourish and let clean waters flow; to nourish starved bodies and feed hungry minds. And to those nations like ours that enjoy relative plenty, we say we can no longer afford indifference to the suffering outside our borders; nor can we consume the world's resources without regard to effect. For the world has changed, and we must change with it.

As we consider the road that unfolds before us, we remember with humble gratitude those brave Americans who, at this very hour, patrol far-off deserts and distant mountains. They have something to tell us, just as the fallen heroes who lie in Arlington whisper through the ages. We honor them not only because they are guardians of our liberty, but because they embody the spirit of service; a willingness to find meaning in something greater than themselves. And yet, at this moment—a moment that will define a generation—it is precisely this spirit that must inhabit us all.

For as much as government can do and must do, it is ultimately the faith and determination of the American people upon which this nation relies. It is the kindness to take in a stranger when the levees break, the selfless-ness of workers who would rather cut their hours than see a friend lose their job which sees us through our darkest hours. It is the 'firefighter's courage to storm a stairway filled with smoke, but also a 'parent's willing-ness to nurture a child, that finally decides our fate.

Our challenges may be new. The instruments with which we meet them may be new. But those values upon which our success depends—honesty and hard work, courage and fair play, tolerance and curiosity, loyalty and patriotism—these things are old. These things are true. They have been the quiet force of progress throughout our history. What is demanded then is a return to these truths. What is required of us now is a new era of responsibility—a recognition, on the part of every American, that we have duties to ourselves, our nation, and the world, duties that we do not grudg-ingly accept but rather seize gladly, firm in the knowledge that there is nothing so satisfying to the spirit, so defining of our character, than giving our all to a difficult task.

This is the price and the promise of citizenship.

This is the source of our confidence—the knowledge that God calls on us to shape an uncertain destiny.

This is the meaning of our liberty and our creed—why men and women and children of every race and every faith can join in celebration across this magnificent mall, and why a man whose father less than sixty years ago might not have been served at a local restaurant can now stand before you to take a most sacred oath.

So let us mark this day with remembrance, of who we are and how far we have traveled. In the year of America's birth, in the coldest of months, a small band of patriots huddled by dying campfires on the shores of an icy river. The capital was abandoned. The enemy was advancing. The snow was stained with blood. At a moment when the outcome of our revolution was most in doubt, the father of our nation ordered these words be read to the people:

"Let it be told to the future world . . . that in the depth of winter, when nothing but hope and virtue could survive . . . that the city and the country, alarmed at one common danger, came forth to meet [it]."

America. In the face of our common dangers, in this winter of our hardship, let us remember these timeless words. With hope and virtue, let us brave once more the icy currents, and endure what storms may come. Let it be said by our children's children that when we were tested we refused to let this journey end, that we did not turn back nor did we falter; and with eyes fixed on the horizon and 'God's grace upon us, we carried forth that great gift of freedom and delivered it safely to future generations.

Thank you. God bless you and God bless the United States of America.

Source: Barack Obama. "Inaugural Address." Office of the Press Secretary, The White House. Available at: https://obamawhitehouse.archives.gov/blog /2009/01/21/president-barack-obamas-inaugural-address

---

Barack Obama's Second Presidential Inaugural Address (January 21, 2013)

On Sunday, January 20, 2013, President Barack Obama was officially sworn in as required by the Twentieth Amendment to the U.S. Constitution. The private ceremony occurred at the White House, where U.S. Supreme Court Chief Justice John Roberts administered the oath of office. The social events for Barack Obama's second inaugural ceremony began on Saturday, January 19, 2013, with a National Day of Service. On Monday, January 21, 2013, the public swearing-in ceremony occurred on the west steps of the Capitol. The ceremony was followed by the customary inaugural parade and various inaugural balls. On Tuesday, January 22, 2013, there was a

National Prayer Service at the Washington National Cathedral. President Barack Obama's second inaugural speech lasted fifteen minutes.

Each time we gather to inaugurate a President we bear witness to the enduring strength of our Constitution. We affirm the promise of our democracy. We recall that what binds this nation together is not the colors of our skin or the tenets of our faith or the origins of our names. What makes us exceptional—what makes us American—is our allegiance to an idea articulated in a declaration made more than two centuries ago:

"We hold these truths to be self-evident, that all men are created equal; that they are endowed by their Creator with certain unalienable rights; that among these are life, liberty, and the pursuit of happiness."

Today we continue a never-ending journey to bridge the meaning of those words with the realities of our time. For history tells us that while these truths may be self-evident, they've never been self-executing; that while freedom is a gift from God, it must be secured by His people here on Earth. (Applause.) The patriots of 1776 did not fight to replace the tyranny of a king with the privileges of a few or the rule of a mob. They gave to us a republic, a government of, and by, and for the people, entrusting each generation to keep safe our founding creed.

And for more than two hundred years, we have.

Through blood drawn by lash and blood drawn by sword, we learned that no union founded on the principles of liberty and equality could survive half-slave and half-free. We made ourselves anew, and vowed to move forward together.

Together, we determined that a modern economy requires railroads and highways to speed travel and commerce, schools and colleges to train our workers.

Together, we discovered that a free market only thrives when there are rules to ensure competition and fair play.

Together, we resolved that a great nation must care for the vulnerable, and protect its people from life's worst hazards and misfortune.

Through it all, we have never relinquished our skepticism of central authority, nor have we succumbed to the fiction that all society's ills can be cured through government alone. Our celebration of initiative and enterprise, our insistence on hard work and personal responsibility, these are constants in our character.

But we have always understood that when times change, so must we; that fidelity to our founding principles requires new responses to new challenges; that preserving our individual freedoms ultimately requires collective action. For the American people can no more meet the demands of today's world by acting alone than American soldiers could have met the forces of fascism or communism with muskets and militias. No single person can train all the math and science teachers we'll need to equip our children for the future, or build the roads and networks and research labs that will bring new jobs and businesses to our shores. Now, more than ever, we must do these things together, as one nation and one people. (Applause.)

This generation of Americans has been tested by crises that steeled our resolve and proved our resilience.   A decade of war is now ending. (Applause.) An economic recovery has begun. (Applause.) America's possibilities are limitless, for we possess all the qualities that this world without boundaries demands: youth and drive; diversity and openness; an endless capacity for risk and a gift for reinvention. My fellow Americans, we are made for this moment, and we will seize it—so long as we seize it together. (Applause.)

For we, the people, understand that our country cannot succeed when a shrinking few do very well and a growing many barely make it. (Applause.) We believe that America's prosperity must rest upon the broad shoulders of a rising middle class. We know that America thrives when every person can find independence and pride in their work; when the wages of honest labor liberate families from the brink of hardship. We are true to our creed when a little girl born into the bleakest poverty knows that she has the same chance to succeed as anybody else, because she is an American; she is free, and she is equal, not just in the eyes of God but also in our own.

We understand that outworn programs are inadequate to the needs of our time. So we must harness new ideas and technology to remake our government, revamp our tax code, reform our schools, and empower our citizens with the skills they need to work harder, learn more, reach higher. But while the means will change, our purpose endures: a nation that rewards the effort and determination of every single American. That is what this moment requires. That is what will give real meaning to our creed.

We, the people, still believe that every citizen deserves a basic measure of security and dignity. We must make the hard choices to reduce the cost of health care and the size of our deficit. But we reject the belief that America must choose between caring for the generation that built this country and investing in the generation that will build its future. (Applause.) For we remember the lessons of our past, when twilight years were spent in poverty and parents of a child with a disability had nowhere to turn.

We do not believe that in this country freedom is reserved for the lucky, or happiness for the few. We recognize that no matter how responsibly we live our lives, any one of us at any time may face a job loss, or a sudden illness, or a home swept away in a terrible storm. The commitments we make to each other through Medicare and Medicaid and Social Security, these things do not sap our initiative, they strengthen us. (Applause.) They do not make us a nation of takers; they free us to take the risks that make this country great. (Applause.)

We, the people, still believe that our obligations as Americans are not just to ourselves, but to all posterity. We will respond to the threat of climate change, knowing that the failure to do so would betray our children and future generations. (Applause.) Some may still deny the overwhelming judgment of science, but none can avoid the devastating impact of raging fires and crippling drought and more powerful storms.

The path towards sustainable energy sources will be long and sometimes difficult. But America cannot resist this transition, we must lead it. We cannot cede to other nations the technology that will power new jobs and new industries, we must claim its promise. That's how we will maintain our economic vitality and our national treasure—our forests and waterways, our crop lands and snow-capped peaks. That is how we will preserve our planet, commanded to our care by God. That's what will lend meaning to the creed our fathers once declared.

We, the people, still believe that enduring security and lasting peace do not require perpetual war. (Applause.) Our brave men and women in uniform, tempered by the flames of battle, are unmatched in skill and courage. Our citizens, seared by the memory of those we have lost, know too well the price that is paid for liberty. The knowledge of their sacrifice will keep us forever vigilant against those who would do us harm. But we are also heirs to those who won the peace and not just the war; who turned sworn enemies into the surest of friends—and we must carry those lessons into this time as well.

We will defend our people and uphold our values through strength of arms and rule of law. We will show the courage to try and resolve our differences with other nations peacefully—not because we are naïve about the dangers we face, but because engagement can more durably lift suspicion and fear.

America will remain the anchor of strong alliances in every corner of the globe. And we will renew those institutions that extend our capacity to manage crisis abroad, for no one has a greater stake in a peaceful world than its most powerful nation. We will support democracy from Asia to Africa, from the Americas to the Middle East, because our interests and our conscience compel us to act on behalf of those who long for freedom. And we must be a source of hope to the poor, the sick, the marginalized, the victims of prejudice—not out of mere charity, but because peace in our time requires the constant advance of those principles that our common creed describes: tolerance and opportunity, human dignity and justice.

We, the people, declare today that the most evident of truths—that all of us are created equal—is the star that guides us still; just as it guided our forebears through Seneca Falls, and Selma, and Stonewall; just as it guided all those men and women, sung and unsung, who left footprints along this great Mall, to hear a preacher say that we cannot walk alone; to hear a King proclaim that our individual freedom is inextricably bound to the freedom of every soul on Earth.

It is now our generation's task to carry on what those pioneers began. For our journey is not complete until our wives, our mothers and daughters can earn a living equal to their efforts.   Our journey is not complete until our gay brothers and sisters are treated like anyone else under the law, for if we are truly created equal, then surely the love we commit to one another must be equal as well.   Our journey is not complete until no citizen is forced to wait for hours to exercise the right to vote.   Our journey is not complete until we find a better way to welcome the striving, hopeful immigrants who still see America as a land of opportunity—until bright young students and engineers are enlisted in our workforce rather than expelled from our country.   Our journey is not complete until all our children, from the streets of Detroit to the hills of Appalachia, to the quiet lanes of Newtown, know that they are cared for and cherished and always safe from harm.

That is our generation's task—to make these words, these rights, these values of life and liberty and the pursuit of happiness real for every American.   Being true to our founding documents does not require us to agree on every contour of life. It does not mean we all define liberty in exactly the same way or follow the same precise path to happiness. Progress does not compel us to settle centuries-long debates about the role of government for all time, but it does require us to act in our time.

For now decisions are upon us and we cannot afford delay. We cannot mistake absolutism for principle, or substitute spectacle for politics, or treat name-calling as reasoned debate.   We must act, knowing that our work will be imperfect. We must act, knowing that today's victories will be only partial and that it will be up to those who stand here in four years and 40 years and 400 years hence to advance the timeless spirit once conferred to us in a spare Philadelphia hall.

My fellow Americans, the oath I have sworn before you today, like the one recited by others who serve in this Capitol, was an oath to God and country, not party or faction. And we must faithfully execute that pledge during the duration of our service. But the words I spoke today are not so different from the oath that is taken each time a soldier signs up for duty or an immigrant realizes her dream. My oath is not so different from the pledge we all make to the flag that waves above and that fills our hearts with pride.

They are the words of citizens and they represent our greatest hope. You and I, as citizens, have the power to set this country's course. You and I, as citizens, have the obligation to shape the debates of our time—not only with the votes we cast, but with the voices we lift in defense of our most ancient values and enduring ideals.

Let us, each of us, now embrace with solemn duty and awesome joy what is our lasting birthright. With common effort and common purpose, with passion and dedication, let us answer the call of history and carry into an uncertain future that precious light of freedom.

Thank you. God bless you, and may He forever bless these United States of America.

Source: Barack Obama. "Inaugural Address," January 21, 2013. Office of the Press Secretary, The White House. Available at: https://obamawhitehouse.archives.gov/the-press-office/2013/01/21/inaugural-address-president-barack-obama

---

Remarks by President Obama on Trayvon Martin (July 19, 2013)

Trayvon Benjamin Martin was born in Florida on February 5, 1995. His parents, Sybrina Fulton and Tracy Martin, divorced in 1999. While visiting his father, Trayvon Martin was killed by a member of neighborhood watch, George Zimmerman, in Sanford, Florida, on February 26, 2012. Martin did not have a criminal record but had been suspended from school. Zimmerman's initial release and arrest generated a national discussion over racial profiling, the role of armed neighborhood watch, and stand your ground laws in the United States. On July 13, 2013, a jury acquitted Zimmerman of murder. In an outpouring of outrage in many cities across the nation, several thousands of people took to the streets in protest of Zimmerman's acquittal. On July 19, 2013, President Barack Obama went to the press room and made public remarks about Trayvon Martin's death and the subsequent acquittal.

July 19, 2013

Remarks by the President on Trayvon Martin

James S. Brady Press Briefing Room

1:33 P.M. EDT

THE PRESIDENT: I wanted to come out here, first of all, to tell you that Jay is prepared for all your questions and is very much looking forward to the session. The second thing is I want to let you know that over the next couple of weeks, there's going to obviously be a whole range of issues—immigration, economics, et cetera—we'll try to arrange a fuller press conference to address your questions.

The reason I actually wanted to come out today is not to take questions, but to speak to an issue that obviously has gotten a lot of attention over the course of the last week—the issue of the Trayvon Martin ruling. I gave a preliminary statement right after the ruling on Sunday. But watching the debate over the course of the last week, I thought it might be useful for me to expand on my thoughts a little bit.

First of all, I want to make sure that, once again, I send my thoughts and prayers, as well as Michelle's, to the family of Trayvon Martin, and to remark on the incredible grace and dignity with which they've dealt with the entire situation. I can only imagine what they're going through, and it's remarkable how they've handled it.

The second thing I want to say is to reiterate what I said on Sunday, which is there's going to be a lot of arguments about the legal issues in the case—I'll let all the legal analysts and talking heads address those issues. The judge conducted the trial in a professional manner. The prosecution and the defense made their arguments. The juries were properly instructed that in a case such as this reasonable doubt was relevant, and they rendered a verdict. And once the jury has spoken, that's how our system works. But I did want to just talk a little bit about context and how people have responded to it and how people are feeling.

You know, when Trayvon Martin was first shot I said that this could have been my son. Another way of saying that is Trayvon Martin could have been me 35 years ago. And when you think about why, in the African American community at least, there's a lot of pain around what happened here, I think it's important to recognize that the African American community is looking at this issue through a set of experiences and a history that doesn't go away.

There are very few African American men in this country who haven't had the experience of being followed when they were shopping in a department store. That includes me. There are very few African American men who haven't had the experience of walking across the street and hearing the locks click on the doors of cars. That happens to me—at least before I was a senator. There are very few African Americans who haven't had the experience of getting on an elevator and a woman clutching her purse nervously and holding her breath until she had a chance to get off. That happens often.

And I don't want to exaggerate this, but those sets of experiences inform how the African American community interprets what happened one night in Florida. And it's inescapable for people to bring those experiences to bear. The African American community is also knowledgeable that there is a history of racial disparities in the application of our criminal laws—everything from the death penalty to enforcement of our drug laws. And that ends up having an impact in terms of how people interpret the case.

Now, this isn't to say that the African American community is naïve about the fact that African American young men are disproportionately involved in the criminal justice system; that they're disproportionately both victims and perpetrators of violence. It's not to make excuses for that fact—although black folks do interpret the reasons for that in a historical context. They understand that some of the violence that takes place in poor black neighborhoods around the country is born out of a very violent past in this country, and that the poverty and dysfunction that we see in those communities can be traced to a very difficult history.

And so the fact that sometimes that's unacknowledged adds to the frustration. And the fact that a lot of African American boys are painted with a broad brush and the excuse is given, well, there are these statistics out there that show that African American boys are more violent—using that as an excuse to then see sons treated differently causes pain.

I think the African American community is also not naïve in understanding that, statistically, somebody like Trayvon Martin was statistically more likely to be shot by a peer than he was by somebody else. So folks understand the challenges that exist for African American boys. But they get frustrated, I think, if they feel that there's no context for it and that context is being denied. And that all contributes I think to a sense that if a white male teen was involved in the same kind of scenario, that, from top to bottom, both the outcome and the aftermath might have been different.

Now, the question for me at least, and I think for a lot of folks, is where do we take this? How do we learn some lessons from this and move in a positive direction? I think it's understandable that there have been demonstrations and vigils and protests, and some of that stuff is just going to have to work its way through, as long as it remains nonviolent. If I see any violence, then I will remind folks that that dishonors what happened to Trayvon Martin and his family. But beyond protests or vigils, the question is, are there some concrete things that we might be able to do.

I know that Eric Holder is reviewing what happened down there, but I think it's important for people to have some clear expectations here. Traditionally, these are issues of state and local government, the criminal code. And law enforcement is traditionally done at the state and local levels, not at the federal levels.

That doesn't mean, though, that as a nation we can't do some things that I think would be productive. So let me just give a couple of specifics that

I'm still bouncing around with my staff, so we're not rolling out some five-point plan, but some areas where I think all of us could potentially focus.

Number one, precisely because law enforcement is often determined at the state and local level, I think it would be productive for the Justice Department, governors, mayors to work with law enforcement about training at the state and local levels in order to reduce the kind of mistrust in the system that sometimes currently exists.

When I was in Illinois, I passed racial profiling legislation, and it actually did just two simple things. One, it collected data on traffic stops and the race of the person who was stopped. But the other thing was it resourced us training police departments across the state on how to think about potential racial bias and ways to further professionalize what they were doing.

And initially, the police departments across the state were resistant, but actually they came to recognize that if it was done in a fair, straightforward way that it would allow them to do their jobs better and communities would have more confidence in them and, in turn, be more helpful in applying the law. And obviously, law enforcement has got a very tough job.

So that's one area where I think there are a lot of resources and best practices that could be brought to bear if state and local governments are receptive. And I think a lot of them would be. And let's figure out are there ways for us to push out that kind of training.

Along the same lines, I think it would be useful for us to examine some state and local laws to see if it—if they are designed in such a way that they may encourage the kinds of altercations and confrontations and tragedies that we saw in the Florida case, rather than diffuse potential altercations.

I know that 'there's been commentary about the fact that the "stand your ground" laws in Florida were not used as a defense in the case. On the other hand, if we're sending a message as a society in our communities that someone who is armed potentially has the right to use those firearms even if there's a way for them to exit from a situation, is that really going to be contributing to the kind of peace and security and order that we'd like to see?

And for those who resist that idea that we should think about something like these "stand your ground" laws, I'd just ask people to consider, if Trayvon Martin was of age and armed, could he have stood his ground on that sidewalk? And do we actually think that he would have been justified in shooting Mr. Zimmerman who had followed him in a car because he felt threatened? And if the answer to that question is at least ambiguous, then it seems to me that we might want to examine those kinds of laws.

Number three—and this is a long-term project—we need to spend some time in thinking about how do we bolster and reinforce our African

American boys. And this is something that Michelle and I talk a lot about. There are a lot of kids out there who need help who are getting a lot of negative reinforcement. And is there more that we can do to give them the sense that their country cares about them and values them and is willing to invest in them?

I'm not naïve about the prospects of some grand, new federal program. I'm not sure that that's what we're talking here. But I do recognize that as President, I've got some convening power, and there are a lot of good programs that are being done across the country on this front. And for us to be able to gather together business leaders and local elected officials and clergy and celebrities and athletes, and figure out how are we doing a better job helping young African American men feel that they're a full part of this society and that they've got pathways and avenues to succeed—I think that would be a pretty good outcome from what was obviously a tragic situation. And we're going to spend some time working on that and thinking about that.

And then, finally, I think it's going to be important for all of us to do some soul-searching. There has been talk about should we convene a conversation on race. I haven't seen that be particularly productive when politicians try to organize conversations. They end up being stilted and politicized, and folks are locked into the positions they already have. On the other hand, in families and churches and workplaces, there's the possibility that people are a little bit more honest, and at least you ask yourself your own questions about, am I wringing as much bias out of myself as I can? Am I judging people as much as I can, based on not the color of their skin, but the content of their character? That would, I think, be an appropriate exercise in the wake of this tragedy.

And let me just leave you with a final thought that, as difficult and challenging as this whole episode has been for a lot of people, I don't want us to lose sight that things are getting better. Each successive generation seems to be making progress in changing attitudes when it comes to race. It doesn't mean we're in a post-racial society. It doesn't mean that racism is eliminated. But when I talk to Malia and Sasha, and I listen to their friends and I seem them interact, they're better than we are—they're better than we were—on these issues. And that's true in every community that I've visited all across the country.

And so we have to be vigilant and we have to work on these issues. And those of us in authority should be doing everything we can to encourage the better angels of our nature, as opposed to using these episodes to heighten divisions. But we should also have confidence that kids these days, I think, have more sense than we did back then, and certainly more than our parents did or our grandparents did; and that along this long, difficult journey, we're becoming a more perfect union—not a perfect union, but a more perfect union.

Thank you, guys.

END

Source: Barack Obama. "Remarks by the President on Trayvon Martin," July 19, 2013. Office of the Press Secretary, The White House. Available at: https://obamawhitehouse.archives.gov/the-press-office/2013/07/19 /remarks-president-trayvon-martin

---

Remarks by President Obama in Eulogy for the Hon. Rev. Clementa Pinckney (June 26, 2015)

On June 17, 2015, a white supremacist killed 9 people including the senior pastor and South Carolina State Senator Clementa C. Pinckney during a prayer service and bible study at the Emanuel African Methodist Episcopal Church. Mother Emanuel, as the church is called, has served as an epicenter for black people during slavery and the civil rights movement. Prior to the shooting, parishioners invited Dylann Roof, the killer, into the church for fellowship. Roof sat next to Pastor Pinckney. Taking his pistol from his fanny pack, Roof began to randomly shoot the victims. When captured after he fled about 240 miles, he confessed to the murders and said he believed the murders would start a race war. He also told investigators that he almost changed his mind about carrying out the murders because the church members showed him tremendous kindness. Clementa Pinckney's funeral was held in the basketball arena at the College of Charleston on June 26, 2015. President Barack Obama eulogized Senator Clementa Pinckney.

June 26, 2015

Remarks by the President in Eulogy for the Honorable Reverend Clementa Pinckney

College of Charleston
Charleston, South Carolina

2:49 P.M. EDT

THE PRESIDENT: Giving all praise and honor to God. (Applause.)

The Bible calls us to hope. To persevere, and have faith in things not seen.

"They were still living by faith when they died," Scripture tells us. "They did not receive the things promised; they only saw them and welcomed them from a distance, admitting that they were foreigners and strangers on Earth."

We are here today to remember a man of God who lived by faith. A man who believed in things not seen. A man who believed there were better days ahead, off in the distance. A man of service who persevered, knowing full well he would not receive all those things he was promised, because he believed his efforts would deliver a better life for those who followed.

To Jennifer, his beloved wife; to Eliana and Malana, his beautiful, wonderful daughters; to the Mother Emanuel family and the people of Charleston, the people of South Carolina.

I cannot claim to have the good fortune to know Reverend Pinckney well. But I did have the pleasure of knowing him and meeting him here in South Carolina, back when we were both a little bit younger. (Laughter.) Back when I didn't have visible grey hair. (Laughter.) The first thing I noticed was his graciousness, his smile, his reassuring baritone, his deceptive sense of humor—all qualities that helped him wear so effortlessly a heavy burden of expectation.

Friends of his remarked this week that when Clementa Pinckney entered a room, it was like the future arrived; that even from a young age, folks knew he was special. Anointed. He was the progeny of a long line of the faithful—a family of preachers who spread God's word, a family of protesters who sowed change to expand voting rights and desegregate the South. Clem heard their instruction, and he did not forsake their teaching.

He was in the pulpit by 13, pastor by 18, public servant by 23. He did not exhibit any of the cockiness of youth, nor youth's insecurities; instead, he set an example worthy of his position, wise beyond his years, in his speech, in his conduct, in his love, faith, and purity.

As a senator, he represented a sprawling swath of the Lowcountry, a place that has long been one of the most neglected in America. A place still wracked by poverty and inadequate schools; a place where children can still go hungry and the sick can go without treatment. A place that needed somebody like Clem. (Applause.)

His position in the minority party meant the odds of winning more resources for his constituents were often long. His calls for greater equity were too often unheeded, the votes he cast were sometimes lonely. But he never gave up. He stayed true to his convictions. He would not grow discouraged. After a full day at the capitol, he'd climb into his car and head to the church to draw sustenance from his family, from his ministry, from the community that loved and needed him. There he would fortify his faith, and imagine what might be.

Reverend Pinckney embodied a politics that was neither mean, nor small. He conducted himself quietly, and kindly, and diligently. He encouraged progress not by pushing his ideas alone, but by seeking out your ideas, partnering with you to make things happen. He was full of empathy and fellow feeling, able to walk in somebody else's shoes and see through their eyes. No wonder one of his senate colleagues remembered Senator Pinckney as "the most gentle of the 46 of us—the best of the 46 of us."

Clem was often asked why he chose to be a pastor and a public servant. But the person who asked probably didn't know the history of the AME church. (Applause.) As our brothers and sisters in the AME church know, we don't make those distinctions. "Our calling," Clem once said, "is not just within the walls of the congregation, but . . . the life and community in which our congregation resides." (Applause.)

He embodied the idea that our Christian faith demands deeds and not just words; that the "sweet hour of prayer" actually lasts the whole week long—(applause)—that to put our faith in action is more than individual salvation, it's about our collective salvation; that to feed the hungry and clothe the naked and house the homeless is not just a call for isolated charity but the imperative of a just society.

What a good man. Sometimes I think that's the best thing to hope for when you're eulogized—after all the words and recitations and resumes are read, to just say someone was a good man. (Applause.)

You don't have to be of high station to be a good man. Preacher by 13. Pastor by 18. Public servant by 23. What a life Clementa Pinckney lived. What an example he set. What a model for his faith. And then to lose him at 41—slain in his sanctuary with eight wonderful members of his flock, each at different stages in life but bound together by a common commitment to God.

Cynthia Hurd. Susie Jackson. Ethel Lance. DePayne Middleton-Doctor. Tywanza Sanders. Daniel L. Simmons. Sharonda Coleman-Singleton. Myra Thompson. Good people. Decent people. God-fearing people. (Applause.) People so full of life and so full of kindness. People who ran the race, who persevered. People of great faith.

To the families of the fallen, the nation shares in your grief. Our pain cuts that much deeper because it happened in a church. The church is and always has been the center of African-American life—(applause)—a place to call our own in a too often hostile world, a sanctuary from so many hardships.

Over the course of centuries, black churches served as "hush harbors" where slaves could worship in safety; praise houses where their free descendants could gather and shout hallelujah—(applause)—rest stops for the weary along the Underground Railroad; bunkers for the foot soldiers of the

Civil Rights Movement. They have been, and continue to be, community centers where we organize for jobs and justice; places of scholarship and network; places where children are loved and fed and kept out of harm's way, and told that they are beautiful and smart—(applause)—and taught that they matter. (Applause.) That's what happens in church.

That's what the black church means. Our beating heart. The place where our dignity as a people is inviolate. When there's no better example of this tradition than Mother Emanuel—(applause)—a church built by blacks seeking liberty, burned to the ground because its founder sought to end slavery, only to rise up again, a Phoenix from these ashes. (Applause.)

When there were laws banning all-black church gatherings, services happened here anyway, in defiance of unjust laws. When there was a righteous movement to dismantle Jim Crow, Dr. Martin Luther King, Jr. preached from its pulpit, and marches began from its steps. A sacred place, this church. Not just for blacks, not just for Christians, but for every American who cares about the steady expansion—(applause)—of human rights and human dignity in this country; a foundation stone for liberty and justice for all. That's what the church meant. (Applause.)

We do not know whether the killer of Reverend Pinckney and eight others knew all of this history. But he surely sensed the meaning of his violent act. It was an act that drew on a long history of bombs and arson and shots fired at churches, not random, but as a means of control, a way to terrorize and oppress. (Applause.) An act that he imagined would incite fear and recrimination; violence and suspicion. An act that he presumed would deepen divisions that trace back to our nation's original sin.

Oh, but God works in mysterious ways. (Applause.) God has different ideas. (Applause.)

He didn't know he was being used by God. (Applause.) Blinded by hatred, the alleged killer could not see the grace surrounding Reverend Pinckney and that Bible study group—the light of love that shone as they opened the church doors and invited a stranger to join in their prayer circle. The alleged killer could have never anticipated the way the families of the fallen would respond when they saw him in court—in the midst of unspeakable grief, with words of forgiveness. He couldn't imagine that. (Applause.)

The alleged killer could not imagine how the city of Charleston, under the good and wise leadership of Mayor Riley—(applause)—how the state of South Carolina, how the United States of America would respond—not merely with revulsion at his evil act, but with big-hearted generosity and, more importantly, with a thoughtful introspection and self-examination that we so rarely see in public life.

Blinded by hatred, he failed to comprehend what Reverend Pinckney so well understood—the power of God's grace. (Applause.)

This whole week, I've been reflecting on this idea of grace. (Applause.) The grace of the families who lost loved ones. The grace that Reverend Pinckney would preach about in his sermons. The grace described in one of my favorite hymnals—the one we all know: Amazing grace, how sweet the sound that saved a wretch like me. (Applause.) I once was lost, but now I'm found; was blind but now I see. (Applause.)

According to the Christian tradition, grace is not earned. Grace is not merited. It's not something we deserve. Rather, grace is the free and benevolent favor of God—(applause)—as manifested in the salvation of sinners and the bestowal of blessings. Grace.

As a nation, out of this terrible tragedy, God has visited grace upon us, for he has allowed us to see where we've been blind. (Applause.) He has given us the chance, where we've been lost, to find our best selves. (Applause.) We may not have earned it, this grace, with our rancor and complacency, and short-sightedness and fear of each other—but we got it all the same. He gave it to us anyway. He's once more given us grace. But it is up to us now to make the most of it, to receive it with gratitude, and to prove ourselves worthy of this gift.

For too long, we were blind to the pain that the Confederate flag stirred in too many of our citizens. (Applause.) It's true, a flag did not cause these murders. But as people from all walks of life, Republicans and Democrats, now acknowledge—including Governor Haley, whose recent eloquence on the subject is worthy of praise—(applause)—as we all have to acknowledge, the flag has always represented more than just ancestral pride. (Applause.) For many, black and white, that flag was a reminder of systemic oppression and racial subjugation. We see that now.

Removing the flag from this state's capitol would not be an act of political correctness; it would not be an insult to the valor of Confederate soldiers. It would simply be an acknowledgment that the cause for which they fought—the cause of slavery—was wrong—(applause)—the imposition of Jim Crow after the Civil War, the resistance to civil rights for all people was wrong. (Applause.) It would be one step in an honest accounting of America's history; a modest but meaningful balm for so many unhealed wounds. It would be an expression of the amazing changes that have transformed this state and this country for the better, because of the work of so many people of goodwill, people of all races striving to form a more perfect union.   By taking down that flag, we express God's grace. (Applause.)

But I don't think God wants us to stop there. (Applause.) For too long, we've been blind to the way past injustices continue to shape the present. Perhaps we see that now. Perhaps this tragedy causes us to ask some tough questions about how we can permit so many of our children to languish in poverty, or attend dilapidated schools, or grow up without prospects for a job or for a career. (Applause.)

Perhaps it causes us to examine what we're doing to cause some of our children to hate. (Applause.) Perhaps it softens hearts towards those lost young men, tens and tens of thousands caught up in the criminal justice system—(applause)—and leads us to make sure that that system is not infected with bias; that we embrace changes in how we train and equip our police so that the bonds of trust between law enforcement and the communities they serve make us all safer and more secure. (Applause.)

Maybe we now realize the way racial bias can infect us even when we don't realize it, so that we're guarding against not just racial slurs, but we're also guarding against the subtle impulse to call Johnny back for a job interview but not Jamal. (Applause.) So that we search our hearts when we consider laws to make it harder for some of our fellow citizens to vote. (Applause.) By recognizing our common humanity by treating every child as important, regardless of the color of their skin or the station into which they were born, and to do what's necessary to make opportunity real for every American—by doing that, we express God's grace. (Applause.)

For too long—

AUDIENCE: For too long!

THE PRESIDENT: For too long, we've been blind to the unique mayhem that gun violence inflicts upon this nation. (Applause.) Sporadically, our eyes are open: When eight of our brothers and sisters are cut down in a church basement, 12 in a movie theater, 26 in an elementary school. But I hope we also see the 30 precious lives cut short by gun violence in this country every single day; the countless more whose lives are forever changed—the survivors crippled, the children traumatized and fearful every day as they walk to school, the husband who will never feel his wife's warm touch, the entire communities whose grief overflows every time they have to watch what happened to them happen to some other place.

The vast majority of Americans—the majority of gun owners—want to do something about this. We see that now. (Applause.) And I'm convinced that by acknowledging the pain and loss of others, even as we respect the traditions and ways of life that make up this beloved country—by making the moral choice to change, we express God's grace. (Applause.)

We don't earn grace. We're all sinners. We don't deserve it. (Applause.) But God gives it to us anyway. (Applause.) And we choose how to receive it. It's our decision how to honor it.

None of us can or should expect a transformation in race relations overnight. Every time something like this happens, somebody says we have to have a conversation about race. We talk a lot about race. There's no shortcut. And we don't need more talk. (Applause.) None of us should believe that a handful of gun safety measures will prevent every tragedy. It will not. People of goodwill will continue to debate the merits of various policies, as our democracy requires—this is a big, raucous place, America is. And there are good people on both sides of these debates. Whatever solutions we find will necessarily be incomplete.

But it would be a betrayal of everything Reverend Pinckney stood for, I believe, if we allowed ourselves to slip into a comfortable silence again. (Applause.) Once the eulogies have been delivered, once the TV cameras move on, to go back to business as usual—that's what we so often do to avoid uncomfortable truths about the prejudice that still infects our society. (Applause.) To settle for symbolic gestures without following up with the hard work of more lasting change—that's how we lose our way again.

It would be a refutation of the forgiveness expressed by those families if we merely slipped into old habits, whereby those who disagree with us are not merely wrong but bad; where we shout instead of listen; where we barricade ourselves behind preconceived notions or well-practiced cynicism.

Reverend Pinckney once said, "Across the South, we have a deep appreciation of history—we haven't always had a deep appreciation of each other's history." (Applause.) What is true in the South is true for America. Clem understood that justice grows out of recognition of ourselves in each other. That my liberty depends on you being free, too. (Applause.) That history can't be a sword to justify injustice, or a shield against progress, but must be a manual for how to avoid repeating the mistakes of the past— how to break the cycle. A roadway toward a better world. He knew that the path of grace involves an open mind—but, more importantly, an open heart.

That's what I've felt this week—an open heart. That, more than any particular policy or analysis, is what's called upon right now, I think—what a friend of mine, the writer Marilyn Robinson, calls "that reservoir of goodness, beyond, and of another kind, that we are able to do each other in the ordinary cause of things."

That reservoir of goodness. If we can find that grace, anything is possible. (Applause.) If we can tap that grace, everything can change. (Applause.)

Amazing grace. Amazing grace.

(Begins to sing)—Amazing grace—(applause)—how sweet the sound, that saved a wretch like me; I once was lost, but now I'm found; was blind but now I see. (Applause.)

Clementa Pinckney found that grace.

Cynthia Hurd found that grace.

Susie Jackson found that grace.

Ethel Lance found that grace.

DePayne Middleton-Doctor found that grace.

Tywanza Sanders found that grace.

Daniel L. Simmons, Sr. found that grace.

Sharonda Coleman-Singleton found that grace.

Myra Thompson found that grace.

Through the example of their lives, they've now passed it on to us. May we find ourselves worthy of that precious and extraordinary gift, as long as our lives endure. May grace now lead them home. May God continue to shed His grace on the United States of America. (Applause.)

Source: Barack Obama. "Remarks by the President in Eulogy for the Honorable Reverend Clementa Pinckney," June 26, 2015. Office of the Press Secretary, The White House. Available at: https://obamawhitehouse.archives .gov/the-press-office/2015/06/26/remarks-president-eulogy-honorable -reverend-clementa-pinckney

Bibliography

Academe. *Bulletin of AAUP* 78, no. 1 (February 1992): 2. https://books
.google.com/books?id=NyIRAQAAMAAJ&dq=Derrick+Bell+believed
+Harvard+should+deliberately+recruit+and+retain+more+minority
+faculty+members

Agiesta, Jennifer. "Most Say Race Relations Worsened under Obama."
CNN, October 5, 2016. https://www.cnn.com/2016/10/05/politics
/obama-race-relations-poll/index.html

Alinsky, Saul. *Rules for Radicals: A Pragmatic Primer for Realistic Radicals.* New York: Random House, 1971.

"America's Fed Up: Obama's Approval Rating Hits an All Time Low, Poll
Shows and Congress on Track to Be the Least Productive." NBC
News, October 5, 2014. https://www.nbcnews.com/politics/first
-read/americas-fed-obama-approval-rating-hits-all-time-low-poll
-n173271

Bacon, John. "Obama Thanks Parkland Shooting Survivors for 'Resilience,
Resolve' in a Handwritten Letter." *USA Today*, March 22, 2018.
https://www.usatoday.com/story/news/nation/2018/03/22/obama
-letter-thanks-parkland-shooting-survivors-resilience-resolve
/448474002/

Ballasy, Nicholas. "Bobby Rush in 2000, Obama a 'Harvard Educated Fool'
Who 'Thinks He Knows All About' the 'Civil Rights Protest.'" *Daily
Caller*, March 28, 2012. https://dailycaller.com/2012/03/28/bobby
-rush-in-2000-obamas-a-harvard-educated-fool-who-thinks-he
-knows-all-about-the-civil-rights-protests/

Balz, Dan, Anne E. Kornblut, and Shailagh Murray. "Obama Wins Iowa
Caucuses." *Washington Post*, January 4, 2008. http://www.washington
post.com/wp-dyn/content/article/2008/01/03/AR2008010304441
.html

Banthin, Jessica, and Sarah Masi. *Updated Estimates of the Insurance Coverage Provisions of the Affordable Care Act.* https://www.cbo.gov/publication/45159

Barnett, Denis. "Obama Makes Impassioned Plea for Clean Energy in Argentina." *Digital Journal,* October 6, 2017. http://www.digitaljournal.com/news/world/obama-makes-impassioned-plea-for-clean-energy-in-argentina/article/504425

Barr, Andy. "The GOP's No-Compromise Pledge." *Politico,* October 28, 2010. https://www.politico.com/story/2010/10/the-gops-no-compromise-pledge-044311

Berry, Mary Frances, and Josh Gottheimer. *Power in Words: The Story behind Barack Obama's Speeches from the State House to the White House.* Boston, MA: Beacon Press, 2010.

Bond-Halbert, Alma. *Michelle Obama: A Biography.* Santa Barbara, CA: Greenwood Press, 2012.

Bryer, Thomas, Jeffery C. Callen, Angela M. Eikemberry, Terrance M. Garrett, Jeanine M. Love, Chad R. Miller, Bethany Stich, and Craig Wickstrom. "Public Administration Theory in the Obama Era." *Administration Theory and Praxis,* 32, no. 1 (March 2010): 118–122.

Burris, Roddie A. "Jackson Slams Obama for 'Acting White.'" *Slate,* September 19, 2007. https://www.politico.com/story/2007/09/jackson-slams-obama-for-acting-white-005902

Butterfield, Fox. "First Black Elected to Head Harvard's *Law Review.*" *New York Times,* February 9, 1990. https://www.nytimes.com/1990/02/06/us/first-black-elected-to-head-harvard-s-law-review.html

Butterfield, Fox. "Harvard Torn by Race." *New York Times,* April 26, 1990. https://www.nytimes.com/1990/04/26/us/harvard-law-school-torn-by-race-issue.html

Butterfield, Fox. "Law Professor Quits until Black Woman Is Named." *New York Times,* April 24, 1990. https://www.nytimes.com/1990/04/24/us/harvard-law-professor-quits-until-black-woman-is-named.html

Calmes, Jackie. "Demystifying the Fiscal Impasse That Is Vexing Washington." *New York Times,* November 15, 2012. https://www.nytimes.com/2012/11/16/us/politics/the-fiscal-cliff-explained.html

Chase, John, and Liam Ford. "Ryan Files a Bombshell." *Chicago Tribune,* June 22, 2004. http://www.chicagotribune.com/news/chi-0406220247jun22-story.html

Chua-Eoan, Howard. "The Queen and Mrs. Obama: A Breach in Protocol." *Time Magazine,* April 1, 2009. http://content.time.com/time/world/article/0,8599,1888962,00.html

Cillizza, Chris, and Aaron Blake. "President Obama Embraces 'Obamacare' Label. But Why?" *Washington Post,* March 26, 2012. https://

www.washingtonpost.com/blogs/the-fix/post/president-obama
-embraces-obamacare-label-but-why/2012/03/25/gIQARJ5qaS
_blog.html

CNN. "Obama to Ratchet up the Hunt for Bin Laden." CNN Politics, November 12, 2008. http://www.cnn.com/2008/POLITICS/11/12/binladen
.hunt/

Cody, Edward. "NATO Backs Obama Afghan Plan but Pledge Few New Troops." *Washington Post*, April 5, 2009. http://www.washington
post.com/wp-dyn/content/article/2009/04/04/AR2009040402594
.html?noredirect=on

Cohen, Tim. "Rough Obamacare Rollout: 4 Reasons Why." CNN Politics, October 23, 2013. https://www.cnn.com/2013/10/22/politics
/obamacare-website-four-reasons/index.html

Cooper, Helen. "Obama Connects with Young Europeans." *New York Times*, April 3, 2009. https://www.nytimes.com/2009/04/04/world
/europe/04prexy.html

Cooper, Helen. "Putting a Stamp on Afghan War, Obama Will Send 17,000 Troops." *New York Times*, February 17, 2009. https://www.nytimes
.com/2009/02/18/washington/18web-troops.html

Corley, Cheryl. "The Legacy of Chicago's Harold Washington." *All Things Considered*, National Public Radio, November 23, 2007. https://
www.npr.org/templates/story/story.php?storyId=16579146

C-SPAN. "Presidential Online Town Hall." March 26, 2009. https://www
.c-span.org/video/?284883-2/presidential-online-town-hall

DeYoung, Karen. "Obama Announces Strategies for Afghanistan, Pakistan." *Washington Post*, March 28, 2009. http://www.washingtonpost.com
/wp-dyn/content/article/2009/03/27/AR2009032700836.html

Dumke, Mike. "Beyond the Base." *Chicago Defender*, February 1, 2004. https://www.chicagoreporter.com/beyond-base/

Dyson, Michael Eric. *The Black Presidency: Barack Obama and the Politics of Race in America*. New York: Houghton Mifflin Harcourt, 2016.

Election Results. *New York Times*. December 9, 2008. https://www.nytimes
.com/elections/2008/results/president/votes.html

Elperin Juliet. "Palin Turns to NYT, Citing Article on Ayers." *Washington Post*, October 4, 2008. http://voices.washingtonpost.com/44/2008
/10/palin-turns-to-nyt-citing-arti.html

Elving, Ron. "What Happened with Merrick Garland in 2016 and Why It Matters Now." National Public Radio, June 29, 2018. https://www
.npr.org/2018/06/29/624467256/what-happened-with-merrick
-garland-in-2016-and-why-it-matters-now

Feltus, William J., Kenneth M. Goldstein, and Matthew Dallek. *Inside Campaign: Elections through the Eyes of Political Professionals. CQ Press*. Thousand Oaks, CA: Sage Publications, 2018.

Ferris, Sarah. "Sanders Campaign, Clinton Attacked Obama on Guns, Too." *The Hill*, January 9, 2016. https://thehill.com/briefingroom -blogroll/265319-sanders-clinton-attacked-obama-on-guns-too

Finnegan, William. "The Candidate: The Political Scene." *New Yorker*, May 31, 2004. https://www.newyorker.com/magazine/2004/05/31/the -candidate-5

Ford, Liam, and David Mendell. "From Keyes, No Congratulations." *Chicago Tribune*, November 4, 2004. http://www.chicagotribune.com /news/ct-xpm-2004-11-05-0411050168-story.html

Frey, William H. "How Did Race Affect the 2008 Presidential Election?" PSC Research Report No. 09-688. *Population Studies Center Publications*, September 1, 2009. http://www.frey-demographer.org /reports/R-2009-2_HowRaceAffect2008Election.pdf

Georgetown University Health Policy Institute. *The Children's Health Insurance Program Reauthorization Act of 2009*. https://ccf .georgetown.edu/wp-content/uploads/2012/02/chip-summary-03 -09.pdf

Gillin, Joshua. "Congress Blocks Obama's Call for New Gun Laws." *Politifact*, January 6, 2017. https://www.politifact.com/truth-o-meter /article/2017/jan/06/congress-blocked-obama-call-gun-control -mass-shoot/

Glanton, Dahleen, Lolly Bowean, and Ted Gregory. "Obama Library Will Be in Chicago." *Chicago Tribune*, May 12, 2015. http://www .chicagotribune.com/news/obamacenter/ct-obama-library-site -announcement-20150512-story.html

Godsey, Melissa Jenna. 2007. https://www.youtube.com/watch?v=4 _oXsljcKaA

Goldberg, Jonah. "Rejection of Identity Politics Is a Part of American History." *Chicago Tribune*, November 30, 2018. http://www .chicagotribune.com/news/columnists/sns-201811291638--tms --jgoldbrgctnjg-a20181130-20181130-column.html

Hamby, Peter, and Jim Acosta. "14 States Sue to Block Health Care." *CNN* March 23, 2010. http://www.cnn.com/2010/CRIME/03/23/health .care.lawsuit/index.html

Harnden, Toby. "Barack Obama's True Colours: The Making of the Man Who Would Be President," August 21, 2008. https://www.telegraph .co.uk/news/worldnews/barackobama/2591139/Barack-Obamas -true-colours-The-making-of-the-man-who-would-be-US -president.html

Harrison, Jenna. Senator Barack Obama's Victory Speech, Full Transcript. ABC News, November 4, 2008. https://abcnews.go.com/Politics /Vote2008/story?id=6181477&page=1

Hayes, Chris. "Obama's Registration Drives." *Nation*, August 13, 2008. https://www.thenation.com/article/obamas-voter-registration-drive/

Hicks, Peter. *Barack Obama: The President for Change*. New York: Rosen Publishing, 2011.

Hopkins, Andrea. "Oprah Draws Iowa Crowds for Democrat Obama." *Reuters News*, December 5, 2007. https://www.reuters.com/article/us-usa-politics-oprah/oprah-draws-iowa-crowds-for-democrat-obama-idUSN0835312820071208

Hulse, Carl. "Obama Sworn in as 44th President." *New York Times*, January 20, 2009. https://www.nytimes.com/2009/01/20/world/americas/20iht-20webinaug2.19522702.html

Inskeep, Steve. Transcript and Video NPR Exit Interview with President Obama. National Public Radio, December 19, 2016. https://www.npr.org/2016/12/19/504998487/transcript-and-video-nprs-exit-interview-with-president-obama

Jackson, David. "Obama to Be Sworn in on Lincoln, King Bibles." *USA Today*, January 10, 2013. https://www.usatoday.com/story/theoval/2013/01/10/obama-inaugural-bible-kennedy-king/1821363/

Janda, Kenneth, Jeffery Berry, and Jerry Goldman. *The Obama Presidency: Year One*. Boston, MA: Wadsworth, Cengage Learning, 2009.

Jarrett, Vernon. "Project Vote Brings Power to the People." *Chicago Sun Times*, August 11, 1992, p. 23.

Johnson, Sasha, Candy Crowley, and Alex Mooney. "Lewis Switches from Clinton to Obama." CNN, February 27, 2008. http://politicalticker.blogs.cnn.com/2008/02/27/lewis-switches-from-clinton-to-obama/

Judis, John B. "The Creation Myth." *New Republic*, September 10, 2008. https://newrepublic.com/article/65874/creation-myth-0

Kaergard, Chris. "Barack Obama's Political Career in Illinois Helped Shaped His Presidency." *Gatehouse Media*, November 11, 2018. https://www.rrstar.com/news/20181111/barack-obamas-political-career-in-illinois-helped-shape-his-presidency

Kantor, Jodi. "Teaching Law, Testing Ideas, Obama Stood Slightly Apart." *New York Times*, July 30, 2008. https://www.nytimes.com/2008/07/30/us/politics/30law.html

Kleine, Ted. "Is Bobby Rush in Trouble?" *Chicago Reader*, March 16, 2000. https://www.chicagoreader.com/chicago/is-bobby-rush-in-trouble/Content?oid=901745

Kornblut, Anne E. "For This Red Meat Crowd, Obama's '08 Choice Is Clear." *New York Times*, September 18, 2006. https://www.nytimes.com/2006/09/18/us/politics/18obama.html

Kornblut, Anne E. "Without Iowa, It's Just a Dream." *Washington Post*, September 27, 2007. http://voices.washingtonpost.com/44/2007/09/without-iowa-its-just-a-dream.html

Kroft, Steve. Interview with Barack Obama. "Obama on Bin Laden: The Full 60 Minutes Interview." CBS News, May 15, 2011. https://www.cbsnews.com/news/obama-on-bin-laden-the-full-60-minutes-interview/

Krulak, Charles C., and Michael R. Lehnert. "First Gitmo Commander: Shut It Down." *USA Today*, February 26, 2016. https://www.usatoday.com/story/opinion/2016/02/23/guantanamo-bay-gitmo-closure-obama-american-values-human-rights-column/80808294/

Lander, Mark, and David E. Sanger. "World Leaders Pledge $1.1 Trillion for Crisis." *New York Times*, April 2, 2009. https://www.nytimes.com/2009/04/03/world/europe/03summit.html

Liasson, Mara. "Clinton Obama Debate Apologize for Misstatements." Morning Edition on National Public Radio, April 17, 2008. https://www.npr.org/templates/story/story.php?storyId=89713246

Lothian, Dan, and Suzanne Malveaux. "Obama: U.S. to Withdraw Most Iraq Troops by August 2010." CNN Politics, February 27, 2009. http://www.cnn.com/2009/POLITICS/02/27/obama.troops/index.html

Mackey, Maureen. "How Barack Obama Amazed His Law School Professor." *Fiscal Times*, July 9, 2014. http://www.thefiscaltimes.com/Articles/2014/07/09/How-Barack-Obama-Amazed-His-Harvard-Law-Professor

Madhani, Aamer. "Obama Unveils Design, Vision for Future Presidential Library." *USA Today*, May 3, 2017. https://www.usatoday.com/story/news/politics/2017/05/03/president-obama-michelle-obama-unveils-design-future-presidential-library/101238328/

Manier, Jeremy. "South Side Residents Overwhelmingly Support to Include Parkland for Obama Presidential Library, Poll Finds." *University of Chicago News*, February 5, 2015. https://news.uchicago.edu/story/south-side-residents-overwhelmingly-support-proposal-include-parkland-obama-presidential

Maraniss, David. *Barack Obama: The Story*. New York: Simon and Schuster, 2012.

McDermott, Maeve. "Obama Cried When Dropping off Malia at Harvard: 'Like Open-Heart Surgery.'" *USA Today*, September 27, 2017. https://www.usatoday.com/story/life/people/2017/09/27/president-obama-cried-while-dropping-off-malia-harvard-like-open-heart-surgery/707475001/

McPhee, Michelle, and Sara Just. "Obama: Police Acted Stupidly in Gates Case." ABC News, July 22, 2009. https://abcnews.go.com/US/story?id=8148986&page=1

Meacham, Jon. "What Barack Obama Learned from His Father." *Time Magazine*, August 22, 2008 https://www.newsweek.com/what-barack-obama-learned-his-father

Moberg, David. "Obama's Community Roots." *Nation*, April 2, 2007. https://www.thenation.com/article/obamas-community-roots/Peter

Montopoli, Brian. "Obama Approves Troop Increase to Afghanistan." CBS News, February 20, 2009. https://www.cbsnews.com/news/obama-approves-troop-increase-in-afghanistan/

Montopoli, Brian. "Obama Freezes Pay for White House Employees, Limits Lobbyists." CBS News, January 21, 2009. https://www.cbsnews.com/news/obama-freezes-pay-for-white-house-employees-limits-lobbyists

Montopoli, Brian. "Obama: Legalizing Pot Would Not Grow the Economy." CBS News, July 19, 2009. https://www.cbsnews.com/news/obama-legalizing-pot-wont-grow-economy/

Mooney, Alexander. "Jesse Jackson: Obama Needs to Bring Attention to the Jena 6." CNN Politics, September 19, 2007. http://www.cnn.com/2007/POLITICS/09/19/jackson.jena6/

Mosendz, Polly. "Dylann Roof Confesses He Wanted to Start a Race War." *Newsweek*, June 19, 2015. https://www.newsweek.com/dylann-roof-confesses-church-shooting-says-he-wanted-start-race-war-344797

Mosk, Matthew. "A $55 Million Month for Obama." *Washington Post*, March 6, 2008. http://voices.washingtonpost.com/44/2008/03/06/a_55_million_month_for_obama.html

Mundy, Liza. *Michelle: A Biography.* New York: Simon and Schuster, 2008.

Mundy, Liza. "When Michelle Met Barack: How Romance in the Sedate Corridors of a Corporate Law Firm Changed Everything for a Woman Who Might Become the Country's First African American First Lady." *Washington Post.* http://www.washingtonpost.com/wp-dyn/content/article/2008/09/26/AR2008092602856_5.html.

National Employment Law Project. "Minimum Wage Basics: Public Opinion on Raising the Minimum Wage." May 2015. https://www.nelp.org/wp-content/uploads/Minimum-Wage-Basics-Polling.pdf

"The New Megachurches: Congregation with Spectacular Structures Spread across the U.S." *Ebony Magazine* 57, no. 2(December 2001): 148–60.

Newton-Small, Jay. "Michelle Obama's Savvy Sacrifice." *Time Magazine*, August 25, 2008. http://content.time.com/time/politics/article/0,8599,1835686,00.html

Norris, Michele. "Obama Shares His Political Vision in *Audacity of Hope.*" *All Things Considered*, National Public Radio, October 16, 2006. https://www.npr.org/2006/10/19/6330677/obama-shares-political-vision-in-audacity-of-hope

Obama, Barack. *The Audacity of Hope: Thoughts on Reclaiming the American Dream.* New York: Three Rivers Press, 2006.

Obama, Barack. "Barack Obama's Acceptance Speech." *New York Times,* August 28, 2008. https://www.nytimes.com/2008/08/28/us/politics/28text-obama.html

Obama, Barack. "Barack Obama's Caucus Speech." *New York Times,* January 3, 2008. https://www.nytimes.com/2008/01/03/us/politics/03obama-transcript.html

Obama, Barack. Congressional Record in 109th and 110th Congress, Congress.Gov. https://www.congress.gov/search?q=%7B%22source%22%3A%22congrecord%22%2C%22search%22%3A%22Obama%20%22%7D&searchResultViewType=expanded

Obama, Barack. *Dreams from My Father: A Story of Race and Inheritance.* New York: Three Rivers Press, 2004.

Obama, Barack. "50th Anniversary of the Selma to Montgomery Marches." White House Press Secretary, March 7, 2015. https://obamawhitehouse.archives.gov/the-press-office/2015/03/07/remarks-president-50th-anniversary-selma-montgomery-marches

Obama, Barack. "Inaugural Address by Barack Obama." White House Press Secretary, January 21, 2013. https://obamawhitehouse.archives.gov/the-press-office/2013/01/21/inaugural-address-president-barack-obama

Obama, Barack. "Keynote Address at 2004 Democratic Party Convention." *Washington Post,* July 27, 2004. http://www.washingtonpost.com/wp-dyn/articles/A19751-2004Jul27.html

Obama, Barack. "Obama's Father's Day Remarks at Apostolic Church of God, Chicago, IL." *New York Times,* June 15, 2008. https://www.nytimes.com/2008/06/15/us/politics/15text-obama.html

Obama, Barack. "Obama's Speech on Race: Obama's Speech on Race in Philadelphia, as Provided by his Presidential Campaign." *New York Times,* March 18, 2008. https://www.nytimes.com/2008/03/18/us/politics/18text-obama.html

Obama, Barack. "Obama's 2013 State of the Union Address." *New York Times,* February 12, 2013. https://www.nytimes.com/2013/02/13/us/politics/obamas-2013-state-of-the-union-address.html

Obama, Barack. "President Obama's Farewell Speech." *Los Angeles Times,* January 10, 2017. http://www.latimes.com/politics/la-pol-obama-farewell-speech-transcript-20170110-story.html

Obama, Barack. "Read President Obama's Commencement Address at Morehouse College." *Time Magazine,* May 19, 2013. http://time.com/4341712/obama-commencement-speech-transcript-morehouse-college/

Obama, Barack. "Remarks by President on New Strategy for Afghanistan and Pakistan." Office of the Press Secretary, March 27, 2009. https://obamawhitehouse.archives.gov/the-press-office/remarks-president-a-new-strategy-afghanistan-and-pakistan

Obama, Barack. "Remarks by President to NAACP Centennial Convention." *U.S. News*, July 19, 2009. https://www.usnews.com/news/obama/articles/2009/07/17/president-obamas-speech-to-the-naacp-centennial-convention

Obama, Barack. "Statement by Senator Obama on Repeal of Jena 6 Conviction." September 14, 2007. http://presidency.proxied.lsit.ucsb.edu/ws/index.php?pid=93165

Obama, Barack. "Text of President Obama's Remarks to African Union." VOA News, July 28, 2015. https://www.voanews.com/a/text-of-president-obamas-remarks-at-the-african-union-/2881236.html

Obama, Barack. "2013 State of the Union, Full Text." *Atlantic*, February 13, 2013. https://www.theatlantic.com/politics/archive/2013/02/obamas-2013-state-of-the-union-speech-full-text/273089/

Obama, Michelle. *Becoming.* New York: Crown Publishing, 2018.

"Obama Narrows Clinton Superdelegate Lead to 1." CNN Politics, May 11, 2008. http://www.cnn.com/2008/POLITICS/05/10/dems.wrap/

"Obama Takes the Lead in Superdelegates." *NBC News*, May 5, 2008. http://www.nbcnews.com/id/24556427/ns/politics-decision_08/t/obama-takes-lead-superdelegates-ap-reports/

Owen, Paul. "Obama Wants to 'Create a Million Young Barack Obamas.'" *Guardian*, March 25, 2018. https://www.theguardian.com/us-news/2018/mar/25/obama-wants-to-develop-a-million-young-barack-obamas

Payne, Ed, Matt Smith, and Tom Cohen. "Report: Healthcare Website Failed Test Ahead of Rollout." CNN Politics, October 23, 2013. https://www.cnn.com/2013/10/22/politics/obamacare-website-problems/index.html

Peters, Charles. "Judge Him by His Laws." *Washington Post*, January 4, 2008. http://www.washingtonpost.com/wp-dyn/content/article/2008/01/03/AR2008010303303.html

Politico Staff. "Wright's Controversial Comments." *Politico*, New York, March 17, 2008. https://www.politico.com/story/2008/03/wrights-controversial-comments-009089

Price, Joann F. *Barack Obama: A Voice of an American Leader.* Santa Barbara, CA: ABC-CLIO, 2009.

Purnick, Joyce, and Michael Oreskes. "Jackson Aims for Mainstream." *New York Times*, November 29, 1987. https://www.nytimes.com/1987/11/29/magazine/jesse-jackson-aims-for-the-mainstream.html

Redding, Robert. "Andrew Young Explains Why He Is Not Supporting Barack Obama." *Redding News Review,* December 5, 2007. http://www.reddingnewsreview.com/newspages/2007newspages/andy_young_explains_why_he_is_no_07_091000299.htm

Remnick, David. *The Bridge: The Life and Rise of Barack Obama.* New York: Vintage Books, 2010.

Reynolds, Gretchen. "A Vote of Confidence." *Chicago Magazine,* January 1, 1993. https://www.chicagomag.com/Chicago-Magazine/January-1993/Vote-of-Confidence/

Rooney, Katie. "Budget Brawl." *Time Magazine,* April 28, 2009. http://content.time.com/time/specials/packages/article/0,28804,1889908_1893383_1893750,00.html

Ross, Brian, and Rehab El-Buri. "Obama's Pastor: Goddamn America U.S. to Blame 9/11." *ABC News,* March 13, 2008. https://www.amren.com/news/2008/03/obamas_pastor_g/

Rovner, Julie, and Jenny Gold. "Obama Lifts Limit on Funding Stem Cell Research." *News and Notes,* National Public Radio, March 10, 2009. https://www.npr.org/templates/story/story.php?storyId=101653356

Rowan, Roy, and Brooke Janis. *First Dogs: American Presidents and Their Best Friends.* Chapel Hill, NC: Algonquin of Chapel Hill, 2009.

Sahadi, Jeanne. "Obama Unveils First Budget Plan." CNN Politics, February 26, 2009. https://money.cnn.com/2009/02/26/news/economy/obama_budget_outline/index.htm

Sakuma, Amanda. "Obama Leaves a Mixed Legacy on Immigration." NBC News, January 15, 2017. https://www.nbcnews.com/storyline/president-obama-the-legacy/obama-leaves-behind-mixed-legacy-immigration-n703656

Saslow, Eli. "The 17 Minutes that Launched a Political Star." *Washington Post,* August 28, 2008. http://www.washingtonpost.com/wp-dyn/content/article/2008/08/24/AR2008082401671.html

Sawano, Nanaho. "Guinier Accepts Law School Tenure." *Harvard Crimson,* January 28, 1998. https://www.thecrimson.com/article/1998/1/28/guinier-accepts-law-school-tenure-plani/

Schieffer, Bob. "Face the Nation Transcripts." *Face the Nation,* October 20, 2013. https://www.cbsnews.com/news/face-the-nation-transcripts-october-20-2013-mcconnell-graham-warner/

Scott, Janny. "In Illinois Obama Proved to be Pragmatic and Shrewd." *New York Times,* July 30, 2007. https://www.nytimes.com/2007/07/30/us/politics/30obama.html

Scott, Janny. "In 2000, a Streetwise Veteran Schooled a Bold Young Obama." *New York Times,* September 9, 2007. https://www.nytimes.com/2007/09/09/us/politics/09obama.html

Scott, Janny. "Obama's Account of New York Years Often Differs from What Others Say." *New York Times*, October 30, 2007. https://www.nytimes.com/2007/10/30/us/politics/30obama.html

Scott, Janny. "Obama's Young Mother Abroad." *New York Times Magazine*, April 20, 2011. https://www.nytimes.com/2011/04/24/magazine/mag-24Obama-t.html

Shapiro, Ari. "Obama Made a Strong First Impression at Harvard." Morning Edition on National Public Radio, May 22, 2012. https://www.npr.org/2012/05/22/153214284/obamas-harvard-days-began-with-exclamation-point

Shear, Michael D. "Obama Pleads for Stricter Gun Laws and Faces Tough Questioning." *New York Times*, January 8, 2016. https://www.nytimes.com/2016/01/08/us/politics/obama-gun-control-town-hall-cnn.html

Shear, Michael D., and Liam Stack. "Obama Says Movements Like Black Lives Matter 'Can't Just Keep on Yelling.'" *New York Times*, April 23, 2016. https://www.nytimes.com/2016/04/24/us/obama-says-movements-like-black-lives-matter-cant-just-keep-on-yelling.html

Shoichet, Catherine, Susannah Cullinane, and Tal Kopan. "U.S. Immigration: DACA and Dreamers Explained." CNN Politics, October 26, 2017. https://www.cnn.com/2017/09/04/politics/daca-dreamers-immigration-program/index.html

Sinclair, Harriet. "Sorry, Trump: Barack Obama Seen by More Americans as Best President in Their Lifetime." *Newsweek*, July 12, 2018. https://www.newsweek.com/sorry-trump-barack-obama-seen-americans-best-president-their-lifetime-1020284

Sinderbrand, Rebecca. "Obama Raises 40 Million in March." CNN Politics, April 3, 2008. http://politicalticker.blogs.cnn.com/2008/04/03/obama-raises-40-million-in-march/

Sink, Justin, and Mike Lillis. "Obama Unveils New Restriction on Assault Weapons, Ammunition." *The Hill*, January 16, 2013. https://thehill.com/homenews/administration/277501-obama-unveils-major-new-proposals-to-restrict-access-to-guns

Smothers, Ronald. "Jackson Declares Formal Candidacy." *New York Times*, November 4, 1983. https://www.nytimes.com/1983/11/04/us/jackson-declares-formal-candidacy.html

Staff Reports. "Obama's Legacy: The First Black President." *Washington Post*, April 22, 2016. https://www.washingtonpost.com/graphics/national/obama-legacy/henry-louis-gates-jr-arrest-controversy.html

Staff, Transcript. "Michelle Obama Full Speech from the DNC 2016." *Washington Post*, July 26, 2016. https://www.washingtonpost.com/news/post-politics/wp/2016/07/26/transcript-read-michelle-obamas-full-speech-from-the-2016-dnc/

Staff Writer. "Barack Obama Presidential Library on Chicago's South Side Would Be an Economic Boom, Study Finds." *University of Chicago News*, May 19, 2014. https://news.uchicago.edu/story/barack-obama -presidential-library-chicagos-south-side-would-be-economic -boon-study-finds

Steinhauser, Paul. "Obama Widens Lead in National Poll." CNN Politics, October 2, 2008. http://www.cnn.com/2008/POLITICS/10/06/poll .of.polls/index.html

Stolberg, Cheryl Gay. "Obama Signs Equal Pay Legislation." *New York Times*, January 29, 2009. https://www.nytimes.com/2009/01/30/us /politics/30ledbetter-web.html

Tatum, Sophie. "Obama Endorses French Presidential Candidate Macron." CNN Politics, May 4, 2017. https://www.cnn.com/2017/05/04 /politics/french-election-obama-endorse-macron/index.html

Thomas, Evan. "Roseland's History." *Chicago Tribune*, June 9, 2006. om /news/ct-xpm-2006-06-09-0606090356-story.html

Thomas, Garen. *Yes We Can: A Biography of President Barack Obama.* New York: Macmillan Publishing, 2008.

Thompson, Cheryl W., Krissah Thompson, and Michael A. Fletcher. "Gates and Police Officer Share Beers with the President." *Washington Post*, July 31, 2009. http://www.washingtonpost.com/wp-dyn /content/article/2009/07/30/AR2009073003563.html

Tiereny, Dominic. "The Legacy of Obama's Worst Mistake." *Atlantic*, April 15, 2016. https://www.theatlantic.com/international/archive/2016 /04/obamas-worst-mistake-libya/478461/

Time Staff. "President Obama's Speech in Charleston Church Shooting." *Time Magazine*, June 18, 2015. http://time.com/3926839/president -obama-charleston-transcript/

Tracy, Jan. "Obama Urged Law School Graduates to Help Fight Poverty." *Boston Globe*, September 25, 2005. http://archive.boston.com/news /local/massachusetts/articles/2005/09/18/obama_urges_alumni _to_help_fight_poverty/

Transcript. "President Obama's Remarks on Donald Trump's Selection." *Washington Post*, November 9, 2016. https://www.washingtonpost .com/news/the-fix/wp/2016/11/09/transcript-president-obamas -remarks-on-donald-trumps-election/

Trice, Dawn Turner. "Far South Side Environmental Activist Hazel John-son and Her Daughter Decided to Stay Here and Fight." *Chicago Tribune*, March 1, 2010. http://www.chicagotribune.com/news/ct -xpm-2010-03-01-ct-met-trice-altgeld-0229-20100228-story.html

Vale, Elizabeth. "Barack Obama and Justin Trudeau Keep Their Bromance Alive; Internet Swoons." *Journal News*, June 7, 2017. https://www .journal-news.com/news/gen-politics/barack-obama-justin

-trudeau-keep-their-bromance-alive-internet-swoons
/NnlURWlv3CiU5QgF9nUq7H/

Wayne, Leslie, and Jeff Zeleney. "Enlisting New Donors, Obama Reaped
$32 Million in January." *New York Times*, February 1, 2008. https://
www.nytimes.com/2008/02/01/us/politics/01donate.html

Weeks, Linto. "A Small Town Mayor vs a Community Organizer." National
Public Radio, September 12, 2008. https://www.npr.org/templates
/story/story.php?storyId=94526145

Whitman, Elizabeth. "Obamacare Website Failure Analysis: Why the
Website Crashed So Often During the 2013 Launch and Mishan-
dled $600 M in Contracts." *International Business Times*, Septem-
ber 15, 2015. https://www.ibtimes.com/obamacare-website-failure
-analysis-why-site-crashed-so-often-during-2013-launch-2097354

Wilgoren, Jill. "Illinois Senator Announces He Will Not Seek Re-election."
New York Times, April 16, 2003. https://www.nytimes.com/2003
/04/16/us/illinois-senator-announces-he-won-t-seek-re-election
.html

Wintour, Patrick. "G20 Summit: U.S. Alone Cannot End Recession, Says
Barack Obama." *Guardian*, April 1, 2009. https://www.theguardian
.com/world/2009/apr/01/barack-obama-g20-global-recession

Wolffe, Richard. *Renegade: The Making of a President*. New York: Crown
Publishing, 2009.

Worley, Will. "Harvard Law Professor Who Taught Barack and Michelle
Obama Says Former First Lady Should Have Been President."
Independent, Monday February 13, 2017. https://www.independent
.co.uk/news/world/americas/us-politics/harvard-law-professor
-charles-ogletree-barack-obama-michelle-former-first-lady-should
-be-us-a7577176.html

Youngman, Sam. "Obama: One of the Longest Serving Dictators Is No
More." *The Hill*, October 20, 2011. https://thehill.com/video/in-the
-news/188863-obama-one-of-the-worlds-longest-serving-dictators
-is-no-more

Index

About the Authors

F. Erik Brooks is dean of the College of Humanities and Social Sciences and director of the Whitney Young Honors Collegium at Kentucky State University. He is coauthor of several books, including *Thurgood Marshall: A Biography, How the Obama Presidency Changed the Political Landscape,* and *The Student Athlete's Guide to College Success.*

MaCherie M. Placide is an associate professor of political science at Western Illinois University. Her research interests include leadership and management in public administration, hiring practices in government administration—particularly within law enforcement—urban politics, and social policy issues.